JUMPING TO CONCLUSIONS

THE FALLING-THIRD CADENCES IN CHANT, POLYPHONY, AND RECITATIVE

JUMPING TO CONCLUSIONS
THE FALLING-THIRD CADENCES IN CHANT, POLYPHONY, AND RECITATIVE

RICHARD HUDSON
Emeritus Professor of Musicology
University of California, Los Angeles

ASHGATE

© Richard Hudson 2006

Richard Hudson has asserted his moral right under the Copyright, Designs and Patents Act, 1988, to be identified as the author of this work.

Published by
Ashgate Publishing Limited
Gower House
Croft Road
Aldershot
Hants GU11 3HR
England

Ashgate Publishing Company
Suite 420
101 Cherry Street
Burlington, VT 05401-4405
USA

Ashgate website: http://www.ashgate.com

British Library Cataloguing in Publication Data
Hudson, Richard, 1924–
    Jumping to conclusions : the falling-third cadences in chant, polyphony, and recitative
    1. Cadences (Music) – History and criticism 2. Gregorian chants 3. Recitative
    4. Counterpoint
    I. Title
    781.2'54

Library of Congress Cataloging-in-Publication Data
Hudson, Richard, 1924–
  Jumping to conclusions : the falling-third cadences in chant, polyphony, and recitative / Richard Hudson.
        p. cm.
  Includes bibliographical references (p.   ) and index.
  ISBN 0-7546-5407-9 (alk. paper)
  1. Cadences (Music)–History and criticism. 2. Music theory–History. I. Title.
ML444.H93 2006 782'.0254–dc22

2005019953

ISBN-10: 0 7546 5407 9

Printed and bound by Athenaeum Press, Ltd.,
Gateshead, Tyne & Wear.

CONTENTS

List of Figures   vi
Abbreviations   vii
Preface   xi

Introduction   1

PART I
THE FALLING-THIRD CADENCES IN
CHANT AND POLYPHONY

1   Gregorian Chant   5

2   Late Fourteenth- and Early Fifteenth-Century Polyphony   15

3   Polyphony from Dufay to Palestrina   27

PART II
THE FALLING-THIRD CADENCES IN
RECITATIVE

4   Monody and Recitative in the Seventeenth Century   41

5   Later Recitative   63

6   The Appoggiatura   113

THE CONCLUSIONS

7   The 4-3-1 Figure in History   183

Bibliography   189
Index   195

LIST OF FIGURES

1 Comparison of the falling-third and repeated-3 cadences
1675–1700   61

2 Principal recitative cadences 1683–1850   64

3 Verbal descriptions of realizations for the brief cadence   71

4 Performance of the V chord in the brief cadences   81

5 Location of the I chord in relation to the voice's first
or single 1   99

6 Performance of the cadential appoggiatura   174

ABBREVIATIONS

AIM	American Institute of Musicology
Bärenreiter	Bärenreiter-Verlag (Kassel and Basle)
BG	*J. S. Bach*: *Werke*, ed. Bach-Gesellschaft (Leipzig: Breitkopf & Härtel, 1851–99; repr., Ann Arbor, MI: J. W. Edwards, 1947)
BWV	*Bach-Werke-Verzeichnis*
CMM	*Corpus mensurabilis musicae* (AIM, 1947–)
DDT	*Denkmäler deutscher Tonkunst*
DM	*Documenta musicologica*, *Erste Reihe* (Bärenreiter)
DO	*G. Dufay*: *Opera omnia*, ed. G. de Van and H. Besseler, *CMM* i (1947–66)
EFM	*Early Fifteenth-Century Music*, ed. Gilbert Reaney, *CMM* xi (1955–83)
ERO	*Early Romantic Operas*, ed. Philip Gossett and Charles Rosen (Garland, 1977–78)
Garland	Garland Publishing (New York and London)
Glixon	Beth Lise Glixon, "Recitative in Seventeenth-Century Venetian Opera: Its Dramatic Function and Musical Language," Ph.D. diss. (Rutgers University, 1985; UM 85-20,360)
HAM	*Historical Anthology of Music*, ed. Archibald T. Davison and Willi Apel (Cambridge, MA: Harvard University Press, 1949–50, repr. 1966)
HG	*Works of George Frederic Handel*, printed for the German Handel Society (Händel-Gesellschaft), ed. Friedrich W. Chrysander (Leipzig and Bergedorf bei Hamburg, 1858–94; repr., Ridgewood, NJ: Gregg Press, 1965–66)
HHA	*Hallische Händel-Ausgabe* (Bärenreiter, 1955–)
HS	*Handel Sources*: *Materials for the Study of Handel's Borrowing*, ed. John H. Roberts (Garland, 1986)
HW	*J. Haydn*: *Werke*, ed. Joseph Haydn-Institut, Cologne (Munich: G. Henle Verlag, 1958–)
IC	*The Italian Cantata in the Seventeenth Century*, ed. Carolyn Gianturco (Garland, 1985–86)
IOB	*Italian Opera 1640–1770*, ed. Howard Mayer Brown and Eric Weimer (Garland, 1977–84)

IOG	*Italian Opera 1810–1840*, ed. Philip Gossett (Garland, 1984–89)
IOR	*The Italian Oratorio 1650–1800*, ed. Joyce L. Johnson and Howard E. Smither (Garland, 1986–87)
JAMS	*Journal of the American Musicological Society*
JW	*Josquin des Prez: Werken*, ed. A. Smijers et al. (Amsterdam, 1921–)
LU	*Liber usualis, with Introduction and Rubrics in English* (Tournai: Desclée, 1950)
MB	*Musica britannica* (London: Stainer & Bell, 1951–; rev. edn., 1954–)
MGG	*Die Musik in Geschichte und Gegenwart*, ed. Friedrich Blume (Bärenreiter, 1949–86; paperback edn., 1989)
ML	*Music and Letters*
MLE	*Music for London Entertainment* (London: Stainer & Bell, 1983–96)
MOS	*Masterworks on Singing* (Champaign, IL: Pro Musica Press)
MQ	*Musical Quarterly*
Murata	Margaret Murata, *Opera for the Papal Court 1631–1668*, in *SM* xxxix (1981)
MW	*F. Mendelssohn-Bartholdy: Werke*, ed. Julius Rietz (Leipzig: Breitkopf & Härtel, 1874–77)
NBA	*Neue Bach-Ausgabe* (Bärenreiter, 1954–)
NG	*The New Grove Dictionary of Music and Musicians*, ed. Stanley Sadie (London: Macmillan, 1980)
NHD	*The New Harvard Dictionary of Music*, ed. Don Mitchell Randel (Cambridge, MA: The Belknap Press of Harvard University Press, 1986)
NMA	*Neue Mozart-Ausgabe* (Bärenreiter, 1955–)
NSA	*Neue Schubert-Ausgabe* (Bärenreiter, 1964–)
OAS	*The Operas of Alessandro Scarlatti*, ed. Donald Jay Grout, in *Harvard Publications in Music* (Cambridge, MA: Harvard University Press, 1974–)
OC	*J. Ockeghem: Collected Works* (American Musicological Society, 1947–)
OH	*The Old Hall Manuscript*, ed. Andrew Hughes and Margaret Bent in *CMM* xlvi (1969–73)
ON	*New Obrecht Edition* (Vereniging voor Nederlandse Muziekgeschiedenis, 1983–)
OUP	Oxford University Press, Clarendon Press

PC	*Leonel Power*: *Complete Works*, ed. Charles Hamm, in *CMM* 1 (1969–)
PMFC	*Polyphonic Music of the Fourteenth Century* (Monaco: L'Oiseau-Lyre, 1956–)
PO	*G. P. Palestrina*: *Le opere complete*, ed. R. Casimiri et al. (Rome, 1939–)
Rackwitz	*Georg Philipp Telemann*: *Singen ist das Fundament zur Music in allen Dingen*, ed. Werner Rackwitz (Leipzig: Verlag Philipp Reclam jun., 1981)
RE	*Gioachino Rossini*: *Edizione critica della opere* (Pesaro: Fondazione Rossini, 1979–)
Rosand	Ellen Rosand, *Opera in Seventeenth-Century Venice* (Berkeley and Los Angeles: University of California Press, 1991)
SM	*Studies in Musicology* (Ann Arbor, MI: UMI Research Press)
TM	*G. P. Telemann*: *Musicalische Werke* (Bärenreiter, 1953–)
UM	University Microfilms (Ann Arbor, MI)

PREFACE

THERE ARE CADENCES which reach their conclusion by jumping downward from the third scale degree to the first. They occur in many different forms of music and in many different periods of music history. They begin in the earliest type of Western music, the chant of the Christian church. They continue in the polyphony of the Middle Ages and Renaissance and appear later in the recitative of the Baroque, Classic, and early Romantic periods. They also occur occasionally in the homophonic music of the nineteenth century and in the blues of the early twentieth.

This book will be mainly concerned with the falling-third cadences in chant, polyphony, and recitative. I first became interested in these cadences in 1975 when Alessandro Scarlatti's opera *Gli equivoci nel sembiante* was performed at UCLA for the forty-first annual meeting of the American Musicological Society. Originally this study was to constitute the opening chapter in a book entitled *The Power of the Third Degree*. As I began to write, however, the sections of this chapter became themselves as large as chapters, and so the history of the falling-third cadences finally seemed complex and interesting enough to deserve a book devoted exclusively to it. Furthermore, such a book provides an opportunity to explore anew some performance problems which have occupied scholars for the last forty years.

Arabic numerals appear throughout the book with several different meanings. Ordinarily they indicate scale degrees. In this way they can identify melodic figures formed by joining the falling third with other notes. Most important is the figure 4-3-1, which may seem at first glance to have an unusual melodic shape, but which becomes finally the most frequent and enduring pattern of them all. Hyphens between the numbers show that the notes belong together in a unified figure.

Beginning with Chapter 4, the same numbers also occur in figured basses. Here numbers such as "4 3" refer not to scale degrees but to intervals above a bass note. In Ex. 4.6*d*, for example, the numbers 4 and 3 above the bass note E indicate that the continuo realization should include the notes A (a fourth above E) and G-sharp (a third above the same note). At the same time 4-3-1 above the voice part refers to scale degrees, where the note A in the key of A minor is 1. The A and G-sharp to which the 4 and 3 refer in the bass are actually scale degrees 1 and 7 and in this case duplicate the pitches in the voice part. In both the examples and the text, numbers connected by hyphens always refer to melodic scale-degrees.

The numbers from figured bass occur also in conjunction with roman chord-numerals. These occur in the conventional way, with the first inversion of a tonic chord, for example, shown as I_6, the second inversion as I_4^6. Uppercase roman numerals stand for major triads, lowercase for minor. The symbol o^7 is a diminished seventh chord. A secondary dominant chord in first inversion which moves to a vi chord is marked "V_6 of vi." Arabic numbers also identify modes, pages, and other items, but these, I believe, will cause no problem. When considering the text associated with a cadence, a word or ending is *feminine* if the accent is on the penultimate syllable, *masculine* if it is on the last. In the few cases in which it is on the third from the last, I will refer simply to an *antepenultimate* accent.

Ex. P Ornamental or nonharmonic tones

Ex. P shows the terminology used for ornamental or nonharmonic tones. A neighbor note moves a step above or below a consonant note and then returns to the same pitch. Double neighbors or changing notes move both above and below. The usual passing tone fills in some interval with stepwise motion. The "leaping" passing-tone (my name) fills in the interval of a fourth, usually beginning by step and continuing with a falling third. It is related to the cambiata, which adds a stepwise note at the end in the opposite direction and thus causes the second note to sound as though it resolves to the fourth. In an échappée, the second note "escapes" from the descending direction in which the first note moves to the third. In an anticipation the dissonant second note is immediately repeated as a consonance. These are all metrically weak notes in contrast to the appoggiaturas in (*h*), where the first is a strong example preceded by a leaping passing-tone, the second a gentler one approached by step. We will be most concerned in this book with the leaping passing-tone in (*d*) and the appoggiaturas in (*h*).

For the sake of the reader who may dip into the book at some point past the beginning, I often refer back to musical examples first presented earlier. This mainly concerns the examples in Chapter 4 and may require some patience from the reader. Persons reading the book from the beginning, however, or already somewhat familiar with its contents, may remember such examples well enough without seeing them again. Most of the examples in Chapter 5 are all together in the middle of the chapter in order to facilitate easier reference.

There are presently no substantial studies in chant or polyphony, as far as I am aware, on either the falling-third cadences or the melodic figures with the shape of 4-3-1. Concerning the rhythmic structure of the recitative cadences, however, I want to acknowledge the pioneering work of Jack Allan Westrup, Sven Hostrup Hansell, Winton Dean, and Michael Collins. There are also important studies on the appoggiatura, including those by Bernhard Paumgartner, Luigi Ferdinando Tagliavini, Charles Mackerras, Erik Smith, Frederick Neumann, and Will Crutchfield, although these deal almost exclusively with internal phrase endings rather than with cadences.

I want to thank my colleague Marie Louise Göllner for help with German translation. I thank the staff of the Walter H. Rubsamen Music Library at UCLA and the Interlibrary Loan Department of the Charles E. Young Research Library. I am grateful, finally, to libraries throughout the world for making books and scores available to me.

R.H.

University of California
Los Angeles

INTRODUCTION

THE FALLING THIRD involved here is the descending interval between scale degrees 3 and 1. This interval occurs at the end of a falling-third cadence or immediately precedes its framework notes of 2 to 1 or 7 to 1. Ex. I shows a familiar example from Handel's *Messiah*. In this case, 3 falls to 1 at the end of the voice part, and the cadential framework of 7 to 1 occurs in the accompaniment. Two problems in this cadence have long puzzled scholars: should the dominant seventh chord in the accompaniment be played as Handel wrote it or should it be delayed for a quarter beat, and should an appoggiatura on scale degree 2 be added before the final note in the voice? An investigation of the history preceding Handel's time reveals some new and unexpected answers to these questions.

Ex. I Handel, *Messiah* (1742), "Comfort Ye," *HHA* I/xvii, 7

The history we will be tracing includes two main periods of development. During the first period, falling-third cadences originate in chant, move along with borrowed chant melodies into Medieval polyphony, and become, finally, a part of the contrapuntal flow of Renaissance music.

During the second period of development, the cadences seem to be reborn, perhaps again influenced by chant, in the recitative of opera, cantata, and oratorio. This development spans the Baroque and Classic periods and extends even into the first half of the nineteenth century. Many examples from this second development are still performed today. We therefore see the falling-third cadences in scores and hear them in performances of works such as Handel's *Messiah*, Bach's *St. Matthew Passion*, Haydn's *Creation*, and Mozart's *Marriage of Figaro*.

Often the cadences in these works have been performed in accordance with the taste of later times. If we want to know how the composers and the musicians of their time performed them, however, we must look not to the future but to the past and to the previous history which produced them. Therefore, we will turn first to the earlier period of development, which begins with the melodies of Gregorian chant.

Part I

THE FALLING-THIRD CADENCES

IN

CHANT AND POLYPHONY

Chapter 1

GREGORIAN CHANT

IN MOST OF THE CADENCES of Gregorian chant scale-degree 2 descends to 1 by step, as in Ex. 1.1. Often 3 precedes the 2. Occasionally 7 ascends to 1 (Ex. 1.2). Some cadences, however, do not move to 1 by step, but leap instead from 3 directly to 1. I have found three hundred and fifty-two examples of this falling-third cadence in the *Liber usualis*.[1] About two-thirds of these involve a minor third from 3 to 1. The falling third may be preceded by scale degree 4 or 2, less often by 1 or 5. When 3-1 follows 4, the special figure 4-3-1 occurs. This pattern of a stepwise descent followed by a leap of a third in the same direction may appear also on other scale degrees (6-5-3 in Ex. 1.3*a*, for example, or 3-2-7 in Ex. 1.3*f*) and in the interior of phrases as well as at the cadences.

Ex. 1.1 Chant cadence ending with 4-3-1 + 2-1:
end of introit antiphon in mode 7 (*LU* 470)

[1] *Edited by the Benedictines of Solesmes, with Introduction and Rubrics in English* (Tournai: Desclée & Co., l950). A survey of the cadences in this source seemed sufficient for the purposes of this study, even though it includes only a selection from the vast repertoire of chants composed in various locations over a considerable span of time. See Frederic W. Homan, "Final and Internal Cadential Patterns in Gregorian Chant," *JAMS* 17 (1964): 66–77, especially the chart of cadences on p. 76; and Willi Apel, *Gregorian Chant* (Bloomington, IN: Indiana University Press, 1970), 263–6.

Ex. 1.2 Chant cadence ending with 4-3-1 + 7-1:
end of Vesper antiphon in mode 1 (*LU* 914)

Ex. 1.3 Chant cadences ending with 4-3-1

The Figure 4-3-1 at Cadence

When 4-3-1 occurs at cadence, however, the initial movement from 4 to 3 seems to promise continued stepwise descent, which is abruptly interrupted by the leap from 3 to 1 and the omission of the usual 2. Ex. 1.3 shows a number of such cadences.

The intensity with which the figure falls onto 1 and thus accentuates this scale degree varies according to a number of factors. Most important is the mode, for its configuration of pitches determines whether the interval between 4 and 3 is a half or whole step and that between 3 and 1 is a major or minor third. The smaller the interval between 4 and 3 and the larger the leap from 3 to 1, the greater the effect. Therefore the pattern with the major third at the end of Ex. 1.3*a* in mode 5 is more striking than the cadence in mode 4 with the minor third in Ex. 1.3*b*. Rhythmically, the leap is strengthened when it is delayed by prolonging one of the notes preceding 1. Although scale degree 4 is seldom treated in this way, the duration of 3 is often extended by repeated notes (*e*). The presence of 3 is also enhanced when it precedes the 4-3-1 figure in Ex. 1.3*c, d, f,* and *g*. In some cases there is the cumulative effect caused by circling around 3 before the cadence. Thus in (*a*) the chant seems to emphasize 3 by extending its length or returning to it often. 3 similarly recurs many times before the cadence in Ex. 1.3*f*, as well as in Ex. 1.2. In all three cases the 3 thus seems to play a prominent role in the structure of the chant.[2]

The 4-3-1 cadence sometimes marks the end of a long melisma, as in Ex. 1.3*a*. When the notes of the cadential figure have text, however, 3 may coincide with an accented syllable, as on the penultimate note of (*b*). In (*d*) the accented syllable of the last two words appears on 3, both words following many repetitions of the reciting tone on A, the fourth step of the mode. In (*e*) the 4-3-1 figure spans the word *firmamentum*, with a three-fold extension of 3 on the accented syllable and with further accentuation given to the penultimate pitch by using 3 also for the preceding unaccented syllable. In general, however, word accent in chant is not marked by greater duration, as shown by the word *Deus* in (*f*). Sometimes the accented syllable falls not on 3 but on the 4 of 4-3-1 (*c* and *g*) or on the final 1. In the latter case, 1 may occur twice to accommodate a two-syllable word with its accent on the first syllable (*f*), or three times for a three-syllable word

---

[2] I am grateful to Richard Crocker for his suggestions regarding this chapter. He prefers to refer to such a structural tone as a "reference pitch," thus avoiding potentially misleading terms such as "dominant" and "mediant." See his book *An Introduction to Gregorian Chant* (New Haven and London: Yale University Press, 2000), 32 and 239.

accented on the first (g). As shown in these examples, both 1's are dotted in the double final 1, but only the last in the triple. The dot is one of the signs that indicate a rhythmic nuance.[3]

The 4-3-1 cadences occur in all the modes, but rarely in 2 and 6, the two modes in which 3 is the reciting pitch in the psalm tone. They show about equal preference for the major and minor third. Most often the pattern is 2-4-3-1, which usually displays the major third, as in Ex. 1.3a, but sometimes the minor (b).[4] Almost as frequent is 3-4-3-1, but this figure favors the minor third (as in c) and rarely occurs in major (g).[5] Less often one encounters 5-4-3-1, usually in the form shown in (e) with a minor third.[6] I have never found 1-4-3-1 or 6-4-3-1, the pattern most popular, as we will see, in later recitative. Occasionally 4-3-1 is followed by 2-1 (Ex. 1.1) or 7-1 (Ex. 1.2), with about half of the examples ending with two 1's in which only the last is dotted (as in Ex. 1.2).[7] I include the cadences in Exx. 1.1 and 1.2 here also because of their similarity to some polyphonic cadences which develop later.

Ornamental Notes

Structural and nonstructural notes in chant may conceivably relate to each other somewhat as they do in later polyphony and homophony. If the final pitch and others that are prominent, along with a cadential progression (2-1,

---

[3] See Crocker, *An Introduction to Gregorian Chant*, 166–72, where such nuances are defined as "subtle variations in rhythmic inflection" (p. 170)—more subtle than the doubled length indicated in *LU* xx.

[4] This formula occurs with a single final 1 mostly in graduals of mode 5; there are also a few in alleluias (*LU* 428, for example) and antiphons (*LU* 516) in modes 4 and 7. The 1 occurs two or three times at the end of antiphons in modes 7 and 8 (*LU* 1209 and 504).

[5] It occurs with a single 1 mainly in graduals (*LU* 499, for example) and usually in mode 3, but also modes 1 and 4. Double and triple 1's most often conclude antiphons in mode 3 (Ex. 1.3f).

[6] There are four examples in introits of mode 1 and another with a double 1 at the end of a Vesper antiphon in mode 8 (*LU* 1339).

[7] 4-3-1-2-1 occurs in graduals (*LU* 1072 and 1207) and other forms in modes 1 and 4; 4-3-1-2-1-1 in communions in modes 6 and 7, also 5 and 8 (*LU* 1365). Thus both major and minor thirds are involved. 4-3-1-7-1-1 concludes antiphons most often in mode 1, but also in modes 2 and 3, and hence all have a minor third.

7-1, or sometimes 3-1), constitute the framework of structure, then the other notes presumably play a different role, that of circling around the structural notes or providing movement between them.

It is thus tempting to hear the 4 in Ex. 1.3*f* as a neighbor note between two 3's, especially since the 4 occurs together with both 3's on a single syllable of text (see Ex. P in the Preface for definitions of the ornamental notes). If the broad movement in (*d*) involves the repeated 4's at the beginning falling finally to the 1 at the end, then the 2 and 4 on *oris* also sound like neighbor notes prolonging 3. Perhaps the 2 and 4 in (*b*) constitute an ornamental figure which could be described as double neighbors or changing notes between two 3's. In (*e*), on the other hand, the descending line tends to make the 3 sound like a passing tone between 4 and 1, one that is left by leap. The final 3 in (*g*) may also seem like such a leaping passing-tone, because of the accented syllable on the preceding 4, and also because it is part of a generally descending line between 5 and the final note.

Perhaps some of the falling-third endings can be interpreted as an ornamental version of a broader 2-1 or 7-1 movement. In (*a*) the last 2 (four notes from the end), for example, may be prolonged and ornamented by the 4 and 3 before resolving to 1, somewhat in the manner of an échappée (2-3-1) but expanded to reach even further (2-4-3-1) as a sort of échappée group. In (*f*) a 7-1 cadence may have been similarly expanded by prolonging the 1 on "*mus*" by means of the group 3-3-4-3. The concept of a concluding 1 whose effect is later prolonged by other notes occurs, of course, in both modal polyphony (see Ex. 3.4*b*) and tonal harmony. One may only wonder if a similar practice applies in chant. There are, on the other hand, some examples, such as the complete antiphon in (*g*), which contain neither a 2 nor 7 to which 4 and 3 could relate.[8]

---

[8] The manner in which any particular person in history heard Gregorian chant must have been heavily influenced by the other music current at the time. Before polyphony, one's ears would have been familiar also with secular monophony. As polyphony later developed, each generation must have heard chant in a somewhat different manner, depending upon the type of polyphonic music it knew. Polyphony quickly developed a concept of consonance and dissonance between intervals and eventually the idea of certain notes relating to others as upper or lower neighbors, passing tones, etc. This may have encouraged the contemporary listener to hear chant in a similar way. When tonality crystallized late in the seventeenth century, new harmonic ways of hearing music emerged and again must have influenced the way one heard the melodies of chant. Whether a particular melodic figure in chant is conspicuous or interesting to a listener might depend, then, upon whether it was familiar or avoided in his contemporary music. We cannot know for sure how anyone in the past heard chant. It is hard to imagine, however, that even the creators of chant did not have some feeling for the way

Other Figures at Cadence

In any event, the concluding figure 4-3-1, however it may be interpreted, contains an unusual leap of a third following a step in the same direction, and modern ears often tend to hear the 3 as an unusual passing tone leaping between 4 and 1. When 3-1 follows scale degree 2 rather than 4, however, the resulting figure 2-3-1 has a subtler effect and 3 is somewhat less conspicuous. Such endings are slightly more numerous than 4-3-1.

Ex. 1.4 Chant cadences ending with 2-3-1

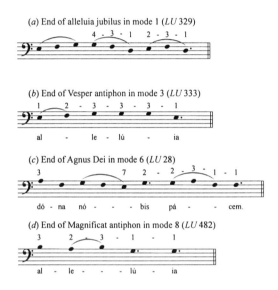

(a) End of alleluia jubilus in mode 1 (*LU* 329)

(b) End of Vesper antiphon in mode 3 (*LU* 333)

(c) End of Agnus Dei in mode 6 (*LU* 28)

(d) End of Magnificat antiphon in mode 8 (*LU* 482)

Two-thirds of them are in modes with a minor third between 3 and 1 (see Ex. 1.4a and b), an interval gentler than the major third (c and d). In addition, 2-3-1 may often be interpreted as a 2-1 progression ornamented by an échappée on 3. As with 4-3-1, the 3 in 2-3-1 may be further emphasized by lengthening it (b), by preceding the 2 immediately with another 3 (d), by giving it an accented syllable (b), or by preceding the accented syllable with another 3 on an unaccented syllable (b again). The cadence may end with a single 1 (a or b), with two 1's in which only the second (c) or both are dotted

some notes relate to others. I have suggested some possibilities. If these are not exactly those conceived originally, then others, which we may not ever know, must apply.

(*d*), or with three 1's. The accented syllable often falls on the first of two dotted 1's (*d*). Most of the 2-3-1 cadences occur in mode 1 or 2. In about half of them 2-3-1 is preceded by 1 (see Ex.1.4*a* or *b*), and the rest appear about equally as 3-2-3-1 (Ex. 1.4*d*), 4-2-3-1, and 7-2-3-1 (Ex. 1.4*c*). Like 4-3-1, 2-3-1 may also lead to 2-1 (Ex. 1.5) or 7-1 (Ex. 1.6).[9]

Ex. 1.5 Chant cadence ending with 2-3-1 2-1: end of offertory in mode 8 (*LU* 439)

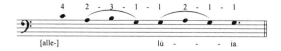

Ex. 1.6 Chant cadence ending with 2-3-1 7-1: end of hymn strophe in mode 1 (*LU* 575)

Far less common than the 2-3-1 and 4-3-1 cadences are two others that incorporate the falling third. 1-3-1 may be preceded by either 2 (Ex. 1.7*a*) or 7 (Ex. 1.7*b*). The concluding 3-1 tends to sound to harmonically conditioned ears as a melodic prolongation of the preceding 1, so that the first 1 of 1-3-3-1 seems like the structural 1 in a basic 2-1 (Ex. 1.7*a*) or 7-1

---

[9] When there is a single concluding 1, 1-2-3-1 occurs mostly in graduals (*LU* 1327) and alleluias of modes 1 and 2; 3-2-3-1 in graduals (*LU* 435), alleluias (*LU* 1208), and other forms in modes 1, 3, 4, and 6; 4-2-3-1 in alleluias (*LU* 1151) and antiphons (*LU* 1094) in modes 1, 4, and 5; and 7-2-3-1 in alleluias (*LU* 790) and antiphons (*LU* 1600) in mode 1. The double 1 with the second dotted appears in modes 1 and 2 and also 5, 6, 7, and 8: sometimes in the Kyrie (*LU* 32) and Agnus Dei (*LU* 59) from the mass ordinary or the communion (*LU* 424) from the proper, and in office antiphons (*LU* 1632) and hymns (*LU* 540). Endings with two dotted 1's or with three 1's and only the last dotted, are mainly in the office antiphons in modes about equally divided between major and minor thirds. I have also found a single example of 6-2-3-1 in an antiphon of mode 4 (*LU* 588) and one of 5-2-3-1 in an antiphon of mode 6 (*LU* 892).

(*b*) cadence.[10] Furthermore, the few examples of 5-3-1 (see Ex. 1.8) outline to us, of course, the notes of a triad.[11]

Ex. 1.7 Chant cadences ending with 1-3-1

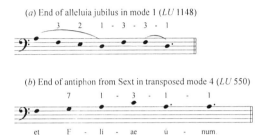

Ex. 1.8 Chant cadence ending with 5-3-1:
end of Vesper antiphon in mode 3 (*LU* 1366)

The Effect of the Figures

In all these cadences the leap between 3 and 1 tends to throw additional accentuation onto the 1. This effect is gentlest in 2-3-1 and 1-3-1, where the preceding movement is in the opposite direction. In 4-3-1 and 5-3-1, however, the steps and the leaps are all in the same direction, so that the energy with which 1 is approached is considerably greater. The 1 may occasionally coincide, as we have noted, with an accented syllable, thus

---

[10] 2-1-3-1 appears in alleluias in mode 1 and always concludes with a single dotted 1. 7-1-3-1-1 ends with a double 1 in which only the last is dotted in two Kyries in mode 1 (*LU* 43 and 51); it concludes with two dotted 1's (as in Ex. 1.7*b*) or with three 1's in which only the last is dotted in some office antiphons in transposed mode 4.

[11] I have located only three examples in office antiphons in modes 3 and 5, all following scale degree 4 and all ending with three 1's (the other two in *LU* 723 and 1503).

increasing the accentuation on 1 even more. The usual 2-1 and 7-1 cadences sound smooth and flowing by comparison. The falling-third cadences seem generally more emphatic. With its distinctive and unusual shape, 4-3-1, it seems to me, is the most striking of them all, especially when the third is major.[12]

* * * * *

Gregorian chant occurs not only in the form of independent monophonic melodies, however, but also as borrowed material in polyphonic music. Evidence of this practice appears in sources of the tenth century, so that eventually polyphony is influenced by many of the traits of chant, including its figures and cadences. We will next explore how the falling-third cadences and especially the 4-3-1 melodic figure emerge in early polyphonic music.

---

[12] There are also simpler melodies with a falling third. The fall from 3 to 1 is sometimes suggested by the tones for readings and prayers. The simplest formula for the office versicles (*LU* 118), for example, commences with a reciting tone on C and falls on the last one or two syllables to A. Although such a chant is too elementary to be reckoned in one of the modes, it does sound, I believe, as though scale degree 3 were being repeated before dropping to 1. See Apel, *Gregorian Chant*, 203–8. Compare with these simple tones the two psalm and canticle tones in which 3 is the reciting pitch: those in mode 2 involving the minor third (*LU* 129 and 208, for example) and those in mode 6 with a major third (*LU* 132 and 211).

Chapter 2

LATE FOURTEENTH- AND EARLY FIFTEENTH-CENTURY POLYPHONY

IT IS AROUND 1400 that falling-third cadences begin to appear with some frequency in polyphony from both England and the Continent. They occur when the falling-third figures are combined with the various elements of polyphonic cadence structure which had developed by the end of the fourteenth century. In earlier Continental music the falling third almost always follows the pitch between the two notes of the third, thus with the shape of 2-3-1, but appearing on other degrees of the scale as well and forming part of the graceful flow of the melody rather than participating in cadence. The same figure occurs also in earlier English music, but far more striking here are those with the shape of 4-3-1.[1] They appear in the Worcester repertory from the late thirteenth to the early fourteenth centuries and in later fourteenth-century sources. In their subtlest form they take the shape of 4-3-1-2, but sometimes they stand out more conspicuously by moving to other pitches, in some cases leaping in the opposite or even the same direction. Usually each note is consonant with the other voices. Occasionally the first (scale degree 4) is dissonant, with the last two belonging to the next chord. In a few striking examples, however, the second note of the figure (scale degree 3, the first note of the falling third) is dissonant. The figure may appear on any degree of the scale and is seldom connected at this time with cadence.[2]

---

[1] According to Philip R. Kaye, in *The "Contenance Angloise" in Perspective: A Study of Consonance and Dissonance in Continental Music, c.1380–1440* (Garland, 1989), 238, the "frequent appearance" of this figure "seems to be an indigenous English trait"; see also 249, 287–8, and 365–7.

[2] For examples of all these variables, see the Sanctus from around 1270 printed as Ex. 4 in the article by Ernest H. Sanders on "Worcester Polyphony" in *NG* xx, 526: figures begin on G at the end of the first line in the top voice, on F a few notes later in the

Cadence Structure Around 1400

Ex. 2.1 shows some of the elements of cadence that had developed before 1400. The basic cadential framework usually consists of two voices pushing from a sixth to an octave (Ex. 2.1a). 2-1 lies below, since this was the usual cadence in the plainchants which often appeared in the tenor. The effect of the 7 in the top voice is sometimes prolonged by lengthening its note value in comparison with those that precede, by repeating it, by circling around it with neighbor notes, or by inserting a 6 before the 1, thus creating an échappée or so-called Landini cadence (b). The 7 itself can be approached by 6 (c) or by 1 (d). Later there is a tendency to emphasize the first 1 in Ex. 2.1d instead of or in addition to a prolonged 7. This 1 can therefore have a longer value and is sometimes associated with the suspension shown in (e). Continuing the tendency to increase the time devoted to cadence, the first 1

Ex. 2.1 Cadential elements around 1400

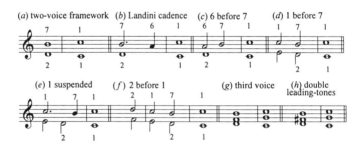

in (d) and (e) can itself be preceded by 2 (f). After 1400 this 2 may also receive additional emphasis. Ex. 2.2a shows how the stream of parallel sixths can expand even further as it falls with the force of gravity toward the final octave on 1.

In addition, Ex. 2.1 also shows how a third voice can be inserted a fourth below the upper (g), sometimes with a sharpened 4 to create a double leading-tone cadence (h). The inner voice from (g) and (h) may then be

middle voice, on G on the second line in the middle voice, and, most striking of all, on G in the middle voice on the last line, where the second note (F) of the figure forms a dissonant seventh interval with the G in the lowest voice and also leaps, after the falling third, another third in the same direction. For other examples from Worcester, see *English Music of the Thirteenth and Early Fourteenth Centuries*, ed. Sanders (*PMFC* xiv). For later examples from the fourteenth century, see *PMFC* xv, xvi, and xvii: the motet, for example, in xv, 114–17.

added above the tenor's 2 also in (a) through (f). If one similarly adds an inner voice a fourth below the top voice in Ex.2.2a, then a series of first-inversion triads results, a texture often employed from the end of the thirteenth century on in the English conductus style.[3]

Around 1400, then, all of these cadential features from the past are occasionally joined by the falling-third figures, which had previously, for the most part, avoided involvement in cadences. Most conspicuous, of course, is 4-3-1, and Ex. 2.2 shows various ways in which the series of sixths in (a) can be modified to include it. The E-flats in parentheses at the beginning of each line indicate that the interval from 3 to 1 may be a major or minor third. (b), (c), and (d) represent an increasing emphasis on 3.

All the notes of 4-3-1 in (b) are consonant. Since the figure lies in the tenor, it is followed by a stepwise movement in the opposite direction to 2; this produces a cambiata-like figure in which 1 seems like an ornament within the stepwise descent from F to D. In (c) all notes of 4-3-1 are again consonant, but now the figure lies in the top voice and moves to 7 rather than 2. In this case the two downward intervals in 4-3-1 are followed by yet another downward step to 7, thus making the 4-3-1 figure more conspicuous. In (d), finally, the 4-3-1-7 movement in the top voice is emphasized even further because 3 is now dissonant against the F below. In all three examples the 1 before 7 is emphasized by a suspension, an emphasis which increases as 1 is leapt to by the falling third (c) and as the first note of the falling third becomes dissonant (d).

There are isolated examples of these cadences even before 1400. Ex. 2.3 from the late thirteenth-century Worcester Fragments follows the model of Ex. 2.2b. There are many chords in first inversion and double leading-tones at the end. Each voice sings the text in this mostly note-against-note conductus style. Interesting for such an early example is the way the melody slows for 2, 1, and 7 in the top voice, joined in this slower movement even by the lowest voice as it reaches 2.

[3] See the article by Sanders on "Cantilena" in *NG* iii, 730, and his Ex. 2a, which includes at the end a series of chords like my Ex. 2.2a with a third voice added between the sixths. See also John Caldwell, *The Oxford History of English Music*, i (OUP, 1991), 47, and his Ex. 14 on 53.

Ex. 2.2 Cadence structures with 4-3-1

Ex. 2.3 4-3-1 cadence from Gloria *c.*1280–90
(*PMFC* xiv, 85, & *HAM* i, No. 57b)

Borrowed Chants

The cadences may have emerged around 1400 because of borrowed chants which contain the figures. I have found two such examples among the earlier pieces of the Old Hall Manuscript, thus probably from the late years of the fourteenth century. The Gloria in Ex. 2.4 places the chant excerpt shown in (*a*) in the tenor (middle voice) of the three-voice setting in (*b*). Since the polyphonic version moves to an internal cadence on C, the figure 2-1-6 in chant becomes 6-5-3 in the tenor, and, when a third voice is added (this time, *below* the tenor), it parallels the tenor in thirds, thus creating 4-3-1 according to the model in Ex. 2.2*b*. In Ex. 2.5, 5-4-2 from a chant Sanctus becomes 4-3-1 in the tenor of a four-voice setting. The voice between the top and tenor is missing in the manuscript; beginning with the second quarter beat of measure 35, however, it no doubt parallels the upper voice a fourth below. If a contratenor had not been added below the tenor, the cadence would probably have resembled Ex. 2.2*b*. With the sustaining of the C below 4 and 3, however, 3 becomes dissonant, forming the interval of the seventh with C. The B or 3 sounds therefore like a leaping passing-tone between C and G. The various modern transcriptions of this passage demonstrate the role of *musica ficta*: in another source the B's in the tenor

Ex. 2.4 2-1-6 figure from Sarum chant Gloria in mode 8 (*OH* iii, 48)
set in polyphony in Old Hall MS (*OH* i, 9)

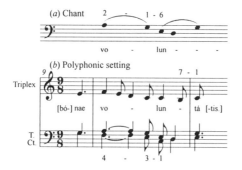

Ex. 2.5 5-4-2 figure from chant Sanctus in mode 5 (*LU* 61)
set in polyphony by Power in Old Hall MS (*OH* i, 358)

are flattened by the editor, producing a minor rather than major third
between 3 and 1.[4]

I have not been able to locate a polyphonic setting which actually
incorporates a 4-3-1 cadence from chant. When the chant is in the tenor, a
cadence such as that in Ex. 1.1 would be required in order to produce the
cadence in Ex. 2.2b. Here 4-3-1 is followed by 2-1.[5] To create cadences
like those in Ex. 2.2c and d, a borrowed chant cadence such as Ex. 1.2 would
have to appear in the top voice. Most of the polyphonic 4-3-1 cadences
seem to emerge independently of the chant *cantus firmus*, but they were
designed, of course, by those who were familiar with the figure from chant
and, in the case of English composers, by those who also knew it from their
own earlier polyphony.

4-3-1 Cadences in the Early Fifteenth Century

Most forceful are those polyphonic cadences in which 4-3-1 precedes 7-1 in
the top voice (Ex. 2.2c and d). Examples appear in the music of both
English and Continental composers. Ex. 2.6a is a cadence by John
Dunstable. Although 3 is consonant, 1 is emphasized not only by the fall
from 3 but also by being repeated and then suspended. 3 is consonant also
in Ex. 2.6b by Bartolomeus Brollo from Italy. In Ex. 2.6c by the English
composer Thomas Damett, however, the 3 on D forms the interval of the
seventh with the sustained E-flat below it, and the cadence concludes,
according to the editor, with double leading-tones. 3 forms the same
dissonance in Ex. 2.6d by the French composer Johannes Legrant; here,
however, 7 rather than 1 is prolonged, in this case by an ornamental form of
the Landini figure in Ex. 2.1b. In Ex. 2.6e by the French composer Estienne
Grossin, 2 appears between 4-3-1 and 7 and tends to soften the effect of the
falling third.

[4] Compare Ex. 2.5 with *The Old Hall Manuscript*, ed. A. Ramsbotham, H. B.
Collins, and Anselm Hughes (Nashdom and London, 1933–38), iii, 77 (printed also in
HAM i, No. 63) in regard to both *musica ficta* and the missing voice.

[5] For a rare example in which the voices in Ex. 2.2b are inverted, see Dunstable's
Sanctus in *MB* viii (revised), 168, m. 95. Here 4-3-1 and 2 are in the upper voice, with 7-
1 below.

Ex. 2.6 4-3-1 in early 15th-century cadences

(*a*) Gloria by Dunstable (*MB* viii, 8)

(*b*) Gloria by Brollo (*EFM* v, 81)

(*c*) Gloria by Damett (*OH* ii, 15)

(*d*) Credo by Legrant (*EFM* ii, 88)

(*e*) Gloria by Grossin (*EFM* iii, 48)

I have located a total of more than fifty 4-3-1 cadences in music from this period. About three-fifths are from English sources, which favor the major third; Continental examples prefer the minor. As we have seen, however, the application of *musica ficta* may, on occasion, alter the pitch of 3. About a quarter of the total have a dissonant 3. In England an equal number have 4-3-1 in the top voice and in the tenor. In Continental cadences about two-thirds favor the top voice. The note preceding 4-3-1 is most often 2 (as in Ex. 2.6*a*, *c*, and *d*), which tends, through the leap from 2 to 4, to make the figure stand out. About equally common, however, are 3 (in Ex. 2.5 and Ex. 2.6*e*) and 5 (Ex. 2.4), both of which move to 4 by step and hence cause 4-3-1 to flow more gently into the melodic line. On rare occasions the preceding note is 1 (Ex. 2.6*b*), an even more dramatic approach than 2.

Ornamental Notes and Rhythm

The precise effect of each 4-3-1 depends also on the note values. Rhythm in this music, as well as for the rest of the fifteenth century, is enormously active. The triple time may imply two groups of three or three groups of two, and the arrangement may be different for each voice, thus creating much syncopation and polyrhythm. The rhythmic relationships between the voices are therefore often complex.

For purposes of illustration, however, I would like to speculate in a tentative way on the effect of rhythm in some of the 4-3-1 cadences. When the preceding note is 2, relatively slow, even notes as in Ex. 2.6*a* may cause the notes 3-2-4-3 to relate together in such a way that 2 and 4 seem like changing notes. In Ex. 2.6*c*, the movement between the two B-flats makes 2 and 3 sound like leaping passing-tones. In (*d*) the shorter notes on 4 and 3 cause 3 to act again as a passing tone. When 3 precedes 4-3-1, the 4 may seem like an upper neighbor (Ex. 2.6*e*, where 2-3-4-3 forms a sort of inverted turn), or slow note values may deprive the preceding 3 of any immediately perceived association with the following note (Ex. 2.5). In Ex. 2.6*b*, the 1 preceding 4 sounds more like an échappée between 2 and 4; the sixteenth notes also seem to throw 4 up into the air so that it can fall more energetically onto 3. In Ex. 2.4, where 5 precedes, the broad swing of melody seems to be the stepwise movement 5-4-3-2-3, in which 1 is an ornamental note between the two 3's. The tremendous energy in the rhythm of this music was no doubt accompanied by an appropriately vigorous manner of performance, especially since most polyphony at this time was still sung by soloists.

The Text

It is not quite so clear what role the text may play. Syllables were not assigned very carefully to specific notes before the late sixteenth century. Furthermore, in many cases the syllables change so seldom that they seem to have little rhythmic impact (as in Ex. 2.4 or 2.5, for example). In Ex. 2.7*a*, as a matter of fact, the text in both voices is completed before the music in the excerpt. In Ex. 2.3, however, the accented syllable of *celéstis* coincides with longer note values. The way the syllables are placed in the upper voice of Ex. 2.6*a* makes the figure 4-3-1 stand out, then adds accentuation to the following suspended 1 by means of the accented syllable of *Dóminus* and the vigorous sound of the letter "*D*." In Ex. 2.6*b* the accented first syllable of *pátris* adds an explosive accentuation with the letter "*p*," which strengthens the rhythmic effect of the note values.[6]

All of the examples in this chapter involve *solo* polyphony, so that each line is executed by a solo performer. Some scholars feel that the two lower lines in works such as those in Exx. 2.6*b*, 2.6*d*, and 2.7*b*, should be played by instruments, presumably two solo instruments of contrasting tone quality. There is growing evidence, however, that medieval polyphony, whether secular or sacred, was performed only by singers.[7] In this case each solo singer would project a distinctive personality which would contrast markedly with the sounds of the other singers. This is part of the medieval

---

[6] All voices sing the same text in Exx. 2.3, 2.4, 2.6*c*, and 2.7*a*. In Ex. 2.5 all have the same text except the textless contratenor. Only the top voice has a text in Exx. 2.6*b*, 2.6*d*, and 2.7*b*. Each of the upper voices has its own text in Ex. 2.9, and the tenor is without text.

[7] In *Performance Practice: Music before 1600*, ed. Howard Mayer Brown and Stanley Sadie (New York: Norton, 1990), see Brown's "Introduction," 3; Christopher Page's "Polyphony before 1400," 90–99; and David Fallows's "Secular Polyphony in the Fifteenth Century," 209–12 and 218 n. 24. See also Christopher Page, "The English *a cappella* Heresy" in *Companion to Medieval and Renaissance Music*, ed. Tess Knighton and David Fallows (New York: Schirmer Books, 1992), 23–9.

ideal of emphasizing the differences between contrapuntal lines.[8] Such a solo method of performance tends to cause the musical elements in individual lines, including the falling-third figures, to stand out with unusual clarity.

Ex. 2.7 2-3-1 in early 15th-century cadences

(*a*) Ballata by Zacharie (*EFM* vi, 138)

(*b*) Rondeau by Libert (?) (*EFM* iv, 36)

Other Cadential Figures

In addition to the 4-3-1 cadences, there are a few, especially in Continental sources, based on 2-3-1. They may likewise have a major or minor third, and the 3 may be consonant or dissonant. In Ex. 2.7a the figure follows scale degree 1, but 3 seems like an échappée between E and D as the music moves in a series of parallel sixths in the manner shown in Ex. 2.2a. 3 precedes 2-3-1 in the texted upper voice of Ex. 2.7b, where 2 seems to be a neighbor note prolonging 3 (the B-flat) as the latter becomes a stunning dissonance against the A below it; the rhythm is brisk and ends with a snappy Landini figure. 2-3-1 is always in the top voice, probably because the 2 and 3 above 1 form a pleasing circular motion with the succeeding 7 below. The resulting 2-3-1-7-1 thus matches the chant cadence in Ex. 1.6.

---

[8] See my article "A Theory of Alternating Attitudes in the Construction of Western Polyphony," *The Music Review* 34 (1973): 221–30.

There are only a few cadences incorporating the 5-3-1 figure. Ex. 2.8 shows one in which 5-3-1 is in the tenor and 7-1 in the upper voice. Perhaps more conspicuous here is the 1-7-5 figure which accompanies 5 and 3 and which is followed by a leap and not a step in the opposite direction. This illustrates the fact that these figures still appear abundantly in the music even outside of the cadence and on any scale degree.

Ex. 2.8 5-3-1 cadence in a Credo by Dunstable
(*MB* viii, 29)

Ex. 2.9 1-7-5 by Hymbert de Salinis
(*EFM* vii, 65) (text omitted)

The figure of the falling third preceded by a descending step occurs now almost as frequently in Continental sources as in those from England. Ex. 2.9 by a Franco-Flemish composer shows that the middle note of such a figure on another scale degree (1-7-5 in this case) can be dissonant just as 3 can in 4-3-1. When 4 is sharpened as a second leading tone moving to 5, it can sometimes be treated just like 7-1: that is, it may be preceded by a note that relates to it as 4-3-1 and may be followed by a Landini figure. The melody in the middle voice of Ex. 2.9 is thus exactly a fourth below the 4-3-1-7-1 which could, as we have seen, appear in the top voice.

$$* \quad * \quad * \quad * \quad *$$

Scale degree 3 is most assertive when it occurs in the upper voice, when it is dissonant with a note below, when it is preceded by 4, when it falls a major third to 1, and when 1 is followed directly by 7. The effect can be enhanced to some extent, by the note which precedes 4, by the rhythm of the notes, and by the placement, accentuation, and pronunciation of the text. 3 is therefore most effective when the complete progression 4-3-1-7-1, as it appears in the chant cadence in Ex. 1.2, lies in the top voice. On other occasions, as we have seen in Exx. 2.4 and 2.5, this progression is broken into two pieces, as it were, so that 4-3-1 appears in a lower voice with 7-1 above.

The falling third preceded by a step above thus adds to the music of the time a special flavor, as do the Landini figure and the double leading-tone. All three of these melodic devices are generally strange to modern ears, and they can all occur equally at cadence or elsewhere. Although the double leading-tones survive only until about 1450, the Landini figure continues until around 1520 and the falling thirds even longer. Thus we will continue to meet the last two devices as we turn now to the music of Dufay, Ockeghem, Josquin, and Palestrina, and to the period between 1450 and 1600.

Chapter 3

POLYPHONY FROM DUFAY TO PALESTRINA

THE FALLING THIRDS continue to be used freely until 1520 and then, for the remainder of the century, are subjected to certain restrictions. The falling-third figures occur in new and increasingly complex ways. Sometimes they are repeated or combined together. Sometimes they appear in new locations within an expanded cadential structure.

The Falling Thirds Preceding 7-1

The falling-third figures all appear abundantly in the music of Guillaume Dufay. Often he combines them with syncopated triple rhythm and a series of first-inversion triads to produce cadences with the framework of Ex. 2.2*b*, *c*, or *d*. Many of them are similar to those in Ex. 2.6*a–d*.[1] He also inserts scale degree 2 occasionally between 4-3-1 and 7 in the top voice, as in Ex. 2.6*e*; sometimes the 2 is emphasized by greater length or some other type of accentuation.

   More complex, however, are examples in which several falling-third figures, on the same or different scale degrees, are joined together as in Ex. 3.1. (*a*) is a fauxbourdon in which only the two outer voices are notated, the third voice to be added a fourth below the upper. The resulting series of chords in first inversion reminds us of the English practice seen in Ex. 2.3.

   In Ex. 3.1*a* an ornamental 6 intervenes between 4-3-1 and 7-1 in the upper voice and 3 is consonant. In addition, the falling third in the top voice

---

[1] See especially the sequences, hymns, and Magnificats in *DO* v, and the secular works in vi.

is accompanied by the same figure on different pitches in the other two voices. By following the upper voice exactly, the inner one forms 1-7-5, the

Ex. 3.1 4-3-1 cadences by Dufay

(*a*) Fauxbourdon from *Magnificat 8. toni* (*DO* v, 83)

(*b*) Sequence *Victimae paschali laudes* (*DO* v, 11)

(*c*) Italian song *Vergene bella* (*DO* vi, 9)

(*d*) Hymn *Hostis Herodes impie* (*DO* v, 43)

(*e*) *Magnificat 5. toni* (*DO* v, 89)

lower one 6-5-3. The first note of the falling third is consonant in the two outer voices, but dissonant, because of the suspension, in the other.

In Ex. 3.1*b*, 4-3-1 in the top voice is imitated, except for the length of the opening D, by the inner voice an eighth beat later. The 3 in the upper voice is dissonant with the D below, whereas the 3 in the inner voice is consonant. In Ex. 3.1*c*, 4-3-1 is incorporated into a melodic sequence following 6-5-3 and 5-4-2. In (*d*) the two statements of 4-3-1 in the outer voices are in imitation a quarter beat apart and each is preceded by the same figure on a different pitch. In (*e*), 2-3-1 in the upper voice moves to 7 while 4-3-1 moves to 2 in the lowest voice; 1-7-5 in the inner part goes to a sharpened 4 to form double leading-tones with the upper voice and a Landini figure doubled in fourths.

Ex. 3.2 4-3-1 cadence by Josquin from *Missa Pange lingua*,
end of first Kyrie (*JW* xxxiii, 1)

The high point of this sort of complexity seems to occur in a late work by Josquin Desprez (d. 1521). Ex. 3.2 shows the long approach to cadence at the end of the first Kyrie in the *Missa Pange lingua*. Both the top voice and the tenor present multiple statements of 4-3-1, with the first two in each case forming overlapping pairs with the other voice. Thus in both measures 13 and 14, 4-3-1 in the top voice overlaps with another 4-3-1 in the tenor. Similarly, the alto and bass each have two or three statements of 7-6-4, with the first and last in each voice making an overlapping pair in measures 13 and 15. In addition, the upper voice concludes and the tenor begins with 5-4-2. Twelve of the figures are thus included in this passage, which generates enormous power through the ostinato effect in the single lines and the imitative action within pairs of voices. This excerpt illustrates Josquin's special interest in voice pairs and in motivic repetition.[2]

---

[2] See Howard Mayer Brown, *Music in the Renaissance* (Englewood Cliffs, NJ: Prentice-Hall, Inc., 1976), 143: "Some motives in the Mass are repeated over and over

Ex. 3.2 also demonstrates the great freedom with which the figures are used. The falling third is major in each 4-3-1 and 7-6-4, but minor in 5-4-2.[3] Scale degree 3 is dissonant in each 4-3-1, as is 6 in each 7-6-4; 4, however, is consonant in each 5-4-2. 2 appears before every 4-3-1; 7-6-4 is approached, however, by 1, 5, or 6, 5-4-2 by 3 or 4.[4] 4-3-1 moves three times to 2, most importantly in measure 15, where it forms a sixth with the top voice, which pushes outward to the octave in measure 16. The other two times, however, 4-3-1 leaps up a third.

The Falling Thirds Following 7-1

Over the course of years cadences tended to expand in length.[5] They sometimes occupy more time before reaching the structural 7 and 2 which resolve to the octave. They often involve a suspension of 2 as in the upper voice in Ex. 3.6a, which resolves to 1 with an anticipation on a short beat in the same way that 7 seems to anticipate itself in Ex. 3.1e. This cadence becomes standard around the time of Josquin, with isolated examples occurring even early in the fifteenth century. Cadences also expand in the other direction, with music continuing on occasion even after the 7 and 2 have resolved. In addition, the 7 and 2 are often accompanied by the scale degree 5 below. This practice begins when the third voice leaps up an octave on 5, as in Ex. 3.1b. During the second half of the fifteenth century this leads to movement in the contratenor from 5 to 1, thus creating the sound of a dominant chord, which becomes itself, of course, an important feature of cadence.

again, a procedure that Josquin customarily adopted to build up a powerful drive to the cadence."

[3] Some editors, however, flatten all the B's, in response, I suppose, to the notated B-flat in m. 14. In this case the third interval in 4-3-1 would, of course, be minor.

[4] The pitches that precede the two figures which begin on the first beat of m. 13 are not actually included in Ex. 3.2.

[5] It may be useful here to define the starting point of a cadence more precisely as that moment when the listener is first aware that he is hearing musical events which he has heard often enough in the past to associate with the approaching conclusion of a musical unit. Such events may be melodic, harmonic, or rhythmic in nature.

Ex. 3.3 4-3-1 after 7 in Power's *Anima mea* (*PC* i, 37)

Exx. 3.3 and 3.4*a* present early fifteenth-century excerpts in which 4-3-1 appears later than usual. In Power's cadence in Ex. 3.3, 4-3-1 follows 7, and its 1 coincides with the resolution of 7 to 1. In Ex. 3.4*a* by the French composer Gilet Velut, 4-3-1 occurs even later, commencing only when 7 moves with the Landini figure to 1. Both examples are brief internal cadences in which 7 is in the lower voice. With the 4-3-1 followed in each case by a rest, the upper voices seem very much like the chant cadences shown in Ex. 1.3*a–e*.

Ex. 3.4 4-3-1 after the final I

(*a*) Motet by Velut (*EFM* ii, 141)

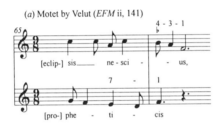

(*b*) Dufay sequence *Rex omnipotens* (*DO* v, 15)

(*c*) Palestrina, *Missa Papae Marcelli*, end of Kyrie (*PO* iv, 171), 1567

Ex. 3.4b shows a far longer extension by Dufay. Following a 5-3-1 figure in the lowest voice, 7 and 2 resolve as usual to 1 at the beginning of measure 51 The music continues, however, with 4-3-1 in the top voice imitated by the lower in a brief plagal dialogue. After both 4-3-1 figures have reached 1, the inner voice provides a final 1-7-5 in which 7 is dissonant and 5 does not move to another note.

In the Palestrina cadence in Ex. 3.4c the harmonic aspect becomes even more conspicuous. In this six-voice setting the structural framework involves 7 (in the top voice in measure 74) and 2 in the second tenor (the D on the third beat of the same measure) both moving to 1 at the beginning of measure 75, as well as the V chord of measure 74 resolving gradually to the I chord in measure 75. This I chord is then prolonged by the IV chord in measure 76, which supports the 4-3-1 figure, moving this time to 2 before resolving finally to 3 in the final I chord in measure 77.

On other occasions the 1 to which the structural 7 and 2 resolve may be accompanied by some lower note other than 1, such as 4, 6, or 3. This creates a deceptive cadence which constitutes a plagal delay of the final I chord. In Ex. 3.5a Dufay resolves 7 to 1 on the last quarter beat of measure 16. 2 in this case is missing, but the D in the lowest voice creates the expectancy of a v-I movement, which is briefly interrupted by the plagal effect of the 4-3-1.[6]

In the cadence by Ockeghem in (b), 7 and 2 at the beginning of measure 216 move to 1 on the last beat. On this beat, however, the 1's are not supported by another A in the voice below, but by a D. This deceptive chordal movement leads to a plagal delay which again concludes with 4-3-1 in the bass.

Far more extensive and complex is the delay in Obrecht's cadence in (c). Here 7 and 2 arrive at 1 on the first beat of measure 109, but the chord is not I but vi. The harmonies circle around IV for two measures before finally reaching I at the beginning of measure 111. In the process the alto voice sings 4-3-1 with a dissonant 3, followed by 7 and a Landini 6 before resolving to 1. The bass repeats 4-3-1, accompanied in the top voice by 6-5-3, and an unusual dissonant combination occurs on the last eighth beat of measure 110. Finally, after the I chord has appeared in measure 111, the alto continues (as in Ex. 3.4b) with the figure 1-7-5.

---

[6] I have added the editorial flat below the E on the last beat of m. 16.

During the first half of the Renaissance, then, the falling-third figures are employed with complete freedom and with increasing complexity both before and following the main structural parts of the cadence. 4-3-1 may appear in any voice, have a major or minor third, have a dissonant or consonant 3, be preceded by 2, 3, 5, 1, or a rest, and be followed by a step or a leap in either direction or even by the rest at the end of a section or composition. The same characteristics apply generally to the numerous examples outside of the cadences. They occur so often that they contribute significantly, it seems to me, to the unique style of the period.

Ex. 3.5 4-3-1 in a plagal delay

(a) Dufay, sequence *Rex omnipotens* (*DO* v, 13)

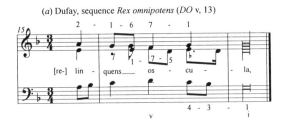

(b) Ockeghem, *Credo sine nomine* (*OC* ii, 64)

(c) Obrecht, *Missa Je ne demande*, Credo (*ON* v, 51)

The Late Renaissance

In medieval music there was, as mentioned in the last chapter, a special interest in the individual lines, which were composed separately, and in differentiating them from one another when combined in polyphony. The Renaissance ideal, on the other hand, was just the opposite: a special interest in what voices do together and a desire to make them like one another in polyphony. The change happened gradually during the period between around 1450 and 1520.

The rhythm changed from complex triple (as in Exx. 3.1 and 3.2) to a more solemn duple (Exx. 3.4c and 3.5c). A chorus superseded soloists in the performance of sacred works, probably a smaller one in Dufay's works in Ex. 3.1, a larger one by the time of Josquin's mass in Ex. 3.2. Instruments could also play along with the voices in works after the time of Ockeghem. If more than one were employed, then they would all be similar to each other in tone quality, so that no single part would sound conspicuously different from the others. *A cappella* performance is associated with Palestrina, and his excerpt in Ex. 3.4c illustrates the trend toward an increase in the number of voices. All voices gradually become equal in activity and all sing the same text, although still in rhythmic counterpoint. The effects of the pronunciation and accentuation of text described for the earlier period thus diminish considerably when several voices sing each line, when instruments join in, when the number of voices increases, and when different voices sing different syllables at the same time.[7] Only in the familiar style, in which voices become like one another rhythmically, can the subtle nuances of text become somewhat more audible.

The chief way in which voices become like one another during the Renaissance, of course, is through imitation. We have seen 4-3-1 imitated between voices in Exx. 3.1b and d, 3.2, 3.4b, and 3.5c. Ordinarily, however, the falling thirds, like the Landini figure, are melodic motives which occur in a single line and cause that line to appear different from the other voices at that moment. Later Renaissance composers tended in general to avoid those devices that would attract attention to a single line—such devices, for example, as ostinato or melodic sequence. They no doubt felt that the most striking of the falling-third figures—those with a dissonant 3 or those followed by a leap, a step in the same direction, or a rest—were too

---

[7] In Ex. 3.4c, for example, each voice sings the syllables of *eleison* at different times, and the second tenor (the one with 4-3-1) sings the full text "*Kyrie eleison.*" The same thing happens in Ex. 3.8.

conspicuous to blend easily into the melodic flow. At the same time there was a general trend to regulate the treatment of dissonance in order to create the feeling of endlessly flowing counterpoint.

Ex. 3.6 Figures with the two-fold suspension formula

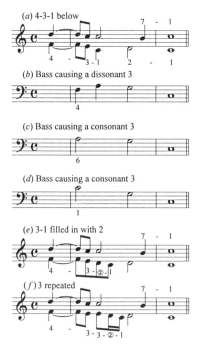

By the time of Palestrina fixed rules governed the behavior of dissonances. They must observe certain note values and must usually be approached and left by step. The only exception is the cambiata, in which the descending second followed by the falling third is itself generally followed by a step in the opposite direction. Occasionally this last note is preceded by a note a step higher.[8] Such figures may occur anywhere in the

[8] See Knud Jeppesen's *Counterpoint: The Polyphonic Vocal Style of the Sixteenth Century*, trans. by Glen Haydon (New York: Prentice-Hall, Inc., 1939), 32, 125, 144–8 (on p. 145 he shows the ancestor of the cambiata as the figure 1-7-5 at the end of a cadence by Obrecht); and *The Style of Palestrina and the Dissonance*, trans. Margaret Hamerik, 2nd. edn. by Edward J. Dent (OUP, 1946; repr., Mineola, NY: Dover Publications, Inc., 1970, 2005), 209-21. For a different point of view, see Carl Dahlhaus, "Die 'Nota Cambiata,'" *Kirchenmusikalisches Jahrbuch* 47 (1963), 115-21.

music, on any scale degree, and with a consonant or dissonant second note. Often, however, 4-3-1, followed now almost always by 2 (or rarely by 3 and 2), occurs at cadences. Ex. 3.6a shows the framework of parallel sixths, most often in the top voice and tenor, which had become a standard feature by the time of Josquin. The upper voice contains two suspensions in succession to provide double braking power to slow the music as it approaches closure. The first suspension is released through a rhythmic anticipation of 1; the second lasts longer and flows more smoothly to the final 1. Ex. 3.6b, c, and d show bass-lines that can occur below (a), producing a dissonant 3 when (a) and (b) are combined, a consonant 3 when (c) or (d) appear with (a).

Ex. 3.7 Palestrina, *Missa Inviolata*, Gloria (*PO* iv, 32), 1567

Ex. 3.7 shows 4-3-1 in its typical location in the tenor voice, followed later by 7-1 in the top, as in Ex. 3.6a. The bass voice follows Ex. 3.6c, in which the 6 is consonant with the tenor's 3. The alto voice parallels the tenor with a 6-5-3 figure, and in this case the 6 in the bass causes 5 to be dissonant and thus requires that the figure be followed by a step in the opposite direction, which is 4. If this 4 is sharpened, then we have a "double" cadence in which the sixth formed by D in the bass and B-natural in the alto push to octave C's just before the 7 and 2 push in turn to their octave on F. In this example, the 4-3-1 is not required to circle to 2 in order to justify a dissonance. It does move to 2, however, to provide the cadential framework of 7 and 2 which can expand to the octave. This had happened previously when 4-3-1 was in the lowest voice and 7 was on top, as in Ex. 2.2b: see Ex. 2.3 from the end of the thirteenth century, Ex. 2.4 from the late fourteenth century, and Ex. 3.1e from the fifteenth.

Before 1520, however, many (and perhaps most) 4-3-1 cadences contained both 4-3-1 and 7-1 in the upper voice, the most conspicuous location possible (see Exx. 2.6 and 3.1). There was thus a long tradition of hearing 4-3-1-7-1 as an unbroken cadential figure. It was only later in the sixteenth century, with composers such as Palestrina, that this melodic progression is regularly broken into two parts, with 7-1 on the top and 4-3-1 moving to 2 below. Only in a few cases, such as Ex. 3.8, are the parts reversed, with 4-3-1 in the top voice and 7 and 1 below. This example also illustrates the less usual resolution of the dissonant 3, which, following the falling third, moves back to 3 before descending to 2 of the cadential framework.

Ex. 3.8 Palestrina, *Missa Ecce sacerdos magnus*, Sanctus (*PO* i, 23), 1554

The 4-3-1 figure was largely confined finally to a particular cadential location in which it must be followed by a specific note. It was thus made to conform to the rules of gentle contrapuntal flow. It could also appear, as we have seen in Ex. 3.4*c*, in cadential extensions, but subject to the same rules of dissonance. The figure could also be dealt with, however, by destroying it. Ex. 3.6*e* shows how easily this could be accomplished: by simply inserting a 2 between the notes of the falling third. This pleasing stepwise progression appears often in late Renaissance cadences. Also frequent is the variant in (*f*), in which 3 is again made conspicuous, but this time by repeating it in sixths with the upper voice and by following it with a sixteenth-note figure.

It is perhaps remarkable, then, that in spite of the popularity of the figures in Ex. 3.6*e* and *f*, the 4-3-1 cadences did continue to thrive and in considerable number.[9] Occasionally 2-3-1 and 5-3-1 could be used in the

[9] For this study I have surveyed a selected group of thirty masses by Palestrina (d. 1594) which were published between 1554 and 1601.

same way, but it was 4-3-1 that was most frequent, because it fit so well into the melodic, harmonic, and rhythmic structure of the late Renaissance cadence.

*   *   *   *   *

The carefully controlled counterpoint of the late sixteenth century marks the end of the first long period in the life of the falling-third figures and the falling-third cadences. Beginning many centuries earlier in monophonic Gregorian chant, they follow chant into polyphonic music and continue to thrive and change as polyphony itself evolves through the course of several centuries. They also continue into the recitative of the seventeenth century, but in ways so new and different that we seem to be dealing here with a separate and distinct period of development.

Part II

THE FALLING-THIRD CADENCES

IN

RECITATIVE

Chapter 4

MONODY AND RECITATIVE IN THE SEVENTEENTH CENTURY

THE FALLING-THIRD CADENCES continued to be heard in Baroque church music in two ways familiar from the past: in Gregorian chant and in the tenor parts of cadences in the *stile antico*. The latter was a modified Palestrina style considered ideal for sacred music and codified finally by Fux in 1725 in his *Gradus ad Parnassum*. Far more conspicuous, however, was the rebirth of the falling thirds in the new styles, especially in the monody and recitative of the opera, cantata, and oratorio.[1] Most of the composers of this new style were Italians brought up in the Catholic church. They were thus familiar with chant and with the music of Palestrina, whose style they learned as part of their education. Many participated themselves as church musicians. When they fashioned a new musical language for a solo voice accompanied by a *basso continuo*, however, they may have been influenced most, although perhaps subconsciously, by monophonic chant—by its recurring figures and cadences and by the speech-like delivery and many repeated notes in the office psalms and canticles.[2]

---

[1] I use the word "monody" to refer to the more or less continuous music for solo voice and continuo in the earlier operas and other forms, and "recitative" when the declamatory style appears in sections separate from the arias in the numbers opera which crystallizes finally around the mid-1670s.

[2] Concerning the continuing influence of Palestrina and his contemporaries on the music of succeeding centuries, see Karl Gustav Fellerer, *Der Palestrinastil und seine Bedeutung in der vokalen Kirchenmusik des achtzehnten Jahrhunderts*: *Ein Beitrag zur Geschichte der Kirchenmusik in Italien und Deutschland* (Augsburg: Dr. Benno Filser Verlag, 1929; repr., Walluf bei Wiesbaden: Dr. Martin Sändig, 1972). Regarding the relationship between the falsobordone and early Baroque monody, see Theodor Göllner, "Falsobordone-Anklänge in Prologen und Auftritten der frühen Oper," *Bericht über den internationalen musikwissenschaftlichen Kongress Bonn 1970* (Bärenreiter, 1971), 179–

The Development of Cadential Types 1600–1675

The new vocal cadences move at first, as in chant, from 2 to 1. The 2 bears the accented syllable and is emphasized musically by greater length, as in Ex. 4.2*a*, or by other means. Only occasionally do cadences end with 7-1.[3] At the same time, the endings in Ex. 4.1*a* and *b*, later called "quasi closes" by Marpurg,[4] emerge to conclude briefer internal phrases.

Ex. 4.1 The quasi closes

These incorporate the falling-third figure and repeated 1's, the first of which accommodates the accented syllable. The 1's are usually followed by a rest. A dominant chord begins with or before the 2 in Ex. 4.1*a* or the 4 in Ex. 4.1*b* and resolves to a I chord precisely with the first 1 in the voice. Either the V or I chord may be in root position or first inversion. Ex. 4.1*a*, which can be compared to the chant cadence in Ex. 1.4*d*, occurs most frequently at first, probably because it can be interpreted as a 2-1 cadence in

---

82; and John Bettley, "North Italian *Falsobordone* and its Relevance to the Early *Stile Recitativo,*" *Proceedings of the Royal Musical Association* 103 (1976–77): 1–18.

[3] See Jacopo Peri, *Le musiche sopra l'Euridice* (Florence, 1600), facs. by Enrico Magni Dufflocq (Rome: Reale Accademia d'Italia, 1934), for many examples of 2-1 cadences. He also uses a great variety of other cadences, including some on 7-1: p. 12 on *ridenti*, for example.

[4] Friedrich Wilhelm Marpurg, *Kritische Briefe über die Tonkunst*, ii (Berlin, 1763; repr., Hildesheim: Georg Olms Verlag, 1974), 357–60, from the issue for 11 September 1762, section 92 entitled "Von den ordentlichen Absätzen oder Quasischlüssen im Recitativ."

which 3 is an échappée.[5]   Starting around 1640, the phrase in Ex. 4.1*b* (compare the chant cadence in Ex. 1.3*f*) appears occasionally, but less frequently than the other.[6] Even less often one can eventually find similar endings with the melodic progressions 5-3-1-1, 7-3-1-1, and 1-3-1-1.

Also around 1640, the repeated-3 cadence in Ex. 4.2*b* appears in both Rome and Venice, accompanied by the basso continuo and its realization shown on the two staves below.[7] This is still a 2-1 cadence, but 2 has been weakened in two ways: first of all, it no longer has the accented syllable, and, secondly, it sings the final unaccented syllable on a comparatively short note-value which is slurred to the final 1.   This method of treating an unaccented syllable had occurred even earlier on a different pitch, somewhat like Ex. 4.3*a*.[8]   In Ex. 4.2*b*, however, it is 3 which dominates—by accompanying the accented syllable, by greater length, and by being anticipated by another 3 on a shorter note (see Ex. 3.6*f* for an earlier example of 3 anticipating itself). The first 3 is dissonant with the root of the IV chord, the second 3 with the D in the realization. Sometimes a simple V chord without a 4 3 suspension accompanies the second 3, in which case 3 is dissonant also with the third of the chord. Some early sources from both Rome and Venice show a trill on the second 3, a feature that may have been applied later, even when not marked, as a matter of performance practice.[9]

---

[5] Peri, *Euridice*, p. 16 on "nell'altrui braccia," and p. 24 on "sfogasse al quanto."

[6] The earliest I have found, with both chords in root position, are in Cavalli's *Didone* of 1641, Act III, sc. ii, mm. 3 and 8 in Glixon, 301.

[7] Note that the 4 and 3 in the basso continuo part of this and other examples are not melodic numbers like those above the vocal melodies, but part of the figured bass, showing intervals above the root of the dominant chord: thus "4 3" in the figured bass represents scale degrees 1 and 7 in the realization (see the explanation in the Preface).

[8] In Peri's *Euridice*, the placing of text seems to make an unaccented 7 on the last syllable of *ridenti* on p. 12, but not on *desio* on p. 35. Stefano Landi makes the unaccented note clear with a slur in *Il Sant'Alessio* of around 1631; see the published version (Rome, 1634; repr., Bologna: Forni, 1970), Act I, sc. i, p. 30 on *foglia*.

[9] The earliest example I know of Ex. 4.2*b* occurs in *L'Egisto* or *Chi soffre speri* by Virgilio Mazzocchi and Marco Marazzoli in 1637; see Act I, sc. ii, printed in Murata, 264. A trill is marked in Luigi Rossi's *Il palazzo incantato* of 1642 in Act I, sc. i (facs. in *IOB* ii, 12ᵛ) and Francesco Sacrati's *La finta pazza* of 1641 (printed in Rosand, 466). This may be the trill which Tosi thought should be on 2 instead of 3: see Pier Francesco Tosi, *Opinioni de' cantori antichi e moderni, o sieno Osservazioni sopra il canto figurato* (Bologna, 1723), facs. as sup. to repr. (Celle: Hermann Moeck, 1966) of Johann Friedrich Agricola's German trans. in *Anleitung zur Singkunst* (Berlin, 1757), 84–5. See also the English trans. by John Ernest Galliard in *Observations on the Florid Song*, 2nd edn. (London: J. Wilcox, 1743), copy in the Special Collections of the UCLA Music Library;

Usually 4 is preceded by 6 as shown in Ex. 4.2*b*, but sometimes by 2 or less often 5. There seems to be a particular interest, in general, in 6 against a IV chord falling somehow to 3 or 2 over a V chord before moving finally to I and 1.

Ex. 4.2 2-1 cadences

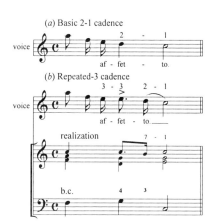

During the first half of the century or so another family of cadences was developing. These are shown in Ex. 4.3*a*, *b*, and *c*. They seem to combine ideas from the other cadences. Ex. 4.3*b* seems to join the 2-3-1 in Ex. 4.1*a* with the unaccented rhythm of Ex. 4.2*b*. In the same way, the 4-3-1 from Ex. 4.1*b* precedes the unaccented figure to produce the cadence in Ex. 4.3*c*. In each case, both 3 and the following 1 are dissonant, the first with the IV chord, the other with V. In comparison with Ex. 4.2*b*, the cadence in Ex. 4.3*c* seems to have simply lowered the fourth and fifth notes in order to change the ending from 2-1 to 7-1. Ex. 4.3*b* and *c* are both cadences with the accented syllable on the 1 preceding 7. The 7 is weakened both musically and textually, whereas the preceding 1 has greater strength because of its longer note value and the effect of the descending leap which precedes it.

modern edn. with almost identical paging (London: William Reeves, 1926), 132–3 and Nos. 6 and 7 on Plate V.

Occasionally other falling-third figures occur in the same construction, with 1-3-1, 7-3-1, or 5-3-1 preceding 7-1.[10] We have already

Ex. 4.3 Cadences in late 17th-century recitative

[10] Ex. 4.3*b* appears in Peri's *Euridice* of 1600, p. 10 on "le voci ei pianti" (the "*ti*" is printed below the 7); other examples are in L. Rossi's *Il palazzo incantato* of 1642 (*IOB* ii, 33ᵛ) and in Claudio Monteverdi's *L'incoronazione di Poppea* of 1642, modern edn. by Alan Curtis (London: Novello, 1989), 82. For Ex. 4.3*c*, see Rossi, *Il palazzo* again, 83ᵛ in Act II, sc. vi, and Cavalli's *Doriclea* of 1645 (Rosand, 642). For 1-3-1 at the beginning, see Landi's *Il Sant'Alessio*, Act I, sc. iii, 42; for 7-3-1, Cavalli's *La Statira* from 1655 or 56, Act I, sc. xv (Glixon, p. 345, mm. 7–8); and for 5-3-1, Cavalli's *Ormindo* of 1644, Act III, sc. iv (Glixon, p. 332, mm. 128–30).

noted similar results in some earlier cadences from the fifteenth century: compare Ex. 4.3*c* with the cadences in Exx. 2.6 and 3.1*a–d*, and Ex. 4.3*b* with those in Ex. 2.7. These earlier cadences were not known, of course, to the Baroque opera composers, so there is no possibility of direct influence.

Each of the cadences on the left side of Ex. 4.3 is also subjected to the remarkable transformation on the right. In comparison to (*b*) the cadence in (*e*) has broken the voice part of (*b*) into two parts: the 2-3-1 remains in the voice, while 7-1 moves to the continuo realization on the staff below. An additional 1 is added in the voice for the final unaccented syllable, producing the melody of Ex. 4.1*a*, with the word accent again on the first 1. Far more frequent in this group of cadences, however, is Ex. 4.3*f*, created by keeping 4-3-1 from (*c*) in the voice, adding another 1 as in Ex. 4.1*b*, and moving the weak 7-1 ending to the continuo realization. In this way the rhythm of Ex. 4.3*c* is preserved in Ex. 4.3*f*, even though the melody has now been divided between the voice and an instrument.[11] In both (*e*) and (*f*) the dissonant 3 resolves to another dissonance on the 1's, and this dissonance finds resolution finally in the 7 of the realization. In Venice the first of the two repeated notes at the end of the voice part in Exx. 4.1*a* and *b* and 4.3*d–f* is occasionally dotted, thus giving a longer duration to the accented syllable.[12]

I have also added the corresponding downward-fourth cadences in Ex. 4.3*a* and *d* and the related cadence in Ex. 4.1*c*. They do not include the falling third, but they involve a similar construction and become enormously popular. In the downward-fourth cadence in Ex. 4.3*d* the first 5 in the voice was often but, as we will see later, not always replaced by 1, as shown to the right. This 1 then acted as an appoggiatura on the accented syllable. Some composers make the method of performance clear by notating the pitches as sung.[13]

---

[11] There are examples of Ex. 4.3*f* in Cavalli's *Erismena* from 1655, Act III, sc. xvi (Glixon, p. 367, mm. 42–3), and Antonio Cesti's *L'Argia* of 1655, Act II, sc. ii (*IOB* iii, 59ᵛ). The latter source also contains on 81ᵛ an example of Ex. 4.3*e*.

[12] See Cesti's *L'Argia* of 1655 (*IOB* iii, 13ᵛ, for example) and *La Dori* of 1661 (*IOB* lxiii, 50ᵛ, 69ᵛ, and 106ᵛ), or Antonio Sartorio's *L'Adelaide* of 1672 (*IOB* viii, 18ᵛ, 100ᵛ, etc.).

[13] For an example of Ex. 4.3*a*, see Peri's *Euridice*, p. 12 on *ridenti*. Ex. 4.3*d* appears in Cesti's *L'Argia* (*IOB* iii, 13ᵛ) on "il pensiero," with the last two notes of the voice part notated as two 5's. As far as I know, however, the earliest example of Ex. 4.1*c* occurs in A. Scarlatti's opera *La Statira* of 1690; see *OAS* ix, p. 122 (m. 4 in No. 69) and p. 129 (m. 2 of No. 71). It may not be coincidental that this is also the earliest opera available to me in which Scarlatti began notating Ex. 4.3*d* cadences with 1-1-5 rather than 1-5-5.

The cadences in Ex. 4.3*d*, *e*, and *f* all allow the voice to finish sooner and thus make way for another character to enter with the I chord in the accompaniment. This presumably permitted a faster pace and more intimate response between characters in an opera. Because of terminology utilized,

Ex. 4.4 Augmented cadences

as we will see later, by theorists, I have labeled them "broken" in distinction to the "unbroken" ones to the left.[14]

Ex. 4.5 Cadence combining Ex. 4.4*a* and *e* from
Carissimi's *Jephte* (1645)

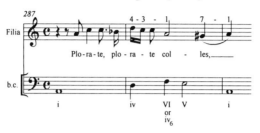

Occasionally the final notes of the cadences in Ex. 4.3*d–f* are augmented in value, in order to produce a more conclusive ending. Ex. 4.4*a* and *b* show such an alteration of Ex. 4.3*c* and *f* respectively, both to be accompanied by Ex. 4.4*d*. Venetian composers often dot the penultimate note of (*b*).[15] Sometimes Ex. 4.4*d* also accompanies the usual broken cadence in (*c*), in which case the chord that in Ex. 4.3*f* occurs on the same quarter beat as the two 1's in the voice is delayed until the following beat.[16] Sometimes the V chord itself is delayed, by moving from IV to vi or IV₆ as

---

[14] Concerning these cadences, see the excellent descriptions, along with examples spanning from early Baroque composers to Handel, in the following articles by Jack Allan Westrup: "The Cadence in Baroque Recitative," *Natalicia musicologica Knud Jeppesen septuagenario*, ed. Bjørn Hjelmborg and Søren Sørensen (Copenhagen: Wilhelm Hansen, 1962), 243–52; "Rezitativ," *MGG* xi (1963), 355–65; "Alessandro Scarlatti's *Il Mitridate Eupatore* (1707)" in *New Looks at Italian Opera: Essays in Honor of Donald J. Grout*, ed. William W. Austin (Ithaca, NY: Cornell University Press, 1968), 136–7; and "Recitative," *NG* xv (1980), 643–8. On p. 644 of the last source, he describes "the practice of cutting off the voice before the cadence and leaving the accompaniment to complete the progression." He also suggests that these cadences originated "where the singer was so overcome with emotion that he could not continue."

[15] Examples of Ex. 4.4*b* with a dotted penultimate note are in Sartorio's *L'Adelaide* of 1672 (*IOB* viii, 43ʳ and 97ʳ). For 5-3-1-1 in the voice, see 35ᵛ and for 2-3-1-1 his *Seleuco* of 1666 (Rosand, 577). For Ex. 4.1*a* and *b* with augmentation and dot, see Cesti's *L'Argia* (*IOB* iii, 7ʳ and 49ʳ).

[16] See Giovanni Antonio Boretti's *Claudio Cesare* of 1672 (Glixon, 81) for Ex. 4.4*c* and *d*. For 2-3-1-1 in the voice, see *Dal male il bene* by Antonio Maria Abbatini and Marco Marazzoli in 1654, Act I, sc. i (Murata, p. 358, m. 52), and also Cavalli's *La Statira* of 1655 or 56 (Glixon, p. 348, mm. 62–3) and *L'Erismena* from 1655 (Glixon, p. 363, m. 54).

in (e), or from IV to I_6 as in (f), by sustaining IV as in (g), or by inserting a rest as in (h). In these cases the first 1 in the voice part of (a), (b), or (c) is not dissonant initially as it is with (d).[17] The early example by Carissimi in Ex. 4.5, which combines Ex. 4.4a with e, suggests that the minor falling third was used at first for its affective value in projecting a mood of lamentation.[18] All of these augmentations in the melody and delays of V cause the cadence to last longer than the brief one in Ex. 4.3f.

The Emergence of Preferred Cadences 1675–1700

Exx. 4.1–4.4 represent, then, the most important types of cadence that developed gradually during the first sixty or seventy years of the century. At first, their diversity was a rich resource for expressing equally diverse emotions. The quasi closes in Ex. 4.1 continue throughout the history of recitative to be used for internal phrases. Eventually, however, some of the other, more final types are preferred over others. It is probably in the mid-1670s that a certain crystallization occurs, with the repeated-3 and unbroken cadences tending to dominate. This was a critical moment in the development of opera, for this was the time when tonality finally crystallized and the time when both recitative and aria finally became clearly separate units in a numbers opera.

Beginning in the early 1680s, however, the broken cadences in Ex. 4.3d, e, and f join and finally, around 1700, replace the unbroken ones in Ex. 4.3a, b, and c and the repeated-3 cadence in Ex. 4.2b. The musically unaccented treatment of the final unaccented syllable in Exx. 4.2b and 4.3a–c thus dies out by the end of the century. Recitative is thereafter left, for the

---

[17] For Ex. 4.4c with g, see Cavalli's *Scipione affricano* of 1664 (Glixon, 73, end of excerpt).

[18] *Historia di Jephte*, ed. Gottfried Wolters (Wolfenbüttel: Möseler Verlag, 1969), p. 29, the Latin text translated on p. 44: "Lament, ye hills." A similar cadence to D follows immediately to the text "mourn, ye mountains." In addition, a cadence joining Ex. 4.4a and d appears on p. 28 shortly before Ex. 4.5, when Jephte says, "Go, my only daughter, and bewail thy virginity." In his opera *Didone* (1641), Cavalli combines patterns similar to Ex. 4.4c and g in the soliloquy in which Didone laments her past behavior and prepares to kill herself. Two such cadences join two others like Ex. 4.1b. They all have a minor falling third and act (Glixon, 134) to unify a section of the scene (included in Glixon, 301–2: the cadences in mm. 3, 8, 18, and 23).

most part, with only 7-1 cadences: those in Ex. 4.3*d–f* and later the augmented one in Ex. 4.4*b*.

Alessandro Scarlatti wrote his first opera, *Gli equivoci nel sembiante*, in 1679, when the first group of cadences was in fashion. Both recitatives and arias are numerous and brief, and both are filled with the repeated-3 cadence. Contrasting with this 2-1 cadence are some that end with 7-1: those in Ex. 4.3*a–c* and similar cadences that commence with 7-3-1 or 5-3-1. Only once does Ex. 4.3*f* occur. In his operas of the 1690s, however, the cadences in Ex. 4.3*d–f* become more numerous and those in Ex. 4.3*a–c* less frequent. By the time of his *Dafni* in 1700 the unaccented cadences in Exx. 4.2*b* and 4.3*a–c* have disappeared, replaced by those in Ex. 4.3*d–f*. He wrote the opera *Il Pompeo* in 1683, during the period of transition between the old and new cadences and at a moment when they were in about even balance. Therefore, this opera presents a great diversity of cadence types and affords a special opportunity to compare them.

Ex. 4.6 shows the most frequent types involving 3 descending to 1. The old cadences at this time were those in Ex. 4.6*a*, *b*, and *d*—those with an unaccented penultimate note slurred to the final 1. Scale degree 3 is conspicuous in (*a*) through its repetition, its length, and its coupling with the accented syllable, and in (*b*) and (*d*) through the falling third, in which a dissonant 3 leaps down to another dissonant note. Furthermore, 4 is often preceded by 6 as in (*a*) and (*d*), creating in both cases a series of four descending intervals, which, compared to the gentler contrary movement in (*b*), provides an impetuous momentum toward the final 1. For brief internal phrases, the patterns in Ex. 4.1 continue.[19]

The new cadences are those in Ex. 4.6*c* and *e*, which, when compared to Ex. 4.6*b* and *d*, retain almost the same rhythm, same melodic pitches, and same chordal harmony, but move the last two notes of the voice part (the 7 and 1) to the continuo realization. These examples also show how a new character can respond quickly over the tonic chord, either after a brief rest (*c*) or with no intervening rest at all (*e*).[20]

---

[19] See *HS* vi, 204[r], second system, for example, where 4-3-1-1 over V₆-I is followed immediately by 2-3-1-1 over V and I. I have changed the value of the opening note in the voice in Ex. 4.6*d* from an eighth to a quarter.

[20] Equally numerous in *Il Pompeo* are the cadences in Ex. 4.3*a* and *d*. For examples, see *HS* vi, 1[r], last system, for (*a*), and 41[v], first system, for (*d*).

Ordinarily the continuo is probably realized in the rhythm shown in Ex. 4.3*d* and *f,* which simply transfers to the new cadences the rhythm of the corresponding old ones in Ex. 4.3*a* and *c.* In Ex. 4.3*e* I have also shown a version of this rhythm which I think would be particularly effective for the

Ex. 4.6 Cadences in Scarlatti's *Il Pompeo* (1683) (*HS* vi)

falling-third cadences: here the repeated 1's in the continuo realization support the two 1's in the voice and, at the same time, give a rhythmic vigor to the rapid resolution of the dissonant 1 to 7. More striking modifications occur on occasion, especially in accompanied recitative, where the accompanying parts are written out. In Ex. 4.7*a*, the 7 in the string parts coincides exactly with the second 1 of the voice, creating a half-step clash. Ex. 4.7*b* shows that this was apparently not offensive, for here the entire dominant chord enters with the second 1 following a rest. There are a number of examples from much earlier in the century in which 1 in the voice sounds throughout the V and I chords in the continuo, as in Ex. 4.8. This sort of polychordal sound may therefore be a possibility in the broken cadences of Ex. 4.3*d–f*. In the Venetian dotted cadences, it would be almost inevitable for the voice's 1 and the continuo's 7 to sound simultaneously, as in Ex. 4.3*f* when the two 1's in the voice have the rhythm of a dotted eighth and sixteenth.

Ex. 4.7 Cadences in accompanied recitative by Scarlatti

The 1680s were also the time when the so-called "Corelli clash" was popular in dance music. This occurs when an upper part descends in dotted rhythm from 2 to 1 over a V chord while a second part moves below it from 1 to 7 in the same rhythm: 7 and 1 both sound together briefly before both move to a unison 1.[21] This is similar to the effect occurring when the voice's final 1 is heard simultaneously with 7 in the instrumental parts of Ex. 4.7a and b.

Ex. 4.8 1 above V in Cavalli's *Le nozze di Teti e di Peleo* (1639), Act III, sc. vi (Rosand, 627–8)

The Theorists

Some writers and theorists eventually describe these cadences and the method of performance. In 1723 Tosi mentions the *cadenze tronche*—those in Ex. 4.3d–f. The "ancient" singers he admires lived during the later years of the seventeenth century when he himself was a popular castrato singer in Italy, Germany, and England—the time, that is, when a great variety of

---

[21] For an early example, see the end of the voice parts in the duet "*Poca voglia di far bene*" from Landi's *Il Sant'Alessio* (printed in *HAM* ii, p. 50 in No. 209). Most of Corelli's examples appear at the end of one or both of the binary sections of the dance movements in his trio sonatas of Op. 2 from 1685; see his *Sonate da camera a tre*, modern edn. in *Historisch-kritische Gesamtausgabe der musikalischen Werke*, ii, ed. Jürg Stenzl (Laaber: Laaber Verlag, 1986), especially the allemandes (pp. 24, 27–8, etc.). In my book *The Allemande, the Balletto, and the Tanz* (Cambridge University Press, 1986), ii, 203, see the final cadences in the allemandes by Domenico Gabrielli (1684): the figure's usual disposition at the end of No. 122b, its inversion at the end of No. 122a. For examples in sarabandes, see my volumes on *The Folia, the Saraband, the Passacaglia, and the Chaconne* in AIM's *Musicological Studies and Documents* 35 (Neuhausen-Stuttgart: Hänssler-Verlag, 1982), ii, 39–40 (the ends of Nos. 56b and 56c by D. Gabrielli in 1684) and 51 (the end of No. 61d by Giorgio Buoni in 1693).

cadences appeared in recitatives such as those in *Il Pompeo*. Tosi states, in
Galliard's translation:

> Much more might still be said on the compositions of recitative in
> general, by reason of that tedious chanting that offends the ear, with a
> thousand broken cadences [*cadenze tronche*] in every opera, which custom
> has established, though they are without taste or art. To reform them all,
> would be worse than the disease; the introducing every time a final
> cadence [*cadenza finale*] would be wrong: But if in these two extremes a
> remedy were necessary, I should think, that among an hundred broken
> cadences, ten of them, briefly terminated on points that conclude a period,
> would not be ill employed.[22]

Ex. 4.9 Galliard's examples of Tosi's cadences
(Pl.V, Nos.1–2)

Galliard adds the illustrations in Ex. 4.9, where his "broken" cadence
in (*a*) matches Ex. 4.3*d* and his "final" cadence is like Ex. 4.3*a* except for
the placement of the final syllables and the augmentation of 7 and 1 shown
in Ex. 4.4*a*. He thus translates *tronca* or its plural *tronche* as "broken," as do
Tosi's other translators. In the Dutch version of 1731 Alençon says that the
Italian *cadenza troncata* is an *afgebrookse cadents*,[23] and Agricola in his
German translation of 1757 refers to *abgebrochenen Cadenzen*.[24]   In
addition, Fux in 1725 writes a *clausula formalis* which is *truncata*.[25]   It thus

---

[22] Tosi, *Opinioni*, 47; Galliard, *Observations on the Florid Song*, 74–5 (see also
Tosi, 80, and Galliard, 127).

[23] J. A. Alençon, *Korte aanmerkingen over de zangkonst, getrokken uit een
italiaansch boek, betyteld Osservazioni sopra il canto figurato di Pier Francesco Tosi*
(Leyden, 1731), copy at the Gemeentemuseum in The Hague, 35–6.

[24] Agricola, *Anleitung zur Singkunst*, 162, 194 (Baird trans., 181, 204).   His
illustration shows a deceptive cadence, which we will consider in the next chapter.

[25] Johann Joseph Fux, *Gradus ad Parnassum* (Vienna, 1725), repr. in *Monuments
of Music and Music Literature in Facsimile*, Ser. 2, xxiv (New York: Broude Brothers,
1966), 278.   His cadence combines the falling fourth in the vocal part of my Ex. 4.9*a*
with the delay of V shown in my Ex. 4.4*d*.

seems to me that *tronca* refers to the fact that the vocal figure in Ex. 4.9*b* and Ex. 4.3*a–c*—that is, the melody in the older cadences at the time of Tosi and such operas as *Il Pompeo*—is either "broken in two" or the final notes are "broken off" in the newer cadences of Exx. 4.9*a* and 4.3d–*f*, so that the part that is broken off, the concluding 7-1, is sounded by the realizing instrument rather than the voice.[26]

The expression *parola tronca*, at least at a later date and perhaps also at the time of Tosi, refers to an Italian word such as *cittade* in which the last syllable has been "cut" or "broken off," leaving it with an accented last syllable: thus *città*.[27] In the *cadenza tronca*, however, the part which is broken off does not disappear, but falls instead into the continuo realization.

[26] A number of modern writers have assumed that *tronca* means "truncated," thus "foreshortened," "abbreviated," or "telescoped," with various explanations of what is truncated and what it is being compared with. For Sven Hostrup Hansell, in "The Cadence in 18th-Century Recitative," *MQ* 54 (1968): 228–48, the *tronca* cadence is truncated by sounding the V chord sooner than it does in the cadence of Ex. 4.4*c* with *h* (a cadence, however, which is preferred at a later date). This idea then appears in Robert Donington, *The Interpretation of Early Music*, New Version (London: Faber and Faber, 1975), 661–4; Kathleen Kuzmick Hansell, *Vorwort* to Mozart's *Lucio Silla* in *NMA* II:5/vii/1, p. xli; and Julianne C. Baird, trans. and ed., *Introduction to the Art of Singing by Johann Friedrich Agricola* (Cambridge University Press, 1995), 26, 273 n. 12. Winton Dean, however, in "The Performance of Recitative in Late Baroque Opera," *ML* 58 (1977): 389–402, suggests, after comparing Galliard's examples (my Ex. 4.9*a* and *b*), that *tronca* may refer not to "the timing of the chords" but to a cadence in which the voice does not "close on the tonic." Michael Collins, finally, comes very close to my own concept in his excellent article "Cadential Structures and Accompanimental Practices in Eighteenth-Century Recitative," pp. 211–32 in *Opera and Vivaldi*, which he edited with Elise K. Kirk (Austin: University of Texas Press, 1984). Although he feels that "broken" is "a quite unfortunate translation" (p. 211), he finally concludes that "*cadenza tronca* does not refer to the bass at all, but rather to the vocal part, which is 'truncated' in that it does not complete the cadence with the bass" (pp. 220–21); after the voice is finished "the accompaniment completes a final cadence of the type singers would have made in the common recitative cadence before the 1790s" (p. 222). He is comparing cadences like those in my Ex. 4.3*f* with others, such as the repeated-3 cadence, in which the voice's 1 coincides with the continuo's I (pp. 211–12). He does not, however, include cadences like my Ex. 4.3*b* and *c*, which perhaps explains why he was puzzled by the word "broken."

[27] The earliest example I can find is in the "tronchi verses" mentioned by Giacomo Gotifredo Ferrari in *A Concise Treatise on Italian Singing* (London, 1818). See his chart printed by Will Crutchfield in "The Prosodic Appoggiatura in the Music of Mozart and His Contemporaries," *JAMS* 42 (1989): 261.

Thus, in this case *tronca* seems also to have the meaning of broken, like a stick, "in two," with both parts still in existence but in a new configuration.[28]

The realization of the continuo is explained by Johann David Heinichen in his *Neu erfundene und gründliche Anweisung . . . zu vollkommener Erlernung des General-Basses* published at Hamburg in 1711.[29] This book is completely different, at least in regard to the cadences, from *Der General-Bass in der Composition* of 1728. Since the earlier book has not been mentioned in recent articles on the subject, it is worthwhile, I think, to devote some attention to it here. Heinichen includes in the book an anonymous cantata with unfigured bass and makes comment on the method of realizing certain passages, such as the three cadences in Exx. 4.10 and 4.11. His comments in all these cadences come at the point, which I have marked with an asterisk, where scale degree 5 appears in the bass.

Ex. 4.10 Heinichen, brief cadence (1711)

The outer voices in Ex. 4.10, which form a cadence much like Scarlatti's in Ex. 4.6*e*, come from Heinichen's score. He describes verbally the realizations which I show on the middle staves. For his preferred realization in Ex. 4.10*a*, "one can make a brief resolution [*kurtze Resolution*]

---

[28] Curiously, Tosi also used the idea of breaking, according to Roger North, to describe the earlier type of rubato, which he called "the breaking yet keeping of time"; see my book *Stolen Time: The History of Tempo Rubato* (OUP, 1994; slightly revised as a paperback, 1997), 44.

[29] Facs. in *DM* xl (2000) and on Microcard No. UR-56 203-9 from the copy at Sibley Music Library, Eastman School of Music. I also consulted a microfilm of the copy at the Library of Congress. For a repr. of the title page, see George J. Buelow, *Thorough-Bass Accompaniment According to Johann David Heinichen*, rev. edn. in *SM* 84 (1986), 19.

of the 4 x" (which are figured-bass numbers, with "x," a sharp sign, being an abbreviation for "3 x," which refers to the sharpened 3). He explains more completely in regard to a similar cadence to B-flat major, that "one can use the customary 4 3 cadence, especially if the brief resolution of the fourth [referring, that is, to the resolution of the figured bass's 4 to 3 or G to F-sharp in Ex. 4.10*a*] is postponed until after the ending of the singer."[30] I presume that he is describing the realization of Ex. 4.3*f*, in which the instruments simply play in the rhythm of the earlier cadence in Ex. 4.3*c*. Theoretically there is a slight overlapping of the voice and the realization for a sixteenth beat, but there is scarcely any other way to resolve the 4 to 3 after the voice and still strike the tonic chord where notated.

Heinichen also suggests the realization in Ex. 4.10*b* as an alternative. Here one can, "with the striking of this note [the D in the bass marked with an asterisk], wait until the voice finishes and then use only 3 [F-sharp] as the cadence to G minor."[31] If the voice sings exactly the notes shown in Ex. 4.10*b*, then this realization does not actually sound much different from Ex. 4.10*a*, since the voice itself supplies the missing 4 or G in the realization.

In his 1728 book three broken cadences occur in a cantata by Scarlatti. The first two are like Ex. 4.3*d*, with the descending fourth from 1 to 5. Each is described as the *gewöhnliche* (familiar) or *bekandte* (well-known) *Recitativ-Cadenz*. In the third one, which ends with 5-3-1-1 in the voice, the "3" or scale degree 7 in the continuo realization should be struck briefly after the end of the voice, as in Ex. 4.10.[32] Earlier in the book he describes

---

[30] The score of the B-flat cadence is on p. 240, the comment on p. 242: "[Hier] kan [man] die gewöhnliche Cadentz 4 3. brauchen, zumahl wenn die Kurtze Resolution der 4te biss nach Endigung der Singe-Stimme verspahret wird."

[31] The cadence in Ex. 10 occurs on p. 251, the description on pp. 253–4: "Bey (π) [the sign I have replaced with an asterisk] kan man eine kurtze Resolution der 4 x machen, oder auch mit Anschlagung dieser Note verziehen biss die Singe-Stimme vorbey, und so dann bloss x brauchen als die Cadentz ins g-moll." Although I feel that Ex. 4.10*b* represents what Heinichen is describing in the second part of his sentence, there is, I suppose, the remote possibility that "diese Note" means "the latter Note," referring to x or 3; in this case, the second half of the sentence could conceivably read: "with the striking of the latter Note [F-sharp] at the place marked [at D in the bass], wait until the voice finishes, and thus use only F-sharp as the cadence to G minor." This would produce the realization in Ex. 5.2*a*, which, as we will see, Telemann recommended for operatic cadences.

[32] *Der General-Bass in der Composition* (Dresden, 1728; repr., Hildesheim: Georg Olms Verlag, 1969), 802 (referring to the cadence on 801), 806, and 824: "Hierdurch wird . . . die Cadenz 4 x praepariret, welche nach Endigung der Stimme pfleget kurtz nachgeschlagen zu werden." It is not as clear as in the 1711 book that it is

three textless 1-1-5 examples like Ex. 4.3d as "the swiftly moving" or "constantly appearing" cadences in recitative.[33]

In 1711 Heinichen also shows the two longer cadences in Ex. 4.11, in which some element has been augmented or delayed in comparison with the briefer type in Ex. 4.10. Ex. 4.11a marks the end of the first recitative in the anonymous cantata. The melody has augmented 1's somewhat like Ex. 4.4b and the bass a VI or iv$_6$ chord as in Ex. 4.4e. Heinichen explains, using figured-bass numbers: "Now the final cadence is at hand, and the familiar resolution of 4.3, to which 5 (or also ♮ ♮) and 8 belong; the resolution of 4 to F-sharp (the major third) can be struck somewhat after the ending of the voice."[34] On the last two quarter beats of the penultimate measure the continuo can then be realized as in the corresponding spot in Ex. 4.4d, changing the D on the third quarter beat of Ex. 4.4d to an E, if desired, to produce a I$_4^6$ chord. In Ex. 4.11b the melody is like Ex. 4.4c, and the concluding continuo chords are again as in Ex. 4.4d. He comments simply that "one can make a small resolution or final cadence with 4.3."[35] Since the resolution here is not brief (*kurtz*) but small (*klein*), it seems to me that my accompaniment on the upper staff of Ex. 4.4d is also appropriate here. Again, as in Ex. 4.11a, a I$_4^6$ chord could precede the V and its 4 3 suspension.

The two cadences in Ex. 4.11 thus have longer duration for purposes of finality, and the V chord is extended, compared to Ex. 4.10, and its resolution to I thus delayed. Hence, I will refer in this book to cadences such as those in Ex. 4.11 as "delayed," those like Ex. 4.10, by contrast, as "brief." Heinichen himself uses the word *kurtz* to refer specifically to the brevity of the figured bass's 3 or x—that is, scale degree 7 in the continuo realization (F-sharp on a sixteenth note in Ex. 4.10a). This, of course, is the crucial pitch which identifies the basic framework of the cadence as 7 to 1.

---

only the resolution of the 4—that is, the 3—which is to be struck after the voice has ended. See Buelow, *Thorough-Bass Accompaniment*, 252, 255, and 267.

[33] *Der General-Bass*, 673-4: "geschwind vorbey gehende Cadenzen"; "im Recitativ alle Augenblick vorkommende Cadenz." The three cadences are printed by Hansell in *MQ* 54 (1968): 242, by Dean in *ML* 58 (1977): 399, and in facs. by Buelow in *Thorough-Bass Accompaniment*, 414.

[34] Heinichen (1711), 232–3: ". . . nun die Final Clausul allhier vorhanden; so ist es die bekandte Resolution der 4 3, worzu 5. (oder auch ♮.♮.) und 8. gehöret; die Resolution aber 4. in das Fis [written as F with a loop, as in the old German letter notation] als Tert. dur, kan nach gefallen bey Endigung der Singe-Stimme etwas nachgeschlagen werden." The score of Ex. 4.11a is on p. 232.

[35] Ibid., 231: ". . . kan man eine kleine Resolution oder Final Clausul machen mit 4.3." Ex. 4.11b is on pp. 229–30.

In addition, he makes very clear that it is the brief structure in Ex. 4.10, rather than one of those in Ex. 4.11, that is the recitative cadence most frequently in use at that time, and that the preferred realization for this structure is that in Ex. 4.10*a*.

Ex. 4.11 Heinichen (1711), augmented cadences which delay V

A completely written out continuo realization for some of these cadence structures appears in 1736 in the *Reglas generales de acompañar* published in Madrid by Joseph de Torres y Martínez Bravo. In a section of the book devoted to the Italian style, he gives two recitative cadences with Spanish texts, one brief, the other delayed. The first has the melody of Ex. 4.3*d* (ending with the falling fourth) and the brief resolution in Ex. 4.10*a*. The continuo accompaniment for the last two syllables is in the dotted rhythm I show in Ex. 4.3*d* and *f*, and, as also in Ex. 4.3*d*, with the continuo's 4 and 3 (or melodic 1 and 7) at the top of the right-hand part. Because of the close connection historically between these cadences and the corresponding unbroken ones in Ex. 4.3*a*–*c*, I suspect that this was indeed the usual rhythm and distribution of notes. His second example is a downward-fourth cadence delayed like Ex. 4.11*b*. In this case the V chord has scale degree 5 at the top of the right-hand part and the figured bass's 4 and 3 in even quarter notes in an inner part below it.[36]

[36] Facs. edn. (Madrid: Arte Tripharia, 1983), 115. In the modern edition and translation by Paul Murphy in *José de Torres's Treatise of 1736* (Bloomington and Indianapolis: Indiana University Press, 2000), the final vocal note in the second example should be transcribed as E and not D. See Collins, "Cadential Structures," 223.

Comparison of the Cadences

The recitative cadences between 1675 and 1700 are all closely related, as we have seen. They thus resemble each other in some ways and differ in others. The seemingly small details in which they differ, however, are highly significant. Fig. 1 points out some of the most important of these differences in the repeated-3 and falling-third cadences. At the top of each column is a diagram showing the melodic and harmonic structures and the way they fit together. Each begins with "2/4," meaning that the melodic pattern commences with either 2 or 4. The continuing quasi closes appear in the first column, followed by the repeated-3 and unbroken cadences—the two types which eventually represent the older practice during this period. The last column shows the broken cadences—the new type developing during the 1680s.

The harmonic framework for all of them is simply V to I, which is modified sometimes for the quasi closes when one or both of these chords is in first inversion. The melodic framework for these quasi closes is essentially 3-1 sung by the voice. In the progression 2-3-1 the 3 may on occasion be interpreted, of course, as an échappée in a 2-1 cadence. In 4-3-1, however, the 3 can often, if not usually, be heard as a sort of leaping passing-tone between 4 and 1. This is especially true when 6 precedes 4, as it often does. The melodic framework for the repeated-3 cadence in the second column is 2 to 1 in the voice, whereas the other two columns involve 7 to 1, performed in the unbroken cadences by the voice, in the broken ones by the continuo realization. The framework 2 in the second column and the framework 7 in the last two ordinarily appear on relatively short note values, as I show in the examples.

The word accent in the repeated-3 cadence occurs on the second of its two 3's. In all the others the accented syllable appears on the first of the last two 1's. The last musically accented 1 in the voice falls in both the quasi closes and the broken cadences on the first 1, but in the other two types on the last note. The chord which coincides with this accented 1 is the tonic in all cases except the broken ones, where it is the dominant. If we assume that the chord preceding V for the cadences in the last three column is IV, as it usually is, then the dissonant notes shown on the last line of Fig. 1 occur. There is only a single dissonant note for the quasi closes, and this note does not bear the accented syllable.

The other three types, however, each have two adjacent dissonant notes, and one of these does coincide with the accented syllable. This significant emphasis on the accented syllable is shown in Fig. 1 by the boxes

Fig. 1 Comparison of the falling-third and repeated-3 cadences
1675–1700

	CONTINUING	OLD		NEW
	Quasi close Ex.4.1*a, b* > 2/4-3-1-1 V$_{(6)}$ I$_{(6)}$	**Repeated-3** Ex.4.2*b* > ⌢ 2/4 3-3 2-1 IV V I	**Unbroken** Ex.4.3*b, c* > ⌢ 2/4-3-1 7-1 IV V I	**Broken** Ex. 4.3*e, f* > 2/4-3-1-1 IV V I
Harmonic framework	V$_{(6)}$-I$_{(6)}$	V-I	V-I	V-I
Melodic framework	3-1 in voice	2-1 in voice	7-1 in voice	7-1 in continuo realization
Word accent	1st 1	2nd 3	1st 1	1st 1
Last musically accented 1 in voice	1st 1	last note	last note	1st 1
Chord with last musically accented 1 in voice	I$_{(6)}$	I	I	V
Dissonant notes	3 with V$_{(6)}$	1st 3 with IV 2nd 3 with V	3 with IV 1st 1 with V	3 with IV 2 1's with V

around the notes on the third and sixth lines. Increased accentuation comes in the second column from the repetition of 3, and in the last two from the leap of the falling third. The relatively less strength with which the closes in the first column reinforce the accented syllable may well account for the fact that they appear usually in less final situations, especially if, in addition, the harmonic progression is weakened by one or more first inversions.

The repeated-3 cadences disappear by 1700 and henceforth almost all recitative cadences have a melodic framework of 7-1. The 2 to 1 framework remains typical, however, for aria cadences, where the word accent occurs on 2 and on a relatively long note, sometimes sustained for a considerable duration or prolonged by written or improvised figuration. The resolution on the final weak syllable coincides, then, with the tonic chord on a strong beat (as in the repeated-3 cadence). Occasionally 7-1 can occur in an aria in a similar manner, but this is a manner contrasting considerably with the rhythmic structure of any of the recitative cadences. By 1700, then, cadence structure was one of the many ways in which the recitative differed from the aria.

Not included in Fig. 1 are the falling-fourth cadences, but a similar comparison would apply to those in Exx. 4.1c and 4.3a and d. These, as well as all the cadences in Fig. 1, may occur in either major or minor. In addition, almost all Italian words have an accent on the penultimate syllable, as shown in Exx. 4.1, 4.2b, and 4.3. The quasi closes and the broken cadences, however, can accommodate other accentuations as well: when the last syllable is accented, the final note in the voice is simply deleted from my examples, leaving the termination of the vocal part on a single 1; when the accent falls on the antepenultimate syllable, the final pitch in the voice is simply repeated one more time.

*   *   *   *   *

By around 1675, then, a process of crystallization begins to operate in the recitative cadences. Out of the enormous variety that had developed before this time, certain ones are selected as preferred types during particular periods of time. This is a process which continues very gradually during the next century as composers decide to restrict the range of possibilities to fewer and fewer types.

Chapter 5

LATER RECITATIVE

As RECITATIVE moves into the eighteenth century it occurs now in more diverse situations. It spreads from Italy to other countries—principally, as far as the falling-third cadences are concerned, to Germany and England.[1] They appear in sacred as well as secular works. The language may still be Italian, even outside Italy, or it may now be German or English. We will continue to be concerned with works of Scarlatti written until 1721. In the first half of the century Keiser, Graupner, Telemann, and J. S. Bach employ the German language in works both secular and sacred. Italian appears in the operatic recitative of Handel and Pergolesi and in later examples by J. C. Bach, Gluck, Haydn, Mozart, and Rossini. English, finally, occurs in the falling-third recitative cadences in the oratorios of Handel.

---

[1] Opera emerged eventually, of course, also in France. Here there was less distinction between recitative and aria, however, with the recitative smoother and more melodic both before and during the cadences. Most cadences end with 2 or 7 over a V chord simply moving to 1 over I. A study of some selected operas of Rameau, Campra, and Charpentier, as well as the secular cantatas in *The Eighteenth-Century French Cantata* (Garland, 1990–91) shows that the only falling-third cadence that occurs with any frequency has the melodic formula 2-3-1-(1), where V coincides with 2 as in the Italian quasi close (Ex. 4.1*a*) when both chords are in root position. See, for example, J.-P. Rameau, *Oeuvres complètes* (Paris, 1895–1924), vi: *Hippolyte et Aricie* (1733), 29, 30, 83, 84, etc., or the cantatas in iii, 51, 59, 71, etc. Occasionally 2-3-1 or 5-3-1 is followed by 7-1 to suggest an unbroken Italian cadence like Ex. 4.3*b*, but with the final syllable of text heard with I; see André Campra's *Les festes vénitiennes* (1710) in *Le pupitre* 19 (Paris: Heugel, 1971), p. 64, mm. 69–70, and p. 260, mm. 356–8. The cadences of Ex. 4.3 appear very rarely and in the works of only a few composers: see the unbroken 4-3-1 7-1 cadences by Jean-Baptiste Stuck in *The Eighteenth-Century French Cantata*, iv, 74 in his first book of 1706, and 60 and 62 in Book 4 from 1714; and the examples by Nicolas Bernier in volume vi of the same set, 14 (for an unbroken 4-3-1 7-1) and 17 (a broken 4-3-1-1 like Ex. 4.4*c* with *d*) from his first book of 1703.

Fig. 2 Principal recitative cadences 1683–1850

	1683–1700	1700–1750	1750–1850
Old	UNBROKEN	BRIEF	AUTHENTIC
New	BROKEN	DELAYED	DECEPTIVE
Defining feature	Melody: location of final melodic fragment	Rhythm: location of V and I chords	Harmony: nature of final chord

4-3-1 cadences

4- 3-1 7-1 IV V I	**UNBROKEN** Ex. 4.3*c*
4-3-1-(1) IV V I	**BROKEN & BRIEF** Ex. 4.3*f*, Ex. 5.1*a* & *b* with *e*
4-3-1-(1) IV ⅔ V I	**DELAYED & AUTHENTIC** Ex. 4.4*c–g*, Ex. 5.1*a* & *b* with *f*
4-3-1-(1) IV ⅔ V X	**DECEPTIVE** Exx. 5.15, 5.16

These representative composers show how recitative changes after 1700. In spite of gradually increasing selectivity, there are many variables at any particular time that affect the precise nature of the cadences. Some of the musical features are more or less constant for a certain period of time, for a certain language, or for secular or sacred music. Others are unique to a certain composer or group of composers. Still others seem to vary systematically over time and hence are involved in a process of evolution. The expression of a special emotion or nuance of meaning to illustrate a text, plot, character, or mood thus involves the concurrence of numerous notated musical elements in addition to the performer's manner of delivery. It will be especially important to note the effect of all these musical variables on the two concluding pitches of the falling-third cadences: scale degree 3 and the note to which it leads—the first or single 1, which coincides with the word accent.

The Basic Structures

Fig. 2 compares the main cadential structures before 1700 with those in the two periods from 1700 to 1750 and from 1750 to 1850. Years, of course, are approximate. During each of the three periods there is an older type which is gradually diminishing in popularity and a newer one which gradually takes its place. To complete the table of cadences, one could also add the repeated-3 cadence as one of the older types in the first column, as well as the quasi closes of Ex. 4.1*a* and *b* during all three periods and Ex. 4.1*c* during the last two. Those listed in Fig. 2, however, are the principal types, whose falling-third versions are given below the table in melodic and chord numerals.

During the late seventeenth century the distinction between old and new involved, as we have seen, the breaking off of the final 7-1 from the melody of the voice part and its relocation in the continuo realization. Since Tosi and his translators referred to the new type as "broken," I have named the old type "unbroken" in contrast. After 1700 this new broken cadence becomes the old type in a new period. The new type which arises to oppose it involves this time not a melodic feature, but the rhythmic location of the framework chords V and I. The brief cadence in the second column is identical to the broken one in the first, but now we must change its name to show its relationship with the new cadence in which V occurs later. I call it "brief," as indicated in the previous chapter, partly because of Heinichen's *kurtze* or brief *Resolution*, but mainly because it occupies less time than the cadence in which V is delayed for a quarter beat. Thus the new broken cadence of the first column becomes after 1700 the old brief cadence of a new period, opposed in its structure to the new delayed cadences. Ex. 5.1 compares the brief and delayed structures, including both the feminine ending on two 1's and the masculine on a single 1.

Ex. 5.1 The most popular 18th-century recitative cadences

The same process occurs then for the period 1750–1850. Now the new delayed cadence of the previous period becomes the old authentic cadence when compared to the new cadences in which the final I chord is changed to a different and thus deceptive chord (indicated by "X" on the last line of Fig. 2). Marpurg shows how this new cadence results when the I chord of an authentic cadence is deleted so that V moves directly to the chord that introduces a new recitative sentence.[2] The deceptive cadence thus usually moves, following the delayed V chord, to vi or VI, to a secondary dominant in first inversion to V or vi, or occasionally to I₆. Perhaps most striking is the movement from a major key to a major VI chord with its root on the flattened sixth degree.[3] In this way the dramatic action can move

---

[2] *Kritische Briefe*, ii, 356.

[3] In the type of deceptive cadence referred to here, of course, V follows the falling third in the voice and a rest in the bass, as depicted in Fig. 2. Marpurg describes this as *elliptisch*, with reference to the omission of the I chord, in contrast to his *ganze*

forward more quickly without waiting for the I chord to intervene. Thus the deceptive cadence facilitates faster presentation of text as did the broken cadence, as we have seen, compared with the unbroken. This is perhaps the reason Giannantonio Banner includes such a deceptive cadence in his examples of the special manner employed in theatrical recitatives.[4] Curiously, Agricola, in his German translation of 1757, gives examples of Tosi's cadences according to his own period: thus his example of the *abgebrochene Cadenz* is a deceptive cadence with V moving to a first-inversion secondary dominant of V, in contrast to his *Endigungscadenz*, which is an authentic cadence with similar structure but ending V-I. Galliard's illustrations in Ex. 4.9 of course, are far closer to Tosi's concept, for they show the new and old cadences from the first column of Fig. 2 rather than those from the third column.[5]

All of the cadences in the second and third columns of Fig. 2 are technically "broken," but by 1700 there was no longer a need for the word simply because there were generally no unbroken ones left for comparison. Similarly, both cadences in the third column are delayed, but since the brief type had by that time considerably diminished in frequency, there was no longer any point in making that distinction. The delayed cadences before 1750, however, employ the variety of ways of delaying V shown in Ex. 4.4*d* through *h*, whereas after mid-century they most often have a rest below the voice's 1's as shown in Exx. 4.4*h* and 5.1*f.*

(complete) *Cadenz*, which ends with V-I. Another type of deceptive cadence would be formed when one substitutes a vi chord for the I$_6$ in my 4.1*b*. Marpurg calls this an *unterbrochne* (interrupted) *Cadenz*, which is one type of quasi close, but one more appropriate in the arioso style (*Kritische Briefe*, ii, 360). The deceptive cadences with the delayed V seem to emerge during the 1730s, with a variety of types, for example, in the recitatives of Pergolesi.

[4] *Compendio musicale*, a MS treatise from 1745, according to Collins, who prints three of the musical examples in "Cadential Structures," 217–18. The work is listed in Gaetano Gaspari's *Catalogo della Biblioteca del Liceo Musicale di Bologna*, i (Bologna, 1890; repr., Bologna: Forni, 1961), 294; the quoted title page includes no date, but the author's name is given as "Giannantonio Banner Padovano or.^{do} Tedesco."

[5] *Anleitung zur Singkunst*, 162. When discussing ornaments employed in falling-fourth cadences on p. 154, however, he notates them with the *brief* structure. See Baird trans., 174 and 180–81.

Performance of the Brief Structure

The brief cadences were described, as we have seen, by Heinichen in 1711 (see Ex. 4.10). Kellner writes out three brief *Final-Cadentzen* in 1732, two with the falling fourth and one with the falling third, but all with "4 x" above the fifth scale degree in the bass. He explains that the thorough-bass "generally plays after the voice ends."[6] Telemann includes two brief falling-third cadences in the recitative section of one of the songs with German texts in his *Singe-, Spiel- und General-Bass-Übungen* from 1733–34. He writes out the continuo realization for the first one as in Ex. 5.2a. In the other one, 5 in the bass coincides with a masculine ending in the voice (a single quarter note on 1 instead of two eighth notes), and the realization includes three or four chord-notes in each hand, with scale degree 5 at the top of each chord. A footnote to both cadences states that "the closes in opera are struck immediately when the singer speaks the last syllables [as he has notated in Ex. 5.2a], whereas in cantatas one generally strikes them afterwards [as I show in Ex. 5.2b and c]."[7]

Ex. 5.2 Realizations of the brief cadence (Telemann, 1733–34)

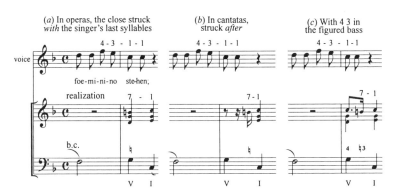

[6] David Kellner, *Treulicher Unterricht im General-Bass* (Hamburg, 1732), copy in Sibley Music Library, Eastman School of Music, repr. on Microcard UR-56 127-9 (University of Rochester Press); and 2nd edn. (Hamburg, 1737; repr., Kultur- und Forschungsstätte Michaelstein, n.d.), 21 (see my Fig. 3 for the German quotation). The second edition contains two sharps added to the second cadence.

[7] Georg Philipp Telemann, *Singe-, Spiel-, und General-Bass-Übungen* (Hamburg, songs published separately during 1733–34, complete edn. 1735; repr., Leipzig, 1983), modern edn. by Max Seiffert (Berlin, 1914), p. 40 in the song "Toback" (see my Fig. 3). An excerpt including my Ex. 5.2a is printed without text in *NG* iv, 697.

By "closes" (*Schlüsse*) Telemann refers, I believe, to the "*kurtze Resolution*" to 3 of the figured bass's 4 in Ex. 5.2*c* or to the melodic figure 7-1 in both (*b*) and (*c*)—the figure which was broken off when the new cadences of Ex. 4.3*e* and *f* were formed from the old ones in Ex. 4.3*b* and *c*. These two realizations for cantata cadences match those by Heinichen in Ex. 4.10. In order to strike these closes after the singer completes the last syllables, scale degree 7 in the realization must occur on a very brief rhythmic value, thus a sixteenth note. The distinction between opera and cantata points out the difference between the conversational style more common in opera and the solo style more frequent in the cantata. Ex. 5.2*b* and *c* do not theoretically occupy any more time than Ex. 5.2*a*, but in the operatic style it would probably be easier to rush on to a new character with the full chords of Ex. 5.2*a* rather than trying to fit in the more detailed rhythm involved in (*b*) or (*c*).

Ex. 5.3 Realizations of the brief cadences (Hahn, 1751)

In addition to Telemann's realizations in Ex. 5.2, Hahn offers in 1751 still another one in Ex. 5.3*a*; here the written-out realization of the V chord is completed on an eighth beat following an eighth rest. He also gives the falling-fourth cadence in Ex. 5.3*b*, which has a realization like Telemann's in Ex. 5.2*a*. For both Ex. 5.3*a* and *b* Hahn explains that "generally the accompaniment should only make the close after the voice has completed its proper descent."[8] He does not distinguish between cantata and opera.

---

[8] Georg Joachim Hahn, *Der wohl unterwiesene General-Bass-Schüler* (Augsburg, 1751), copy in the Music Division, Special Collections, of the New York Public Library, prose description on p. 57 (see my Fig. 3), the example on pp. 58–9. The D in the bass of Ex. 5.3*a* is given incorrectly in the source as C, and the excerpt in Ex. 5.3*b* has no text.

Now, it has been assumed that Telemann was referring in his comment about cantatas to the delayed cadence in which the final 1 or 1's in the voice are unaccompanied and only later followed by the continuo's V and I. Since the brief and delayed cadences are indeed the two principal types during the period 1700 to 1750 (see Fig. 2), and since J. S. Bach almost always notates the delayed type in *his* cantatas, it is tempting to conclude that Telemann was comparing the brief and delayed types.[9] A number of factors, however, strongly suggest that instead of this, he was contrasting different methods of realizing the continuo part in the brief cadence—the methods I show in Ex. 5.2.   These factors include the traditional language for describing the realizations, the notation in actual musical works by Telemann, and the problems of substituting a delayed cadence for one which is notated as brief.

To deal first of all with the prose descriptions, I show in Fig. 3 the comments by theorists from Heinichen to Hahn. At the top are those in which the figured bass's x or 3 (or scale degree 7) occurs on a sixteenth note following the voice's last 1, either when the bass is figured with 4 3 (Exs. 4.10*a*, 5.2*c*) or when one waits, after striking the root of the V chord before playing only the x or 3 (Exs. 4.10*b*, 5.2*b*). Below are those in which the full V chord appears with the voice's first 1 (Exs. 5.2*a*, 5.3*b*) or in which the root of the chord coincides with the first 1, the rest of the chord with the second (Ex. 5.3*a*).   On the left is the portion of each quotation which identifies *what* happens, on the right, the portion which tells *when* it should happen. In some cases this has required rearranging the order of the words in the sentence or relevant portion of a sentence. Telemann apparently knew Heinichen when they were both in Leipzig between 1702 and 1705. He most certainly was later well acquainted with his thorough-bass book of 1728 and probably also with the earlier one from 1711. He likewise knew Kellner's book of 1732, for he himself wrote the foreword to the second edition of 1737. Both this work and Heinichen's book of 1728 were widely known and respected in musical circles.

---

[9] This is assumed in all recent writings on the subject. See Westrup, "The Cadence in Baroque Recitative" (1962), 248 and his Ex. 13; Hansell in *MQ* 54 (1968): 244 n. 45; Donington, *The Interpretation of Early Music* (1975), 661–4; Dean in *ML* 58 (1977): 394; Williams in *NG* iv (1980), 697–8 and his Ex. 17; Westrup in *NG* xv, 644; and Collins, "Cadential Structures" (1984), 214 and his Ex. 4.

Fig. 3 Verbal descriptions of realizations for the brief cadence

THE EVENT	THE TIMING

The figured bass's x or 3 on a sixteenth note following voice's last 1
(Exx. 4.10, 5.2*b*, *c*)

Heinichen (1711) p. 242
 Die kurtze Resolution der 4ᵗᵉ   *wird biss nach Endigung der Singe-Stimme*
                  verspahret.

Heinichen (1728) p. 824
 Die Cadenz 4 x,   *welche nach Endigung der Stimme pfleget*
                  kurtz nachgeschlagen zu werden.

Kellner (1732) p. 21
 Der General-Bass   *nachzuschlagen pfleget, wann die Singe-*
                  Stimme geschlossen.

Telemann (1733–34) p. 40
 Die Schlüsse in Cantaten   *pfleget man nachzuschlagen [nachdem]*
                  der Sänger die letzten Sylben spricht.

The V chord with the voice's 1's
(Exx. 5.2*a*, 5.3*a*, *b*)

Telemann (1733–34) p. 40
 Die Schlüsse in Opern   *werden so fort angeschlagen, wann der*
                  Sänger die letzten Sylben spricht.

Hahn (1751) p. 57
 Der Bass, [um] den Schluss zu machen,   *pfleget erst nachzuschlagen, dann da*
                  die Sing-Stimme durch ihr artiges
                  Fallen sich schon geschlossen.

When the x or 3 occurs on a sixteenth note, the excerpts in the right column all agree that something happens "after the end of the voice," "when the voice closes," or "after the singer speaks the last syllables." That which happens is described most accurately by Heinichen in 1711: it is the brief *resolution* of the 4—that is, the 3—which is postponed until the voice is finished. Later explanations are less precise, but usually include some form of the word *nachschlagen*. Thus, what is played after the voice finishes is "the cadence 4 x," "the thorough-bass," or "the close," the last two meaning, apparently, some part of the accompaniment or the realization. By the time of Telemann's book of thorough-bass exercises in 1733–35, this cadence had become so frequent and familiar in recitative that it probably did not require as precise a definition as it did in 1711.

The comments on the lower part of Fig. 3 are made completely clear by accompanying realizations written out in score (Exx. 5.2*a* and 5.3). For Telemann, the close in this case occurs while the last syllables are being sung. For Hahn, the accompaniment plays the close "after the voice descends," thus following the falling third or fourth and during the voice's last syllables. Hahn continues to use the verb *nachschlagen*, which is associated with the other realizations at the top of Fig. 3. His comment, however, refers not only to a dominant triad simultaneous with the bass's root note, but also to the situation in Ex. 5.3*a* in which the voice supplies the interval of a fourth for an eighth beat before the dominant triad is completed.

The second factor leading me to conclude that Telemann describes the different realizations of the brief cadence lies in his own scores. All of the cadences in the many church cantatas in his *Harmonischer Gottes-Dienst* of 1725–26 are notated as brief. Also brief are all the cadences in the two secular cantatas from before 1750 which are available to me.[10] In his opera *Socrates* from 1721, most of the cadences are, again, brief, but about sixteen percent of them do have a delayed V chord. He delays V, however, in a number of ways: most often by continuing below the voice's final 1 or 1's the previous IV, ii$_5^6$, or IV$_6$ chord, or by placing a rest at this point. Occasionally he also places under the voice's 1's a I$_4^6$ or I$_6$ chord (see Ex. 5.12*a*). Thus only six percent of the cadences in this opera are actually notated with a rest under the voice's 1's, as J. S. Bach usually does and as

---

[10] *Harmonischer Gottes-Dienst* (Hamburg, 1725–26), copy at the British Library (H.71.b.). See *Tirsis am Scheidewege*, ed. Klaus Hofmann (Bärenreiter, 1981), and *Kanarienvogel Kantate*, ed. Werner Menke (Bärenreiter, 1977). These two cantatas have not yet appeared in the complete works.

became common in the delayed cadence generally after 1750.[11] There were thus several types of delayed cadence available for those rare occasions that required a special sense of finality or emphasis. Other composers of the period, such as Scarlatti, Keiser, and Handel, likewise overwhelmingly favor the brief cadence, but occasionally notate one of the delayed types.[12] Like the numerous brief cadences, they were certainly easy enough to notate. In any event, changing a brief cadence in a cantata to a delayed one would require further instructions from the composer concerning the method of delay.

This consideration leads to the third factor acting against the assumption that Telemann preferred delayed cadences in cantatas. In order to achieve this result, the performer would have to change the notated rhythm of hundreds of Telemann's cadences. Extending each brief cadence by the value of a quarter beat would create measures of 5/4. Italian and German recitative, however, is carefully crafted to fit into measures of four quarter beats. The vocal line, to be sure, is expected to flow freely with a speechlike declamation. To periodically change the continuo part to 5/4, however, would seem to be a rhythmic disturbance of quite a different order from the rhythmic flexibility expected of the singer.

There is certainly no indication in Telemann's notation to suggest such a practice. He does carefully align all the notes in the instructional source from which Ex. 5.2a comes, but elsewhere, as in the cantatas from 1725–26 and 1744, there is no attempt at all for vertical alignment. As in most manuscripts and printed sources of the period, a whole note in the bass is simply written in the middle of a bar; the first of two half notes appears approximately below the second quarter note in the voice. In most cases the penultimate bass note on scale degree 5 in the cadences therefore occurs considerably to the left of the voice's first 1; occasionally it lies between the

---

[11] See Telemann's *Der geduldige Socrates* in *TM* xx, p. 47, m. 13 for scale degree 4 sustained below 1; p. 62, m. 10 for 6; p. 49, m. 8 for scale degree 3 below 1; p. 257, m. 6 for 5; and p. 15, m. 21 for a quarter rest.

[12] See Scarlatti's *Griselda* (*OAS* iii, 191, m. 14) for V delayed by sustaining a V$\frac{4}{2}$ chord below the voice's 1-1; and Keiser's *Passion nach dem Evangelisten Markus*, ed. Felix Schroeder in *Die Kantate* 152 (Stuttgart-Hohenheim: Hänssler-Verlag, 1967), end of Nos. 7 and 9, and m. 11 of No. 19 for V delayed by a rest, a ii$\frac{6}{5}$ chord, and i$_6$, respectively. See also Handel's *Hercules*, Act II (*HG* iv, 113) for V delayed by a rest. Dean prints the last example in *ML* 58 (1977): 399, to suggest that Handel intended thereby to emphasize the word *jealousy*.

two 1's and only rarely to their right.[13] From our point of view, such a lack of concern for alignment would seem as much a disadvantage to the contemporary continuo player as it is to us.

For all these reasons, then, it seems to me that Telemann intended that all his cadences, whether notated as brief or delayed, should be performed as written. There was a certain variety among his notated delayed cadences. If I am correct, there was also, as he demonstrated in Ex. 5.2, variety in the continuo realizations of the brief cadence.

The brief cadences decline in frequency during the second half of the century, although a few still occur in the 1760s in operas by Gluck and late works by Telemann. As late as 1752 Quantz still seems to be describing the brief structure when he writes that "in all cadences of theatrical recitatives, whether accompanied or secco, the bass must begin its two notes, which consist of a descending leap of the fifth, under the last syllable" (referring perhaps to the second 1 in a feminine ending, as in Ex. 4.7b, or to the single 1 in a masculine ending, as in Ex. 5.3b).[14] There are even a few examples of brief cadences which are deceptive.[15]   Eventually, however, the brief structure was considered unsatisfactory.   In 1762 Marpurg prints a brief downward-fourth cadence in which he finds three errors. Although none of his objections would apply necessarily to the brief falling-third cadences, he feels that it is not good to anticipate V by omitting the rest.[16] He thus refers

---

[13] *Harmonischer Gottes-Dienst* was engraved by Telemann himself. See pp. 72, 145, 173, and 207 in the first volume, for example, for the bass's 5 to the left of the first 1; pp. 19, 57, and 75 for 5 between the two 1's; and pp. 132 and 146 for 5 to the right of both 1's. Sometimes even the barlines do not line up, as on pp. 109 and 159. See also his *Musicalisches Lob Gottes in der Gemeine des Herrn* (Nuremberg: Balthasar Schmid, 1744), copy in the British Library (H.71.). Similar misalignment occurs in Heinichen's book of 1711 and in MSS of Scarlatti's *Il Pompeo* in *HS* vi and Keiser's operas in *HS* i–iii. Not so badly aligned is Handel's autograph score of *Tamerlano* in *IOB* xxvii. Bach, on the other hand, more carefully aligns the notes: see *NBA* I/iv, pp. VII and IX, for examples of recitative in manuscript.

[14] Johann Joachim Quantz, *Versuch einer Anweisung die Flöte traversiere zu spielen* (Berlin, 1752), 3rd edn. (1789; repr. in *DM* ii [1953]), 272. I have followed part of Edward R. Reilly's translation from *On Playing the Flute*, 2nd edn. (New York: Schirmer Books, 1985), 292.

[15] See the progression V-I₆ in the 4-3-1 cadences from Handel's *Orlando* of 1733 (*HHA* II/xxviii, 62, 91, 124, and 163), as well as in the descending-fourth cadences in Telemann's *Der Tag des Gerichts* from 1762 in *DDT*, 1. Folge, xxviii, 64; and Handel's *Serse* from 1738 in *NG* xv, 644.

[16] Marpurg, *Kritische Briefe*, ii, 352–3 (4 Sept 1762). He objects that with the brief cadence (his Ex. 2 on p. 353) one cannot explain the unusual harmonic movement from V$^4_2$ to V in the continuo (see Heinichen's 1728 book, pp. 673 and 674 n., concerning

to "the rest," for after mid-century the authentic and deceptive cadences (see Fig. 2) are now usually delayed by means of a rest below the voice's final syllable(s). Therefore when Haydn mentions in 1768 that in a certain accompanied recitative "the accompaniment should not enter until the singer has quite finished his text, even though the score often shows the contrary," he is not referring to cadences at all, since at this date they are almost all delayed in the notation.[17]

In the 1790s, finally, writers begin to suggest that when one finds a notated brief cadence in an older work, one should change it to the delayed type with a rest below the voice's final notes. In his thorough-bass book of 1791 Türk shows three downward-fourth cadences: the first with V directly below the voice's last accented syllable, the second with a rest below it, and the last with I_6. "If the bass is underlayed as in the first example," he explains, "one [that is, the continuo player] usually waits, in spite of this [notation] until the singer has completely finished the phrase [as in his second example]. However, according to circumstances one can [as in the final example] also enter during the singing." In the second edition of his book in 1800 he describes the brief cadence in his first example as "incorrectly underlayed," but admits that he himself had included such a cadence in a cantata published in 1782, even though he "now considers it incorrect."[18]

---

the same problem), that the I chord in his example ends on weak beat 4 of the measure, and that it is a short note tied to a longer note. He also rejects a cadence like my Ex. 4.4c with d (his Ex. 1 on p. 353).

[17] Joseph Haydn, *Gesammelte Briefe und Aufzeichnungen*, ed. H. C. Robbins Landon and Dénes Bartha (Bärenreiter, 1965), 58; trans. by Robbins Landon from *The Collected Correspondence and London Notebooks of Joseph Haydn* (London: Barrie and Rockliff, 1959), 9. Haydn refers specifically to his later oratorio/cantata *Applausus* from 1768 and to a situation in which the final two repeated pitches of a vocal phrase overlap in the score with vigorous orchestral figures (see *HW* xxvii/2, p. 12 on the word *Metamorphosis*). The cadences in the work are all delayed, and in only one of them (p. 169) does the final syllable of a word accented on the antepenultimate syllable coincide with the V chord in the strings. In any case, Haydn's comment does not seem to me to refer to the *brief* cadences at all, as assumed in Donington, *The Interpretation of Early Music* (1975), 661.

[18] Daniel Gottlob Türk, *Kurze Anweisung zum Generalbassspielen* (Halle and Leipzig, 1791), copy in Sibley Music Library, Eastman School of Music, repr. on Microcard UR-59 201-6 (University of Rochester Press), 263: "Sollte . . . der Bass so untergelegt seyn, wie hier bey d) [his three examples are labeled d), e), and f)], so wartet man dessen ungeachtet gewöhnlich, bis der Sänger seinen Satz völlig vorgetragen hat e). Jedoch kann man in dem Beyspiele f) nach Umständen noch während des Singens einfallen . . ." See also his *Anweisung zum Generalbassspielen*, 2nd edn. (Halle and

Ex. 5.4 Converting a brief cadence to delayed in Handel's *Jephtha*
(Callcott, 1792)

1782 is very late for a composer to write a brief cadence, and 1791 is very late to publish a book on thorough-bass. For the most part, the only brief cadences still around by 1791 would occur in works which had been written much earlier and were still performed. Few Baroque works with brief cadences survived this long—only the works of Handel, especially *Messiah*. It is mainly in later performances of Handel's oratorios, then, that the practice arose of "correcting" the brief cadences, of converting them into the sort of cadence that later audiences preferred to hear. In 1792 Callcott shows the transformation in Ex. 5.4, "remembering," he says, "to let the voice part be entirely finished before the two last notes are struck in the bass." His unidentified cadence actually comes from the end of a recitative in Handel's oratorio *Jephtha* (from around 1752), where it is accompanied by sustained strings.[19] In *The Singer's Guide* published around 1800, Peter Urbani shows how to perform an excerpt from the end of "Comfort Ye" from Handel's *Messiah*. Handel originally wrote the accompanied brief cadence shown as Ex. I in the Introduction, whereas Urbani simply places a quarter rest below the voice's last syllable and shifts the two cadence chords over to beats 2 and 3 of the measure (see Ex. 6.23*b* in the next chapter).[20] In

Leipzig, 1800; repr., Amsterdam: Fritz Knuf, 1971), 339: "unrichtig untergelegt," and 340 n.: "erkläre ich es jetzt für unrichtig." The examples and the explanation occur also in a *neue verbesserte Ausgabe* (Vienna: S. A. Steiner, 1822), copy in the Special Collections of the UCLA Music Library, 298.

[19] John Wall Callcott, *Explanation of the Notes, Marks, Words, &c Used in Music* (London, preface dated 1792), copy in the Library of Congress repr. on microfiche in *Musical Dictionaries*, Series I (Washington, DC: Brookhaven Press, 1976), 17. See *Jephtha*, Act III, sc. i in *HG* xliv, 189.

[20] Concerning Handel's original notation, see *Das Autograph des Oratoriums "Messias,"* ed. with preface by Friedrich Chrysander, 3 vols. (Hamburg, 1889–92), repr. as *Handel's Messiah: The Original MSS in Facsimile* (New York: Da Capo, 1969); and *Handel's Conducting Score of Messiah*, with introduction by Watkins Shaw (London:

spite of the method of performance, however, this cadence continued to be notated sometimes as in Ex. I. Therefore, when Mendelssohn includes a brief falling-third cadence in his arrangement of Handel's *Israel in Egypt* around 1846, I presume he intended that it be performed as Callcott, Urbani, and Türk suggested.[21]

The full score of *Messiah* was first published in 1767, with later editions appearing periodically until our own time. The earlier editions print the falling-third cadence at the end of "Comfort Ye" as Handel wrote it. This occurs, for example, in Clarke's piano/vocal score published early in the nineteenth century.[22] When Friedrich Chrysander began editing the works of Handel in 1858 for the complete edition published for the German Handel Society by Breitkopf & Härtel in Leipzig, he likewise printed the brief cadences as Handel wrote them. When he reached the oratorio *Samson* for the tenth volume in 1861, however, he acknowledges "the aid of the oldest English pianoforte arrangement by Dr. Clarke, . . . which has been followed—with justice, though in rather too servile a manner,—by all later English pianoforte editions," but adds:

> I have introduced an innovation in the accompaniment of the cadence of the recitative (viz.[he gives the sign for a fermata]), by which the discrepancy, hitherto existing, between the printed accompaniment and the actual performance, is most simply removed.[23]

In succeeding volumes of this set, the brief cadences, whether secco or accompanied, show the V chord shifted to the right and, before Volume 50, also a fermata below the final accented syllable in the voice. The shift and

---

Scolar Press for the Royal Musical Association, 1974). For more on the book by Peter Urbani (Italian singer and composer 1749–1816), see n. 91 in the next chapter.

[21] G. F. Handel, *Israel in Egypt . . . in Vocal Score, edited, and the pianoforte accompaniment arranged, by Felix Mendelssohn Bartholdy* (London and New York: Novello, Ewer and Co., n.d.), copy in UCLA Music Library, 35: the cadence with the text "even darkness, which might be felt," which concludes the chorus "He Sent a Thick Darkness." Mendelssohn died in 1847, and this arrangement was first published as part of the series "Novello's Cheap Oratorios" or "Novello's Octavo Editions of Oratorios"; see *The Musical Times* 3 (1850): 294 and 316. Ewer was part of the firm's name between 1867 and 1898.

[22] John Clarke-Whitfeld, *The Messiah . . . arranged for the Piano-forte or organ* (London: Jones & Co., 1835), apparently originally published before 1808 (see *NG* iv, 449). For a French version with the brief cadence, see *Le Messie . . . reduit pour piano et chant par F. Gasse* (Paris: Marquerie Frères, 1840). Copies of both works are in the Special Collections of the UCLA Music Library.

[23] *HG* x, p. XI.

the fermata thus occur at the end of "Comfort Ye" in *Messiah*, which, although edited by Chrysander, appeared as Volume 45 after his death.

Similar practice continues, generally, in succeeding editions of Handel's works. In the new *Hallische Händel Ausgabe* published by Bärenreiter, operas and oratorios published through 1971 shift the V chord slightly to the right, but usually omit the fermata. This method appears in the final cadence of "Comfort Ye" in the full score published in 1965. In the piano/vocal score of 1972, however, the V^7 chord is exactly with the voice's 1, as Handel wrote it. Most of the subsequent scores during the 1990s continue this practice, and finally J. Merrill Knapp explains in 1993 in connection with an opera by Handel:

> It must be emphasized that cadences in most Italian operas of the early eighteenth century were executed on the first beat of the final bar and not after the singer had finished singing, as was true later in the eighteenth century.[24]

The same general transition can be observed in the full or piano/vocal performing editions of *Messiah*. A fermata appears below the accented 1 in "Comfort Ye" from the edition by Shaw in 1959, a fermata in parentheses in the scores of Coopersmith in 1947 and 1950 and the reprint in 1989 of the score by Mann.[25] The V chord is shifted but the fermata is missing in the editions by Mann in 1966 and 1983.[26] The V^7 occurs exactly with the voice's final 1, however, in scores by Prout (1902), Spicker (1912), Burrows (1987), and Shaw (1992).[27] It is Watkins Shaw who finally explains the change in his revised score:

> In 1959 [the date of his original edition] the long-standing convention was unchallenged whereby, despite the strict notation of the bar, the cadence chords at the ends of recitatives were held up until after the soloist had finished. . . . Subsequently this convention was challenged by J. A. Westrup [in his article in 1962].

---

[24] *HHA* II/13: *Flavio, Re de' Langobardi*, p. XVII.

[25] Piano/vocal score by Watkins Shaw (London: Novello, 1959; repr. 1966); J. M. Coopersmith, piano/vocal (New York: Carl Fischer, 1947) and full score (Carl Fischer, 1947, 1950); Alfred Mann, full score (New York: Dover).

[26] Alfred Mann, full score in *Documents of the Musical Past*, No. 6 (New Brunswick, NJ: Rutgers University Press).

[27] Ebenezer Prout, full score (New York: G. Schirmer, preface dated 1902); Max Spicker, piano/vocal score (New York: G. Schirmer); Donald Burrows, piano/vocal score (London and New York: Edition Peters).

> . . . Handel's contemporary Telemann . . . drew a distinction
> between cadences in opera (non-postponed) and cantata (postponed). . . .
> This brings up the awkward question of which category *Messiah*, with
> obvious operatic roots, belongs to.

He concludes, however, that the performers are therefore "free," in the case
of each particular cadence, "to decide for themselves," since it is a "matter
of taste" and "individual judgement."[28]

In the complete works of Telemann, this same freedom of choice is
exercised by the editor in 1967 and 1969 in the operas *Socrates* and *Damon*.
In the church cantatas (1953), however, every one of the numerous brief
cadences has a fermata below the accented 1 and the V chord shifted to the
right.[29] In 1961 Mozart's arrangement of *Messiah* in the *Neue Ausgabe*
shows the V^7 chord moved to the right at the end of "Comfort Ye." Mozart
himself, however, may have written the cadence in 1789 as a very late
example of the brief type, for he had earlier included two brief downward-
fourth cadences in his own opera *Lucio Silla*.[30] In the earlier volumes of the
complete works of Fux, the V chord is shifted and two small slanting lines
placed below 1 on the top line of each staff of the continuo realization. This
is to offer the possibility for either a brief or delayed performance, even
though the application of the latter "seems doubtful with Fux." In later
volumes from 1976 to 1996, however, the cadences are printed as Fux wrote
them, but with the suggestion that one occasionally delay the V.[31]

---

[28] Watkins Shaw, rev. piano/vocal score (London: Novello, 1992), p. vii.

[29] *TM* xx: *Der geduldige Socrates* (1721), ed. Bernd Baselt (who was associated
later with *HHA*), 100, for example, where V is with 1 in m. 31, but marked for delay by a
fermata in m. 33; *TM* xxi: *Der neumodische Liebhaber Damon* (1724), ed. Bernd Baselt;
and *TM* ii–v: *Harmonischer Gottes-Dienst*, ed. Gustav Fock.

[30] *NMA* X:28/I/ii: *Der Messias*, K 572 with German text, ed. Andreas
Holschneider, 9. The full score was first published in 1803, at which time performers
probably did follow Callcott's advice in Ex. 5.4. For a piano/vocal arrangement, see the
modern edn. (Bärenreiter, 1989), ed. Ernst R. Barthel. For *Lucio Silla*, K 135, see *NMA*
II:5/vii, ed. Kathleen Kuzmick Hansell (1986), p. 293, m. 50, and p. 297, m. 115. See
also p. XLI of the *Vorwort* concerning Tosi's *cadenza tronca* and other ideas from Sven
Hansell's article of 1968.

[31] See *Johann Joseph Fux: Sämtliche Werke*, IV/1: *La fede sacrilega nella morte
del Precursor S Giovanni Battista* (1714), ed. Hugo Zelzer (1959), p. XI: musical
examples showing the editorial notation and the brief and delayed performances that may
result, even though for the latter "ihre Anwendung bei Fux eher zweifelhaft scheint." See
also V/1: *Julo Ascanio, Re d'Alb*a (1708), ed. Hellmut Federhofer (1962), p. X. Even in
V/5: *La decima fatica d'Ercole* (1710) published in 1996, in which the little lines are

In the Gluck complete works, the Vienna version of the opera *Ezio* (1992) shows an asterisk on each brief cadence and a footnote reading "Kadenzierung nachschlagend." In the Prague version of the same opera (1990), however, the root of the V chord appears with the accented 1, but the realizations contain unusual harmonies: in one case, V^7 with the first 1 and I_4^6 with the second, moving, after the voice has finished, to a I_6 chord; in another case, a I_4^6 below both 1's, moving later deceptively to V_3^6 of V.[32] In the opera *Telemaco* published earlier in 1972, the root of the V chord is again below the accented syllable, but on one occasion a I_4^6 chord occurs with both 1's, followed by I in root position. These strange I_4^6 chords are no doubt an attempt to avoid the dissonance between the voice's scale degree 1 and the accompaniment's scale degree 7, but I know of no historical evidence to support the practice. Two other brief cadences in the modern edition of *Telemaco*, on the other hand, are harmonized in a more authentic way, with I_4^6 below the first 1 moving to V below the second.[33]

The recordings available to me mirror the same changes in performance practice. In 1980 Christopher Hogwood performed the brief cadence at the end of "Comfort Ye" as Handel notated it. This was done also in 1983 by Gardiner and in 1988 and 1989 by Pinnock and Parrott.[34] *Messiah* recordings from before 1980 include a rest in the accompaniment with the voice's 1, followed usually by more rest and then ponderous and deliberate chords on V^7 and I. Sometimes this older practice continues even into the 1990s.

This performance history has been accompanied by a long series of explanations which state that something in the accompaniment is to be played after something in the voice. We have already noted in Fig. 3 the earliest such statements. Türk in 1791 and Callcott in 1792 describe the situation in Ex. 5.4. Later writers and editors repeat the essential elements of this method of performance: it is the last two chords (the V and I) which are to be played after the voice has completely finished, thus necessitating a rest in the accompaniment during the quarter beat which begins with the voice's accented 1. Thus in 1953 we read: "In den Rezitativen werden die

---

omitted and V coincides with 1, Federhofer recommends on p. IX "anstelle von simultanen, gelegentlich die ebenso zeitgemässen nachschlagenden Kadenzen."

[32] *C. W. Gluck: Sämtliche Werke*, Vienna version (1763) in iii/24, ed. Gabrielle Buschmeier; Prague version (1750) in iii/14, ed. Gabrielle Buschmeier and Hanspeter Bennwitz, p. 265, m. 6, and p. 183, m. 15, respectively.

[33] Ibid., i/2: *Telemaco* (1765), ed. Karl Geiringer, p. 79, m. 29; p. 111, m. 32; and p. 112, m. 58.

[34] See footnote 10 in the next chapter for specific recordings by these conductors.

Kadenzakkorde natürlich nachgeschlagen," and as late as 1992: "Kadenzierung nachschlagend."[35]   These numerous statements between 1711 and 1992 must, as we have seen, be read with great care. Most are in German, and most include the word "nachschlagen." They must all be carefully analyzed, however, and understood in the historical context in which they occur.

Fig. 4 Performance of the V chord in the brief cadences

	1680s–1790	1791–1860	1861–1971	1972–1997	the future?
Written	V with accented 1	V with accented 1	fermata & shifted V	fermata or V with accented 1	always V with accented 1
Performed	always as written	V delayed by rest	V delayed by rest	as brief or delayed, as preferred by performer or editor	always as written

The history of the performance of the brief cadence can then be summarized by identifying four periods from the past (see Fig. 4). First of all, from its origin in the 1680s until around 1790, the bass was played as written, with freedom in secco recitative granted to the keyboard player to vary the realization to the extent shown in Exx. 5.2 and 5.3. Secondly, from around 1791 to 1860 a brief cadence in an older work was notated as the composer wrote it, but the performer altered the structure so that it became a delayed cadence, as in Ex. 5.4. By this time performers were no longer concerned much with thorough-bass, and performing editions simply printed a simple chordal realization for the pianist to play. Thirdly, from 1861 to

---

[35] The first is from *TM* ii: *Harmonischer Gottes-Dienst*, ed. Gustav Fock, p. IX; the second from Gluck's *Sämtliche Werke*, iii/24, ed. Gabrielle Buschmeier, p. 86, for example.

about 1971, fermatas and shifted chords made the delayed alteration more apparent to the performer. In a fourth period, from around 1972 to perhaps 1997 or so, some brief cadences are notated and presumably to be performed as written, while others in the same opera, cantata or oratorio continue to be marked for delay.

Now we are ready, I believe, for a new period in this performance history, one in which every composer's cadences will be performed—at least in regard to the basic rhythmic structure—as they are notated. Winton Dean has strongly suggested "that when Handel wrote a foreshortened [brief] cadence he meant it."[36] I think we can add now that when Telemann wrote such a cadence, he also meant it.   And I know of no evidence to even suggest that when *any* composer before 1791 notated a brief cadence, he did not want it performed exactly in that manner, whether in an opera, a cantata, or in any other work.   The performer never had the choice, let alone the obligation, to change the basic structure.   During the Baroque period the composer wrote out the *basso continuo* with the intention that it be played and not altered by the performer.   The keyboard player had considerable freedom, but that was confined to the realization, which itself offered a wide range of variety.   We may or may not want to hear brief cadences in performances today, but that is a different matter of audience preference. Historically, however, I feel that there is no question that composers who wrote brief cadences—with the falling third or the falling fourth—wanted them performed that way, and that it is incorrect in modern editions of their works to indicate any alteration whatsoever under any circumstances.

The Bass Figures in the Brief Cadences

Some sources, such as the cantatas in Heinichen's books, include no figures at all. Others are carefully and thoroughly figured. Most lie somewhere in between, with only some of the cadences marked. We have already noted four different realizations for the brief secco cadence. One involves the figures 4 3, 4 x, 4 ♯, 4 ♯3, or 4 3♯, or 4 ♮ above the bass's scale degree 5, which supports the penultimate chord of the cadence. Only rarely is 5 written above the 4, and occasionally the seventh is added. This is the classic early type shown by Heinichen in Ex. 4.10*a* and the one evolving directly from the corresponding unbroken cadence of Ex. 4.3*c*. The other three do not

---

[36] "The Performance of Recitative in Late Baroque Opera," *ML* 58 (1977): 398.

include 4, but only an x, a sharp, a natural, or, if no chromatic alteration of 3 is required, nothing at all above this bass note.[37]   These include the realization of Telemann in Ex. 5.2*a* and Hahn in Ex. 5.3*b*, in which the entire dominant chord occurs simultaneously with the first or single 1; that described verbally by Heinichen in Ex. 4.10*b* and Telemann in Ex. 5.2*b*, where the 3 by itself is delayed until after the second 1; and that of Hahn in Ex. 5.3*a*, where the three right-hand notes are delayed by an eighth rest and thus sound simultaneously with the second 1. Telemann includes the natural sign above the bass's 5 (or G) in Ex. 5.2*a*, whereas Hahn prints no figures in Ex. 5.3. It is possible, I suppose, that even when only a sign for 3 is marked, the continuo player had the option of adding a seventh or even preceding it with 4.   4 and 3 were apparently sometimes both heard together, for Gasparini says in 1708 that when the penultimate cadence chord "calls for both seventh and major third, the fourth, as an acciacccatura, is added between the major third and the fifth."[38]   In addition, Bach sometimes marks ⁴₃ below the two 1's of a feminine ending, probably intending that the second 1 be heard simultaneously with the full dominant triad.[39]

In the realization in Ex. 5.2*a*, the figured bass's natural sign occurs precisely with the bass note. In Ex. 5.2*b* and *c*, however, 3 is actually played slightly later.   One might think that this later sounding of 3 might be depicted in the score by placing the sign to the right rather than directly above the bass note, as I have done in Ex. 5.2*b* and *c*. Because of the serious

---

[37] MSS of numbers operas generally have no key signature for recitatives. Cantatas, on the other hand, usually do: see Telemann's *Harmonischer Gottes-Dienst* of 1725–26 and some of the examples by Gasparini, Giovanni Bononcini, and Scarlatti in *IC* vii, x, and xiii, as well as the cantatas of Bach and Handel. When there is a key signature, the figures above the bass's 5 naturally take account of this fact.

[38] Francesco Gasparini, *L'armonico pratico al cimbalo* (Venice, 1708), repr. in *Monuments of Music and Music Literature in Facsimile*, Ser. 2, xiv (New York: Broude Brothers, 1967), 94; trans. by Frank S. Stillings and ed. by David L. Burrows as *The Practical Harmonist at the Harpsichord* (New Haven, CT: Yale School of Music, 1963), 82. His examples show the seventh of the chord on top and "all the notes . . . are played together at a single stroke" (p. 92; trans., p. 80). This chord then resolves to a tonic chord which includes scale degree 7 as a mordent to be played "on, or rather a little before the beat and released immediately" (p. 91; trans., p. 80). See *NHD*, 3; and Sven Hansell in *MQ* 54 (1968): 230–31 .

[39] See the cantata *BWV* 16 (1726) in *BG* ii, 192 (in *NBA* I/iv, 123, the ₃ is incorrectly placed). For the same progression in masculine endings, see *BWV* 115 (1724) in *BG* xxiv, 131, and *BWV* 199 (Weimar version, 1714) in *NBA* I/xx, 4. The last work is dated 1713 in *MGG*, 2nd edn., *Personenteil*, i, 1438. I have generally taken dates for Bach's vocal works, however, from the *Bach Compendium*, ed. Hans-Joachim Schulze and Christoph Wolff, i: *Vokalwerke* (Leipzig and Frankfurt: Edition Peters, 1985–89).

misalignment described above between the voice part and the bass, however, this does not occur. Therefore, in the cantatas of the *Harmonischer Gottes-Dienst,* for example, Telemann regularly places the symbol for 3 directly above the bass note, even though it is to be played after the singer's last syllable. Thus in general, when 3 alone is indicated in a score, it could apparently indicate theoretically any of the realizations in Ex. 5.2 or 5.3.

Most cadences occur in secco recitative, and here, of course, the figures are more important than in accompanied recitative, where the melody instruments, in effect, perform the realization. In most cadences the bass's scale degree 5 occurs precisely with the first or single 1 in the voice. In accompanied recitatives, the noncontinuo instruments either play the V or V^7 chord with the first 1,[40] or play the figured bass's 4 with the first 1 and 3 with the second (Ex. 4.7a). Occasionally the bass note alone occurs with the first 1, and the other instruments play, after an eighth rest, with the second 1. In this case the continuo figures are 4 3, with the 4 coinciding with the voice's first 1 and the 3 with a dominant chord played by all the instruments.[41] Sometimes both the bass note and the other instruments are delayed by an eighth rest, as we noted in Ex. 4.7b. There are even a few secco examples of such an eighth-rest delay.[42]

Surveying the manuscript sources from around 1680 to 1750, then, one can get some idea of how the bass figures change over the course of time. Those sources which include marks at cadence generally show a preference for 4 3 during the earlier period from about 1680 to 1700, and for only a sharp sign thereafter. Scarlatti carefully writes "4 3" for almost every brief cadence in *Il Pompeo* of 1683 and in most of his other operas and cantatas. Only rarely, however, does he indicate a required sharp for the 3.[43]

---

[40] For both masculine and feminine endings, see the MS presumably supervised by Keiser of *La forza dell virtù* (1700), *HS* ii, 135, 137, and 138.

[41] See the autograph of Scarlatti's *Telemaco* (1718) in *IOB* xxiii, 13[r] in Act I, sc. i, and two examples in Act II, sc. ix.

[42] See the MS of the revised version in 1739 of Porpora's opera *Semiramide Riconosciuta* in *IOB* xxx, Act I, 44 (two examples) and 92; Act II, 19; and Act III, 28, 31, and 38. See also Porpora's *Oratorio per la nascita di Gesù Cristo* (1748) in *IOR* xx, 8[r] (accompanied) and 127[v] (a secco trio in which 3-1-1 in one voice coincides with 1-1-5 in another). See also Wagenseil's *Ariodante* of 1745 in *IOB* lxxiii, 19[r], 62[v], 74[r], and 79[r] for examples in which the voice's two 1's are quarter notes; and Nicola Logroscino's comic opera *Il governatore* (1747), *IOB* xlii, 18[r]. In these same sources V is delayed sometimes by an eighth rest also in the brief downward-fourth cadences.

[43] See *HS* vi and vii for the operas *Il Pompeo* and *Dafni* (1700), *IOB* xxiii for *Telemaco*. Figures from the MSS seem to be faithfully followed in the modern editions

From 1680 to around 1705 other composers of Italian opera, such as Pasquini and Stradella, occasionally mark 4 3 or 4 3♯, but only for one to ten cadences in each opera.[44] The same practice occurs in oratorios[45] and cantatas of the period.[46] During this early period most of the falling-third cadences still tend to be unbroken (as in Ex. 4.3*a–c*) or with the repeated 3 (Ex. 4.2*b*), both types usually marked with 4 3. Because of the close connection historically between these two types, the increasing number of brief broken cadences were no doubt simply marked the same way to indicate a similar continuo realization. At this time the falling-fourth cadences were also marked with 4 3.

One later composer continues to mark 4 3 or 4 3♯ for some of his brief cadences, but ♯, 3, or 3 ♮ for others. Leonardo Leo indicates some sort of 4 3 for eleven cadences in his *Catone in Utica* of 1729, whereas four others are marked with only 3. In the later arrangement of the opera prepared for Handel in 1732, there are four 4 3 cadences and three with only a symbol for 3. Such careful distinction between the two types is unique in the repertoire available to me. It gives evidence, I would think, of an unusual sensitivity to the different affective qualities of the two realizations.

After 1700, however, when the brief structure had become the principal type of cadence (see Fig. 2), almost all penultimate bass notes are either unmarked or marked with a symbol for 3 rather than 4 3. When marked, a sharp or natural sign usually appears above or below the note. There are isolated cases of the sharp even earlier.[47] After 1700 it appears

in *OAS*. For some of the cantatas, see *IC* xiii, and for oratorios, *Gli oratorii di Alessandro Scarlatti*, ed. Lino Bianchi (Rome: Edizioni de Santis, 1964–), i–iv.

[44] See Pasquini's *L'Idalma* (1680) in *IOB* xi, Act I, 24[r] or 103[v], for example (and eight others in the same opera); Stradella's *Moro per amore* (before 1682), *IOB* x, Act III, 5[r] (and three others); Bernabei's *L'Ascanio* (1686), *IOB* lxvi, 210; Pollarolo's *Gl'inganni felici* (1696), *IOB* xvi, Act II, sc. ii, p. 2 (and three others); and Mancini's *Gl'amanti generosi* (1705), *IOB* xviii, 14 and 18.

[45] For a very early example, see Pasquini's *Sant'Agnese* (1671), *IOR* viii, 86[r]. For later ones, see Lanciani, *Santa Dimna, figlia del re d'Irlanda* (1687), *IOR* vi, 28[v] (and four others); Colonna, *La caduta di Gierusalemme* (1688), *IOR* v, 16[r], 24[v] (two 1's on a dotted quarter and eighth note), and 116[r] (two quarter notes); Perti, *Agar*, *IOR* iv, 36[r]; and Ziani, *Il sacrifizio d'Isacco* (1707), *IOR* x, 8[r] (and at least eight others).

[46] See examples of Gasparini in *IC* vii, 49; and Giovanni Bononcini in *IC* x, 108.

[47] See Pallavicino, *L'Amazzone corsara* (1686), *IOB* xiii, 16[r] and 46[v]; Draghi, oratorio *Jephte* (1687), *IOR* ix, 32[v]; and G. Bononcini, Serenata (1693), *IC* x, 145, 155, 208, 221, and 234.

sometimes in a few cadences within a single opera[48] or oratorio.[49] Many brief cadences, however, are left unmarked, even those requiring chromatic alteration.

More numerous are the signs in Handel's Italian operas. In his composing score for *Tamerlano* in 1724, for example, he marks a sharp or natural above the bass's 5 in twenty-three brief cadences. Three of these are accompanied, the rest secco; three move deceptively to I_6, one to VI, the rest to the usual tonic. In the same opera, however, twenty-seven similar places are left unmarked, even though fourteen of them require a chromatic change. There are also nineteen falling-fourth cadences marked with a sharp or natural.[50] A similar practice occurs in most of Handel's thirty-nine operas from *Almira* of 1704 through *Deidamia* of 1740–41. The number of cadences marked with a sharp or natural sign ranges from one to twenty-three per opera, the number which need a sign but are unmarked, from around three to nineteen. There seems to be no apparent reason why some are marked and others not. In all of his operas I have found four hundred and forty brief cadences with a sharp or natural, and only one with a $\frac{5}{4}$#.[51] Although the original sources for his secular cantatas from 1707 to 1709 are less reliable, they generally show a similar pattern: in sixty cantatas, nine brief cadences have a sharp and only one has 4#.[52]

Other languages usually follow the same practice. In Handel's twenty-four oratorios and similar works in English from 1718 to 1757, two hundred and fifty-three brief falling-third cadences are marked with a sharp

---

[48] G. Bononcini, *Il trionfo di Camilla* (1696, MS copied around 1700), *IOB* xvii, 15^v (and twenty-nine others); A. M. Bononcini, *Griselda* (1718–19), *IOB* xxi, 206^r; Gasparini, *Il Bajazet* (1719), *IOB* xxiv, Act II, 19^r (and six others, most of them early examples of the deceptive resolution of V to I_6, VI, or V_6 of V; Leo, *L'Olimpiade* (1737), *IOB* xxxvi, 63, 182, 338, 402.

[49] Bencini, *Il sacrificio di Abramo* (1708), *IOR* xv, 22^r, 71^v, etc.; Galuppi, *Adamo ed Eva* (1747), *IOR* xix, 102^v; and Porpora, *Oratorio per la nascita di Gesù Cristo* (1748), *IOR* xx, 8^r and 127^v.

[50] *IOB* xxvii. For the sharp sign in falling-third cadences, see 12^r and 13^r, for example; for the natural, 82^v; for a deceptive cadence to I_6, 70^r, and to VI, 43^r; for an accompanied one, 51^v.

[51] In *Silla* (1713), *HG* lxi, 1. A comparison of the MS of *Tamerlano* in *IOB* xxvii with the edition in *HG* lxix shows that Chrysander follows the original sources very carefully. Therefore, I have felt confident in deriving statistics from the other operas in his set.

[52] In *HG* li, 143 (in Cantata No. 67). For a sharp, see p. 134, for example, or *HG* l, pp. 3 and 16, or *HG* liiA, p. 79. At the same time, there are eighty-nine unmarked cadences in the cantatas that need a chromatic leading-tone.

or natural, eighty-eight more require the sign but are unmarked; in the same works two hundred and forty-two falling-fourth cadences have a sharp or natural, whereas seventy-eight that need a sign do not have one.[53] I found no 4 3 among these works at all. Somewhat more diverse is the treatment in German works, depending on the composer. Handel's Passion of 1716 contains sixteen brief falling-third cadences marked with a sharp or natural.[54] Although Keiser seldom includes figures at cadence, the manuscript of his *Nebucadnezar* of 1704 contains one secco example with a sharp and two others with a 7 as well as a sharp or natural.[55] Only seven of the numerous secco cadences in his opera *Die grossmütige Tomyris* from 1717 have a sharp.[56] J. S. Bach favors delayed cadences, but he does have at least eleven brief ones in church cantatas between 1714 and 1726; nine of these are figured with some form of 4 3: either 4♯ or ♮ (sometimes with 3 replaced by a sharp).[57] In this regard, he therefore follows the practice of Scarlatti rather than that of Handel and Keiser. Telemann, on the other hand, prefers the sharp or natural by itself, marked a few times in his operas, but included every time it is required in the many brief cadences in his published cantata collection of 1725–26 as well as in his *Singe-, Spiel-, und Generalbass-Übungen* of 1733–35.[58]

---

[53] Marked cadences are most numerous and diverse in the oratorio *Joseph* (first performed in 1744): five are accompanied, four are in a duet with a falling fourth, two are deceptive to I6, one is deceptive to VI, and twenty-eight move to the usual tonic; see *HG* xlii, 12, 140, 179, and 230, for example.

[54] *HG* xv: *Der für die Sünden der Welt gemarterte und sterbende Jesus* (Brockes' Passion).

[55] *HS* iii, 209, 212, and 223. There are no figures in the MSS of his *Adonis* (1697), *Janus* (1698), *La forza della virtù* (1700), or *Claudius* (1703) in *HS* i–iii.

[56] Modern edn. by Klaus Zelm (Munich: G. Henle Verlag, 1975), 132, 146, etc. I found no marked examples in *Masagniello furioso* of 1706 in *Das Erbe deutscher Musik*, 1. Reihe, lxxxix.

[57] For the first, see *BWV* 23 (1723) in *NBA* I/viii/1, 82; *BWV* 27 (1726) in *BG* v/1, 228; *BWV* 33 (1724) in *NBA* I/xxi, 49; and *BWV* 199 (Leipzig version, 1723) in *NBA* I/xx, 26 and 38. For the other, see *BWV* 8 (1724) in *NBA* I/xxiii, 160; *BWV* 16 (1726), *BG* ii, 192 (incorrectly marked on *bauen* in *NBA* I/iv, 123); *BWV* 115 (1724), *BG* xxiv, 131; and for a sharp instead of 3, *BWV* 199 (Weimar version, 1714), *NBA* I/xx, 4 (no figures, however, appear on page 16). As we will see in the next chapter, Bach also has five brief cadences with an appoggiatura.

[58] *Der geduldige Socrates* (1721) contains two brief secco cadences marked with a sharp; see *TM* xx, 167 and 222; two more occur in *Der neumodische Liebhaber Damon* (1724), *TM* xxi, 125, 217. Concerning the other works, see footnotes 7 and 13 in this chapter.

In the brief cadences of Scarlatti and other earlier composers, as well as in the examples by Bach, the 4 coincides with the first 1 in the voice, with the 3 presumably delayed until after the second 1, as described, as we have seen, by Heinichen and demonstrated by Torres: thus with 4 and 3 on a dotted eighth note and sixteenth, as in Ex. 4.10a. In one case Bach actually places the 4 directly below the voice's first 1 and the sharp sign clearly to the right of the second.[59] On the other hand, when only 3 appears, as in the works of Handel, Telemann, and most of the later composers, this then indicates, if taken literally, one of the three realizations in Ex. 5.2a and b and Ex. 5.3. The notation, however, does not differentiate between them.[60]

Function

From a theoretical point of view, the cadences functioned according to both physical location and grammar. Baroque writers emphasize the distinction between church, chamber, and theatrical music. To a certain extent, each style had its own place of performance, method of composition, type of text, manner of delivery, practice of ornamentation, instrumentation, type of recitative, and appropriate cadences.

During each of the periods in Fig. 2, the cadences that occupy the least amount of time are favored for the faster pace of theatrical productions. Thus, in the first period before 1700, the broken would be preferred in opera over the unbroken (Tosi and Galliard); during the next period, the brief over the delayed (Quantz) or the simple chordal realization in Ex. 5.2a over the 4 3 appoggiatura in Ex. 5.2b and c (Telemann); and, in the final period, the deceptive over the authentic (Agricola, Banner). These faster paced cadences were not confined to the theater, however, for the brief ones, for

---

[59] *BWV* 33 in *NBA* I/xxi, 49. I presume that this modern edition follows the original source in this regard. Bach aligns notes vertically in his MSS far more accurately than the other composers discussed here. See, however, the feminine ending in *BWV* 27 in *NBA* I/xxiii, 232, where 4 and the sharp lie directly below the two 1's. For the same progression in masculine endings, see *BWV* 199 (Leipzig version) in *NBA* I/xx, 38, and the accompanied example in *BWV* 23, *NBA* I/viii/1, 82.

[60] In his *Musicalisches Lob Gottes* of 1744, Telemann states in the *Vorrede* that he uses diagonal lines to indicate when the right hand is to rest. Unfortunately for us, he does not use it for the cadential situation in Ex. 5.2b or Ex. 5.3a, but rather, as shown by his Ex. tt, when eighth-note arpeggios, for example, occur in the left hand.

example, appear between 1700 and 1750 in numerous church cantatas by Telemann as well as in the secular chamber cantatas in Heinichen's books.

From the rhetorical point of view, cadences often correspond to the punctuation in the text. A number of writers identify a "final" cadence, with the implication that other currently existing cadences serve some other purpose. Tosi wrote the passage quoted in Chapter 4 during the period represented by the middle column of Fig. 2. He yearned, however, for the situation in the first column, which existed when he was at the high point of his own vocal career and when the singers and the style of singing he admired the most were currently in fashion. Therefore he recommended that instead of using every time a broken cadence (Galliard's in Ex. 4.9*a*), unbroken ones (Ex. 4.9*b*) should be employed "at periods which end a sentence." From the singer's point of view, the unbroken cadences, in which the voice's concluding 1 coincides exactly with the continuo's I chord, offer more opportunity for improvised embellishment over the V chord. He mentions the possibility of a shake on the penultimate syllable or an appoggiatura on the last one (applied, for example, to the cadences in Ex. 4.3*a–c*). He believed, however, in moderate embellishment added "without injuring the time." After describing the 2-1 and 7-1 melodic cadences, he says that "in airs for a single voice, or in recitatives, a singer may choose which . . . pleases him best." The church recitative, however, "yields more liberty to the singer than the other two [the theater and chamber], particularly in the final cadence."[61]

Early in the period covered by the middle column of Fig. 2, Heinichen makes different distinctions. His final cadences, as we saw in the preceding chapter, show the augmentation of some concluding element from his brief cadences in Ex. 4.10. In his *Final Clausul* in Ex. 4.11*a* he increases the value of the voice's last two notes, whereas in the *kleine Resolution oder Final Clausul* in Ex. 4.11*b* it is the V chord which is extended, thus delaying its resolution to I. Later in the same period, however, Kellner's three examples of *Final-Cadentzen* are all brief.[62]

Other writers during the same period refer to punctuation in a more detailed and systematic way. In 1737 Mattheson explains how melody should fit the text. The end of a paragraph requires a complete cadence (*gäntzliche Cadentz* or *Endigungs-Schluss*)—that is, a broken one with a delayed V chord—, the end of preceding sentences, any type of V-I cadence (*förmliche Cadentz* or *Schluss*). The colon should also receive the latter, but

---

[61] Tosi, *Opinioni*, 42, 80, 84–6, 88; Galliard, *Observations*, 68, 126, 133–5, 138.
[62] *Treulicher Unterricht im General-Bass* (1732), 21.

the semicolon "must never have any type of V-I cadence, much less a complete one." In an example of recitative, he shows a brief falling-third cadence for a colon and, at the end, a falling-fourth cadence in which V is delayed by an extension of the previous VI or iv$_6$ chord.[63]

Fux outlines a somewhat different catalog of punctuation in 1725. When there is a period at the end of a sentence and the recitative continues on the same topic, one employs the same cadence one would for the colon. For the latter, he shows two quasi closes: one with 2-3-1-1 like Ex. 4.1a, the other with 4-3-1-1 and both chords in first inversion. However, when "another speech is immediately introduced" (as in my Ex. 4.6c or e, where a new character must enter quickly), one uses a *clausula formalis* which is usually *truncata*. We can now translate this terminology as "a V-I cadence which is usually broken." His example shows a falling fourth on two eighth notes in the voice and a continuo part which sustains V and delays its resolution (rhythmically like Ex. 4.4d with c). "To make a finish," however, one uses a 2-3-1-1 quasi close like Ex. 4.1a when both chords are in root position.[64] Also from this period comes a manuscript treatise by Stölzel from around 1739. His *Final Clausuln* are brief cadences with the falling third or fourth in the voice; his colon matches a quasi close with 4-3-1-1

---

[63] Johann Mattheson, *Kern melodischer Wissenschafft* (Hamburg, 1737; repr., Hildesheim: Georg Olms Verlag, 1976), 74–87, repeated with only slight changes in *Der vollkommene Capellmeister* (Hamburg, 1739), repr. in *DM* v (1954), 182–91 (see especially 182 and 190–91). Curiously, the colon which concludes the brief masculine falling-third cadence to the text "Wohnplatz ab" on p. 85 of the earlier work has been changed, apparently incorrectly, to a semicolon on p. 190 of *Der vollkommene Capellmeister*. Note that in Ernest C. Harriss's translation in *SM* 21 (1981), 383–97, *gäntzlich* is given as "full" or "complete," but *förmlich* is sometimes "formal" and at other times "full." It is important, however, to distinguish carefully between the two types of cadence, for Mattheson says that both are *förmlich* but only one is complete.

[64] *Gradus ad Parnassum*, 277–8; Latin text trans. in Hansell, "The Cadence in 18th-Century Recitative," *MQ* 54 (1968): 234–6. The word *clausula* had earlier referred to the melodic formulae of individual voices: thus, the tenor clausula (scale degree 2 to 1), discant clausula (7 to 1), etc. Early in the 17th century the expression *clausula formalis* emerges to indicate harmonic (V to I) rather than melodic construction, and eventually this is replaced by the word *cadence*. *Clausula* generally refers to melody and *cadence* to harmony. See the article "Kadenz und Klausel" in *MGG* vii (1958), 406–11. Kellner, in his *Treulicher Unterricht im General-Bass*, equates the "Cadentz oder Formal-Clausul" on p. 22, and on p. 23 shows the four melodic clausulae that make up the I-V-I progression of the *Cadentz*.

over V_6-I and his comma, various quasi-like closes including 2-3-1-1 over V_2^4-I_6.[65]

The writers between 1700 and 1750 thus all deal in different ways with the two cadences listed in the middle column of Fig. 2. The most complete and conclusive cadence for Heinichen and Mattheson was the delayed type; for Kellner and Stölzel it was the brief. Fux used the delayed type when one character was finished and another immediately followed, but for the end of the recitative he preferred a quasi close with both V and I in root position. This diversity of opinion was also reflected in the contemporary musical scores, where the most conclusive spots are marked sometimes by the brief type, at other times by the delayed. The brief cadence for a period or exclamation point occurs at the end of a recitative in Exx. 5.5 (by Scarlatti in 1710 [Exx. 5–16 are printed together in the middle of this chapter]), 5.7 (Keiser in 1717), 5.12c (Telemann in 1721), and Ex. I in the Introduction (Handel in 1742); the delayed one, on the other hand, appears in the middle of a recitative for a semicolon or a period in Exx. 5.9 and 5.10 (J. S. Bach in 1724) and at the end of the recitative in Ex. 5.11 (Bach in 1726) for a question mark. For both composers and theorists, the falling third and falling fourth seem equally appropriate at either a final or internal cadence.

During the next period (the last column in Fig. 2) terminology changes once again to mirror new cadence structures. For Agricola in 1757 the *Endigungscadenzen* are V-I cadences with a falling third or fourth and with the V delayed by a rest during the voice's 1-1. Internal cadences are deceptive (*abgebrochen*), with V not moving to I.[66] In 1762 Marpurg explains that the first can appear during the course of the recitative as well as the end, but the other, of course, only in the middle. These two cadences occur when the subject matter has concluded or presumably, especially in the case of the deceptive type, when a new character enters. When the subject continues or the text has a colon, semicolon, or comma, the quasi closes are used.[67] In 1764 Scheibe characterizes the delayed authentic cadence as *völlig* or *ganz*, the other, like Agricola, as *abgebrochen*. He felt that recitative could be made less monotonous by a variety of cadences, by avoiding too many, especially at every period sign, and by carefully

---

[65] Gottfried Heinrich Stölzel, *Abhandlung vom Recitativ* (MS at Vienna, Gesellschaft der Musikfreunde), 135–6, repr. by George Joseph Skapski as Plates V and VI on pp. 124–5 of "The Recitative in Johann Adolph Scheibe's Literary and Musical Work," Ph.D. diss. (University of Texas, 1963; UM 64-3,814); see also pp. 138–9.

[66] *Anleitung zur Singkunst*, 162; Baird trans., 180–81.

[67] *Kritische Briefe*, ii, 349ff, especially 355–6 and 365.

following the sense of the words.[68] In Sulzer's *Theorie der schönen Künste* of 1774 the *Schlusscadenz* is again the authentic cadence of Agricola, Marpurg, and Scheibe; less conclusive sentences should end with a quasi close like my Ex. 4.1*c* or one of the various types of deceptive cadence. For the latter, seven different chords are given to which V may go from a major key and five more from a minor key.[69]

There is naturally more agreement during this period on the role of the two cadences in the third column of Fig. 2. The deceptive cadence, by its very nature, must move forward rather than rest. It is often referred to as *abgebrochen* or "broken"—the translation which Agricola made for Tosi's *cadenza tronca* but incorrectly illustrated with the deceptive cadence of column 3 rather than the true broken cadence of column 1.

The Vocal Melodies

The falling-third figures may occur in the major or minor mode. In the major mode the fall, of course, involves the interval of a major third. In the minor mode scale degree 3 is flattened, resulting in a falling minor third. In this mode, 6 is also flattened in those figures that include this scale degree. During the period from 1700 to 1750 there is about an equal number of examples in each mode. Only Handel seems to show a preference for minor. Between 1750 and 1800, however, there is about a three to one preference for the major mode, mirroring the general practice in Classic music. In

---

[68] Johann Adolph Scheibe, "Abhandlung über das Recitativ," *Bibliothek der schönen Wissenschaften und der freyen Künste*, xi (Leipzig, 1764), 242–6; see the falling-third cadences with delayed V in the score on pp. 249–50, 256, and 260. See also Skapski, "The Recitative in Scheibe's Work," 209–12.

[69] Johann Georg Sulzer, *Allgemeine Theorie der schönen Künste*, ii (Leipzig, 1774), 942–53: article "Recitativ." Sulzer presumably wrote the first part of the article (to p. 946), but the author of the rest is uncertain (perhaps Johann Philipp Kirnberger or Johann Abraham Peter Schulz); see Skapski, "The Recitative in Scheibe's Work," 275–6 n. 23, and *NG* xviii, 365. In the *Allgemeine Theorie*, see p. 949 and the first line of Ex. XXIV for final cadences with the falling third and fourth, the second line of Ex. XXIV for quasi closes, and p. 950 and Exx. XXVII and XXVIII for the deceptive types in major and minor. On p. 950 the author discusses an excerpt from a cantata by Scheibe to illustrate the use of too many final cadences and another from a work by Carl Heinrich Graun to show the correct method. He seems to delight in ridiculing Scheibe's compositions and in proving that they do not follow the rules Scheibe himself advocated (Skapski, 275–89).

Italian almost all endings are feminine, as shown in Ex. 5.1*a*. The more abrupt masculine endings (Ex. 5.1*b*) are far more numerous, however, in German and English. The possibility of softening the endings by means of ornamentation will be discussed in the next chapter. For comparison, Ex. 5.1*c* and *d* give the corresponding endings for the falling fourth.

The falling third is far more frequent from 1700 to 1750 than it is later. Its frequency in relation to the falling fourth varies somewhat from composer to composer. For Keiser, Graupner, and Telemann the falling thirds represent about sixty percent of the total number of cadences, whereas for Scarlatti's later works from 1695 to 1721 and for J. S. Bach they are only about forty percent, and for Handel only about thirty. During the next period there is a steady decline, with the falling thirds about twenty percent for Mozart and about ten percent for Gluck, Haydn, and Rossini.[70] There is a dramatic decrease in the total number of cadences of any kind in recitative. The tiny phrases of Scarlatti give way eventually to longer spans of declamation in the Classic period.

The melodies which precede the falling third are most diverse with Scarlatti, but gradually become more limited until the domination finally of 6-4-3-1 in the Classic period. The process of evolution begins with a variety of pitches before 3. By 1750 most of them are gradually eliminated, leaving 4, preceded itself by different pitches. Finally, the pitches preceding 4 are themselves gradually limited and then reduced to a single pattern: the 6 leading to 4-3-1 in Ex. 5.1*a* and *b*.[71] This occurs in examples by Gluck, Paisiello, and Haydn. A few cadences with 1-4-3-1 still occur in recitatives of J. C. Bach, Mozart, and Rossini, but the conquest of 6-4-3-1 is finally almost complete.

Occasionally two pitches are united with a 4-3-1 to produce a pleasing melodic shape. The figure 5-1-4-3-1 occurs in Keiser's brief cadence in Ex. 5.7 and J. S. Bach's delayed one in Ex. 5.9. Ex. 5.8 by Graupner shows 6-1-

---

[70] In *Kritische Briefe* ii, 352 (from 1762), Marpurg states that the feminine falling fourth cadences were in general more frequent in the secular style than those with the falling third (referring to his examples on p. 351). See my note 31 in Chapter 6.

[71] The late works of Scarlatti contain a number of cadences with 2-3-1 and 5-3-1, even a few with 1-3-1 or 7-3-1. His overwhelming preference, however, is for 4-3-1, with this figure preceded most often by 6, 1, or 3, occasionally by 2, and rarely by 5 or 7. Keiser sometimes uses 7-3-1, but usually 4-3-1 preceded by 6 or 2, sometimes by 1, 3, or 5. Graupner confines himself almost exclusively to 4-3-1, but still with a variety of preceding pitches. J. S. Bach occasionally employs 7-3-1, but most often 4-3-1. He seldom approaches 4 with 6, however, preferring instead 1 or occasionally 5 or 2. Telemann, on the other hand, prefers to move to 4 after 6 or 2, sometimes after 1 or 3, and rarely after 5. Handel shows a similar practice, favoring 6, 1, or 2 before 4.

4-3-1, and Ex. 5.6 by Keiser has 6-2-4-3-1. Bach sometimes ascends from 7 to 1 before falling to 4-3-1 as in Ex. 5.10, and Keiser and Telemann sometimes leap from 4 to 6 before falling again to 4-3-1. Such figures seem to be favored by these composers who are setting the German language in their recitatives. Their gently circling or undulating figures contrast markedly with the more active downward leaps in 6-4-3-1.

Although scale degree 3 is almost never repeated, 4 often is and sometimes 6. The 4 recurs twice in Exx. 5.14 and 5.15, five times in Ex. 5.16. Keiser, Mattheson, Graupner, Telemann, and Handel sometimes repeat 6 in the pattern 6-6-4-3-1, with the 6-6-4-3 on even eighth notes. 6 recurs three times in Ex. 5.5, and in Ex. 5.14 seems to repeat four times if the D is perceived as a sort of mordent. Such repetition happens most often in the 6-4-3-1 melody. The German figures in Exx. 5.6 through 5.11, on the other hand, usually avoid repeated pitches (except, of course, the final 1 in a feminine ending). Repetition therefore occurs most often in recitatives in Italian, thus in works of Scarlatti, Handel, Gluck, Haydn, Mozart, or Rossini.

Sometimes the melodic formula seems to be split between two or more phrases. See Ex. 5.5 by Scarlatti, in which the penultimate phrase concludes with 6 repeated and then the complete 6-4-3-1 melody occurs in the final phrase. In such cases, the arrival of 6 coincides with the IV chord in the harmony, creating a powerful feeling of expectation. A similar situation occurs when the penultimate phrase ends on 4 over a subdominant chord, with the entire 6-4-3-1 following in the last phrase (Mozart's cadence in Ex. 5.15). Sometimes the 6-4 is split by a rest from the 3-1 as in Ex. 5.14 by Haydn, or from the 4-3-1 as in Rossini's cadence in Ex. 5.16. The 6 or 4 at the end of the penultimate phrase is itself often approached in a flowing manner: see the 3-4-5 which precedes the first 6 in Ex. 5.5, and the 3-2-1 which swings up to 4 at the beginning of Ex. 5.15. Occasionally 6 is preceded by 5-6-♭7. These penultimate phrases often constitute the ascending half of an arch shape which is completed, finally, by the plunging descent of 6-4-3-1. The 6-4-3-1 cadences seem to require a more sensitive approach, so that their two downward leaps will not sound too awkward. The descent is sometimes slowed down and thus softened by neighbor notes, such as 6-5-6 preceding 4-3-1, or by repeating 4 or 6, as we have seen. The German figures in Exx. 5.6–5.9, on the other hand, do not need a preceding phrase, ornamentation, or pitch repetition to complete a melodic design, since they already possess an interesting and pleasing shape.

Occasionally the falling third is combined with the falling fourth in a recitative duet. In Ex. 5.13, 2-4-3-1-1 combines with 1-5-5 to lead to a feminine ending. The 6-4-3-1 in Ex. 5.12*c* joins a 1-5 fall in a masculine ending. Ex. 5.12*b* links 3-4-3-1 (the first 3 occurs before the excerpt) with 1-1-5 for another feminine cadence.

Rhythm

Scale degree 3 in the falling third invariably appears in a weak rhythmic position: the second eighth or the fourth sixteenth of a quarter beat. The strongest rhythmic pulse is on the first or single 1 at the end. A secondary strong point is the note preceding 3, usually 4.

The smoothest possible rhythm occurs in most of the German cadences of Keiser, Telemann, J. S. Bach, and Handel. Here the four notes preceding the final 1(s) are simply even eighth notes, as in Ex. 5.6, 5.7, 5.9, or 5.10. Graupner is an exception, for he usually dots one of the four notes—either the first, the third, or both. When the third one is dotted, as in Ex. 5.8, 4 receives greater accentuation and 3 is reduced. This creates a sparkling fall to 1, since 3 and 1 are now united in a vigorous rhythmic motive. Although Keiser also dots an eighth note occasionally, most of these German composers use the gentle approach to cadence, perhaps because it is particularly appropriate for solemn sacred music. Telemann, on the other hand, favors the four even eighth notes in his operas as well as his church cantatas.

Some composers, such as J. C. Bach, Gluck, and Rossini, employ the smooth as well as more varied rhythms. Lively rhythms are more usual, however, in the cadences of Scarlatti, Pergolesi, Haydn, and Mozart. Frequent is the sprightly rhythm of an eighth followed by two sixteenth notes. It appears immediately before 1 in Ex. 4.6*e* in the last chapter. It occurs a beat earlier in Ex. 5.16 and in both positions in Ex. 5.15. The rhythm often accompanies 4-4-3 in the melody, sometimes 6-4-3. The same pitches may sometimes occur on three sixteenth notes that follow a sixteenth rest.

Such rests can add considerable rhythmic vitality. Occasionally the "dotted" rhythm is notated as an eighth and sixteenth note separated by a sixteenth rest. At other times parts of the melody are delayed by a rest and thus given greater rhythmic presence. The second eighth rest in Ex. 5.5 acts to bind the last five notes in a common rhythmic motive; the rest in Ex. 5.14 joins the last three together. The rests in Ex. I help to produce a sense of great dramatic power.

Ex. 5.5 Scarlatti, *La principessa fedele* (1710),
Act III, sc. x (*OAS* iv, 166)

Ex. 5.6 Keiser, Marcus-Passion (1717?), Parte prima, No. 21, m. 13

Ex. 5.7 Keiser, *Die grossmütige Tomyris* (1717), Act I, No. 1, p. 11

Ex. 5.8 Graupner, Church cantata No. 6 (1729), *DDT* li-lii, 129

Ex. 5.9 J. S. Bach, Church cantata *BWV* 153 (1724), *NBA* I/iv, 211

Ex. 5.10 Bach, Church cantata *BWV* 134 (1724), *NBA* I/x, 80

Ex. 5.11 Bach, Church cantata *BWV* 32 (1726), *NBA* I/v, 151

Ex. 5.12 Telemann, *Socrates* (1721)

(*a*) Act II. sc. i, *TM* xx, 100

(*b*) Act III, sc. iii, *TM* xx, 211

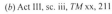

(*c*) Act II, sc. vii, *TM* xx, 143

Ex. 5.13 Handel, *Rinaldo* (1711), Act III, sc. xiii, *HHA* II/iv/1, 191

Ex. 5.14 Haydn, *Lo speziale* (1768), Act I, sc. i, *HW* XXV/3, 25

Ex. 5.15 Mozart, *Lucio Silla* (1772), Act II, sc. ix, *NMA* II:5/vii, 296

Ex. 5.16 Rossini, *L'italiana in Algeri* (1813), Act II, sc. xi, *RE* I/xi, 498

A broader sense of rhythm concerns the positioning of the cadence in relation to the strong and weak beats of a measure. The I chord falls on the beat following the voice's first or single 1 for the brief ending, a beat later for the delayed. Fig. 5 shows where I occurs when the first 1 is on each of the four beats. When 1 is on beat 2, for example, I follows in the brief ending on beat 3, in the delayed on beat 4. Scarlatti places 1 on any of the four beats in his brief cadences, but somewhat favors 2 and 4, beats which allow the I chord to fall on strong beats 3 and 1. In Ex. 4.6c, the 1's are on the second beat, I on the third; in Ex. 4.6e, the 1's on beat 4 are followed by I on beat 1 of the next measure. In Ex. 4.7a, however, the 1's on beat 3 force I onto beat 4, and in Ex. 5.5, 1 on beat 1 leads to I on beat 2. All composers after Scarlatti, however, place the 1's almost exclusively on beat 1 or 3. This means that in the brief cadences generally preferred before 1750 the I chord appears on weak beats 2 and 4. For 1 on the first beat followed by I on the second, see Ex. 5.12c, and for 1 on the third beat and I on the fourth, see Exx. 5.6, 5.7, and 5.8.

Fig. 5 Location of the I chord in relation to the voice's first or single 1

Beat of measure for voice's first or single 1	Beat of measure for I chord	
	Brief cadence	Delayed cadence
2	3	(4)
4	1	(2)
1	2	3
3	4	1

J. S. Bach favors the delayed cadence, however, so that the same beats for the voice's 1 create strong beats for I. Thus in Exx. 5.9 and 5.10, 1 on beat 1 enables I to appear on beat 3, and in Ex. 5.11, the 1's on beat 3 result in I on the strong first beat of the following measure. This is also true after 1750, when the delayed cadences, whether authentic or deceptive, become the principal type. See Ex. 5.14 by Haydn for the 1's on beat 3, the I on beat

1, as well as the deceptive cadence by Mozart in Ex. 5.15 with the 1's on beat 1 and VI, to which V resolves, on beat 3. In the right-hand column of Fig. 5, I have shown the I chord on beats 4 and 2 in parentheses, because they almost never occur in the delayed cadences. Occasionally, as in Ex. 5.16, additional time is inserted between the 1's and the V chord, causing the chord following V to fall upon the first beat of the next measure.

Stölzel, in his treatise from around 1739, requires the voice to end with its 1's on a strong beat (thus beat 1 or 3) in his brief cadences. The I chord would therefore fall on beat 2 or 4.[72] In the delayed cadences, according to Marpurg in 1762, the final note in the bass "must not fall on a weak, but on a strong beat." His examples show I on beat 1 or 3.[73]

Concerning the rhythmic effect of the continuo, finally, we have already noted the dotted resolution of 1 to 7 (the figured bass's 4 to 3) in the realization of the brief cadences (Ex. 4.3) and the augmentation which can delay the arrival of the V chord (Ex. 4.4). Also significant is the harmonic rhythm preceding the V chord, especially the duration of the usual IV or IV$_6$ chord. This chord may last from one to as many as ten quarter beats, but most often two, before moving to V in the brief structure or before being terminated by the rest in the delayed. Scarlatti shows variety in his brief cadences, with IV spanning usually one, two, or three beats (Ex. 5.5). Keiser, Graupner, Telemann, and Handel prefer two beats (Exx. 5.6, 5.8, 5.12c, and 5.13), but Graupner and Handel also frequently employ four. In the delayed cadences of J. S. Bach, IV is sustained either one or two beats before reaching the rest. In the former case (Exx. 5.9 and 5.10), a rapid harmonic rhythm invigorates the measure preceding the voice's 1. In the delayed cadences after 1750, J. C. Bach, Haydn, and Rossini extend IV for either two or four beats; Gluck favors four, Mozart two, four, or six.

In the later cadences, the usual rest below the voice's 1 sometimes extends back into the previous measure. In Ex. 5.14 Haydn adds a half rest, and in Ex. 5.16 Rossini increases the rest another measure and three-quarters. In both these examples, the extended rest in the orchestral accompaniment allows the voice to be projected with conspicuous and dramatic presence. Although rests are not ordinarily included in the brief

---

[72] Skapski, "The Recitative in Scheibe's Work," 99–100, especially 100 n. 184.

[73] *Kritische Briefe*, ii, 353. See also Scheibe, "Fortsetzung der Abhandlung übers Recitativ," *Bibliothek der schönen Wissenschaften und der freyen Künste*, xii (Leipzig, 1765), 17; and Skapski, 220.

cadences at all, Telemann occasionally does place a quarter rest below the voice's 4-3 or even extends the rest back another one or two quarter beats.[74]

Harmony

The subdominant chord that precedes the cadential V chord may be in root position or first inversion. Both possibilities occur frequently in cadences by Scarlatti, Graupner, Handel (but more in root position), and J. C. Bach (more in first inversion). Keiser, Mattheson, and Telemann show overwhelming preference for root position. J. S. Bach favors first inversion (as in Exx. 5.9 and 5.10), but sometimes moves from IV to IV_6. In the Classic period Gluck, Haydn, and Rossini have more in root position, Mozart more in first inversion. When speaking of the root position of IV on a bass note of scale degree 4, I include also ii_6 and ii_5^6, and, for the IV_6 on a bass note of 6, also ii_3^4. As a matter of fact, one often encounters an unfigured bass at cadences, so that the person realizing the basso continuo must be guided to some extent by the requirements of the vocal line in determining the precise chord to play.

 Although chords of subdominant color usually precede V in both the brief and delayed cadences, other chords occasionally appear. Seventh chords in second and third inversion and diminished seventh chords may occur. A few of these different chords appear throughout the entire history from Scarlatti to Rossini. Scale degree 4 can also support a V_2^4 chord or IV followed by V_2^4, and in the minor mode a diminished seventh chord. On the natural or flattened sixth degree, one sometimes finds vi or VI (and iv_6 to VI, or VI to iv_6) as well as a diminished seventh chord (marked o^7 in Ex. 5.11). Keiser has a i_6 chord with scale degree 3 in the brief cadence in Ex. 5.7. Bach harmonizes the same 5-1-4-3-1 melody differently in Ex. 5.9, with the I_6 followed by IV_6. Telemann employs the i_6 chord in the delayed cadence of Ex. 5.12a, where it replaces the rest which later becomes more common at this point. Even less common are other bass pitches preceding V: 2 with ii or ii^o (indicating a diminished triad), vii^o_6, or, in minor, o^7; or even scale degree 5 with V^7, or 1 with I. Sometimes the raised fourth degree supports a diminished seventh chord.

---

[74] See especially the *Frankfurter Festmusiken* from 1716 in *TM* xvi, 59 (m. 81), 117 (mm. 7–8), 131 (mm. 10 and 13), etc.; and xvii, 96 (mm. 9, 11, and 15).

The last line of Fig. 1 in the preceding chapter shows, as we have noted, the dissonant notes for the brief cadence when IV precedes V. In the delayed cadence the voice's 3 is still dissonant with the IV chord, but the 1's no longer occur with the V chord, but with a rest. The 1's, of course, are consonant with the usual IV or IV_6 chord on the preceding beat. There is a question, however, concerning what the ear hears harmonically during the rest. Ordinarily, one assumes that a chord continues in effect throughout succeeding rests. In this case one would imagine the IV or IV_6 chord sustained as the voice sings its 1 or 1-1. On the other hand, the same recitatives also contain numerous examples of the falling-fourth cadences. In this case a melody like Ex. 5.1c is heard with the accompaniment in Ex. 5.1f. During this rest, the voice sings 1-5, notes which surely suggest to the ear a change to a I_4^6 chord rather than a continuation of the IV on the preceding beat. When one hears the falling third in Ex. 5.1a, then, I wonder if the 3 and 1 may sometimes sound like an anticipation of a I_4^6 chord. Perhaps the lingering effect of the preceding IV chord as well as the suggestion of a change to a I_4^6 combine to create an ambiguous response during the rest, favoring one or the other in specific cases. The greater the distance between the IV and the V, the more one erases the impression of IV and the more likely one is to hear I_4^6 (see Exx. 5.14 and 5.16). In addition, the first inversion of IV is probably more likely to be felt more keenly during the rest, as in Exx. 5.9 and 5.15.

When some other chord replaces IV or IV_6 before V, the dissonances, of course, change. In Ex. 5.7, for example, scale degree 3 is consonant and 4 is dissonant above the i_6 chord, whereas in Ex. 5.9 it is the 3 which is dissonant. If the V in Ex. 5.7 had been delayed by a rest, the voice's 1 would also have been consonant with the preceding i_6. Bach writes an intense 7-3-1 cadence in Ex. 5.11. Here the colorful diminished seventh chord provides a consonant support for the 7 in the voice, but both 3 and 1 are dissonant with it. The power of this dissonant 3 becomes further intensified by leaps both toward and away from it. Perhaps here, again, the ear imagines during the rest the I_4^6 chord that appears on the following beat. The expressive minor third in the voice contrasts dramatically with the major third in the final tonic chord.

The deceptive cadences, finally, often conclude with chord progressions which anticipate harmonic practice of a later period. The progression V-VI or the modulation from the key of A major to F major in Ex. 5.15, for example, constitutes the seed which grows into the Romantic idea of moving between keys a third apart.

Combined Melody of the Voice and the Accompaniment

In the broken cadences, whether brief or delayed, the concluding V and I chords contain pitches which combine with the voice's formula to produce together the overall cadential melody. As we noted in the last chapter, the vocal melody in the unbroken cadences (Ex. 4.3c) was broken or split into two parts in the broken type, with one part remaining in the voice, the other moving to an instrument (Ex. 4.3f). Ex. 5.17 puts the two parts back together, so to speak, so that one can see the entire melody.

Ex. 5.17 Cadential melodies formed by the voice (downward stems) and accompaniment (upward stems)

The opening vocal part is shown with downward stems to distinguish it from the concluding instrumental part with upward stems. For the same purpose the two parts are also shown an octave apart, although they often appear at the same octave level. In the left column are the brief cadences, in the right, the delayed. Two basses are given in (g) and (h) for the brief type, the first with the rests which are more usual in accompanied recitative.

A study of accompanied recitatives and continuo realizations written out by theorists shows that 7-1 occurs in the top voice of V-I about seventy percent of the time (as shown in Ex. 4.3). This is true for brief as well as delayed cadences, masculine as well as feminine, falling third as well as falling fourth, and accompanied as well as secco. Ex. 5.17a gives what must be the natural and original form for the brief cadences, especially for secco recitative (see Ex. 4.3d–f). As we saw in the last chapter (Ex. 4.7a), the 7 may be delayed until the second half of the beat as in Ex. 5.17b, but both parts of the combined melody are still recognizable. Sometimes the 7 of the accompaniment coincides exactly with the 1's of the voice, as in Ex. 5.17c, in which case the flow of melody is somewhat obscured. In the usual delayed cadence of Ex. 5.17i, on the other hand, the two halves of the combined melody do not overlap and can therefore both be heard very clearly.

Sometimes other pitches occur as the high notes of the instrumental V and I chords. When they are 5-3 or 5-5 (Ex. 5.17d and j), 7-1 appears in an inner voice and, if it uses the dotted rhythm shown in (a), can still be perceived as the second half of the joint melody. Other pitches might act in a similar way, but tend to have more melodic presence of their own. Thus, 4-3 (Ex. 5.17e and k) and 2-3 (f and l) seem to attract attention away from 7-1 in an inner voice, especially if 7-1 is not distinguished by a different rhythm. 4-3 becomes more prominent in an accompanied recitative if the 4 commences during the IV chord and then continues as the common note in V^7. 2 to 3 makes a logical melodic conclusion by itself, as seen in Ex. 4.7b.

Very rare, however, is 2 to 1 over V and I. Even in the brief cadences 2-1 would, in a sense, be contradicting the manner in which the falling third approaches 1. In the delayed cadence (m), however, additional problems arise. If 2 is added by the composer or the performer as an appoggiatura to one of the two final 1's in the voice, then its repetition by the accompaniment would probably sound unsatisfactory. In addition, if the IV chord in Ex. 5.17n is in root position, then the fifth interval formed by the F in the bass with the voice's final 1 on C (Ex. 5.17m) would be parallel to the fifth created between the bass's G and the instrument's 2 on D. Mozart does indeed have such an example in *The Marriage of Figaro* (see Ex. 6.29).

Following a IV chord in the strings, the voice continues without accompaniment and finally, still unaccompanied, makes a 6-4-3-1-1 cadence, after which the strings play V to I with the melody 2-1. Perhaps in this case the many rests in the accompaniment tend to decrease the effect of the bass note on scale degree 4, or perhaps this is an example of the listener imagining a I$^6_4$ chord below the voice's 1-1.[75]

There is a strong yearning for the 1 following the falling third to resolve in the accompaniment to 7. Usually 7 is provided as the highest pitch of the V chord. Even when it is not, however, the ear strives most earnestly, I think, to find it in some inner voice.

The Instruments

In "plain" or "simple" recitative (*recitativo semplice*)—the type later called *secco*—a viola da gamba, cello, or double bass usually plays the notated bass-line while a keyboard (or occasionally plucked-string) instrument plays the bass-line as well as a realization of the chords (often indicated by a figured bass). The "accompanied" type of recitative, on the other hand, includes also other instruments, often a full string orchestra, which require the exact notation of the pitches to be performed. At the time of Scarlatti, most recitative was simple, with the accompanied type occurring only rarely for very special or emotional moments. As time went on, however, accompanied recitative gradually became more frequent until, by the nineteenth century, it was the principal type.

The examples of simple recitative in this and the previous chapters probably all involve either the harpsichord or the organ as the realizing instrument—the former in the secular music in the theater or chamber, the latter in the sacred music in church. Both instruments can alter the sound of a chord by changing the number of notes played, as well as their spacing and octave level. The organ has the natural ability to sustain sound for long periods of time, but requires rests or "silences of articulation" to clarify rhythmic figures or changes of harmony. The harpsichord, on the other hand, has a percussive attack and can make detailed rhythms very clear; it cannot, however sustain the notes of a chord the way an organ can. Each instrument compensates for its lack by developing special techniques.

---

[75] *NMA* II:5/xvi, 509 in Act IV, sc. x.

The chords on a harpsichord can be prolonged by arpeggiation, a process which also acts to soften the percussive quality. Pasquali describes in 1757 how to perform the chords:

> Care must be taken not to strike abruptly, but in the harpeggio way, laying down the fingers in the chords harp-like, i.e. one after another, sometimes slow, other times quick, according as the words express either common, tender, or passionate matters.
>
> For example: for common speech a quick harpeggio; for the tender a slow one; and, for any thing of passion, where anger, surprise, etc. is expressed, little or no harpeggio, but rather dry strokes, playing with both hands almost at once.
>
> The abrupt way is also used at a *punctum* or full stop, where the sense is at an end.

He actually writes out the continuo realization for the recitative in a cantata, showing not only the pitches of the chords, but also the arpeggiation in small notes. He shows a single chord arpeggiated both down and then up; in a long sweep up; or sometimes down, up, and then down again. Almost all the chords are arpeggiated except the V and I chords following the rest in three delayed cadences (two with a falling third, one with a falling fourth). These two chords are left with their pitches vertically aligned, to indicate the "abrupt way."

A IV chord which precedes the cadential V and lasts for some time, as in Ex. 5.5, could, then, depending on the meaning of the text, be arpeggiated, with the succeeding V and I abrupt. The same might apply to the IV$_6$ in Ex. 5.15, with the following V short. Each of Pasquali's recitative sentences begins with a rolled chord, which starts, on occasion, before the notated position of the bass note. I presume, although he does not mention it, that in a deceptive cadence such the one in Ex. 5.15, the V is abrupt, but the following chord, since it begins a new musical sentence, is not. Even though a new voice enters in Ex. 5.15 with the VI chord and with a rapid rhythmic figure, the chord might still be arpeggiated very quickly, beginning before the voice enters and thus helping the singer find the F-natural.[76] Chords may also be prolonged by repetition, and Scarlatti's tied C in the bass of Ex. 5.5

---

[76] Nicolo Pasquali, *Thorough-Bass Made Easy* (Edinburgh, 1757), 2nd edn. (London, 1763; repr. with an introduction by John Churchill, OUP, 1974), 47–8 for the quotation, Plates XXIV, XXVII, and XXVIII for the cadences in his cantata. Peter Williams includes excerpts in *NG* iv, 695, and in his *Figured Bass Accompaniment*, i (Edinburgh: The University Press, 1970), 56.

may be an indication of such a practice. Perhaps here the chord is struck in one manner on the second beat, then repeated in the same or another manner on the third.[77] A chord may also be sustained on the harpsichord by breaking its notes into Alberti-like figures or by rapidly alternating two of its notes.[78]

Arpeggiation, of course, is not used on the organ. Here the problem is not the sustaining, but the separation of the chords. Occasionally rests are included in the continuo notation. More often the organist is simply expected to articulate the chords clearly and in accordance with their musical sense. The silences of articulation between the chords may therefore vary considerably from the imperceptible to the bold. A staccato touch would probably occur on the V chord when it appears alone before the I in a delayed cadence, as in Ex. 5.10. It might be more gentle when I$^6_4$ intervenes (Ex. 5.9). When the chords preceding V change on every quarter beat, they require a certain separation as well (Ex. 5.9 again).

In the brief cantata cadence of Ex. 5.6, the V chord would probably include the usual 1 to 7 dotted figure shown on the middle staff of Ex. 4.10a. In this case the four-note vertical combination played on the third quarter beat of Ex. 5.6 would probably sound for about an eighth of a beat, followed by a sixteenth rest and then scale degree 7 on a sixteenth note in the upper voice, with this pitch itself separated by a very brief silence of articulation from the final I chord. A soft 8′ Gedackt on the manual and soft 16′ and 8′ flutes in the pedal could speak promptly and probably give a crisp precision to this *kurtze Resolution*. This sort of articulation is common to all wind instruments, of course, and is similar to the insertion of consonants in speaking or singing. For the organ, however, which cannot control volume through touch, this is the chief means of expressive playing. One does not ordinarily think in terms of "rests" or silences, but rather of a continuous flow of music which is animated rhythmically to one degree or another.

The harpsichord, however, could probably more easily accompany such a brief cadence with rhythmic vigor and precise clarity in the dotted figure. Perhaps this is one of the reasons why J. S. Bach preferred the delayed cadence in the cantatas which would be accompanied by the organ

---

[77] See *OAS* iii: Scarlatti's opera *Griselda*, ed. Donald Jay Grout, p. 11 of the Introduction: "These tied notes are plainly in the autograph and are scrupulously reproduced in the copies. Tentatively, they may be interpreted as a direction or reminder to the cembalist to repeat a chord either literally or in a different position—but this interpretation is by no means certain." See also Peter Williams, *Figured Bass Accompaniment*, i, 44.

[78] Ibid., 35–6.

in a church (Exx. 5.9–5.11).   Another reason might be the longer reverberation times in a church, which might blur a brief cadence played by an organ. This might be especially true for a Gothic structure which had been rearranged to fit a Protestant service. Bach's Thomaskirche in Leipzig, on the other hand, apparently had a relatively short reverberation time, as did also the usual opera house.[79]

Occasionally chords are separated far more than they would be in the usual style of organ playing.[80]   Contemporary writers show examples for both organ and harpsichord in which a sustained basso continuo is realized by inserting between the chords substantial rests of a quarter beat or longer. In some cases the complete chord is thus affected; at other times only the upper parts are short, while the left hand or organ pedal sustains the bass pitch as notated.   In 1733–34 Telemann shows a realization in which the upper voices in the right hand (or sometimes in both hands) are reduced to quarter notes over bass notes which last for two, four, or six quarter beats.[81] "Organs are seldom purely tuned," writes C. P. E. Bach, so that "in recitatives with sustained accompanying instruments, the organ holds only the bass in the pedals, the chords in the hands being lifted soon after they are struck."[82]   Kollmann states in 1799 that even the sustained bass notes in secco recitative "should in general not be held to their full length."[83] Sometimes the same procedure is recommended for the organ realization in accompanied recitative as well.

[79] See *NG* i, 58–9.

[80] See Arthur Mendel, "On the Keyboard Accompaniments to Bach's Leipzig Church Music," *MQ* 36 (1950): 339–62, for descriptions of the detached organ style by Albert (1640), Niedt (1706), Heinichen (1711), Voigt (1742), Hahn (1751), Petri (1767), Schröter (1772), and Adlung (1783).

[81] Telemann, *Singe-, Spiel- und General-Bass-Übungen*, 39–40: recitative section of "Toback." On p. 41 he shows arpeggios (up or both up and then down) for the harpsichord and states that the organ, in contrast, plays all the notes at the same time. Note that the three words "auf der Orgel" in the title of Telemann's book in the excerpt in *NG* iv, 697, Ex. 17, do not appear in the facsimile or the modern edition.

[82] *Versuch über die wahre Art das Clavier zu spielen*, ii (Berlin, 1762; repr., Leipzig: Breitkopf & Härtel, 1969), 316; see the trans. by William J. Mitchell in *Essay on the True Art of Playing Keyboard Instruments* (New York: Norton, 1949), 422, and by Mendel in *MQ* 36 (1950): 355. See Peter Williams, *Figured Bass Accompaniment*, i, 62–3, 93–5; and Patrick J. Rogers, *Continuo Realization in Handel's Vocal Music*, in *Studies in Music*, No. 104 (Ann Arbor, MI: UMI Research Press, 1989), 109–22.

[83] Augustus Frederic Christopher Kollmann, *An Essay on Practical Musical Composition* (London, 1799; repr., New York: Da Capo, 1973), 80.   For an illustration from Kollmann's *Second Practical Guide to Thorough-Bass* (1807), see *NG* iv, 697, Ex. 16.

There are two main types of accompanied recitative. In the earliest type, strings simply sustain the notes of the chords. Since such an accompaniment was rarely used, it contrasted markedly with the more numerous secco recitatives in the same work. Its warm and sensual sound gave special prominence to certain situations or characters (the witches in Purcell's *Dido and Aeneas*, for example, or the figure of Jesus in settings of the Passion). In the later type, sections for unaccompanied voice alternate with independent sections, often energetic and dramatic, for orchestra alone. This *recitativo obbligato* appears in Rossini's cadence in Ex. 5.16, where the vocal portion of the cadence is totally unaccompanied and the orchestra plays the two concluding chords. In some cases orchestral chords may sound with the voice, as in Ex. I in the Introduction, or alternate with sections that use a secco accompaniment (Ex. 5.14).

The final two chords in Exx. I, 5.14, and 5.16 would receive the proper rhetorical emphasis, I presume, if the strings all played with successive down-bows. This would also automatically ensure the brief but important break between the two chords which throws accentuation onto the second. This is probably William Boyce's intent in Ex. 6.17 when he marks these two chords with vertical strokes and the word *forte*.[84] In both secco and accompanied recitative, the cello and double bass, according to Quantz, execute the final two notes (scale degrees 5 to 1) "by a short accent with the lowest part of the bow and take both notes with down-strokes."[85]

The Strength of 3 and Its Relation to the Accented 1

The effect of these cadences depends largely upon how conspicuous scale degree 3 is. The power of 3 then determines the nature of the fall to 1 and the impact, finally, on the final syllable. The presence of 3 is determined, in turn, by the cumulative effect of all the structural, melodic, harmonic, rhythmic, and other musical factors we have just considered.

From the point of view of structure, the longer cadences seem to me to make the entire cadential drama more conspicuous, for they allow the listener time to absorb and respond in greater detail to each succeeding

---

[84] See also the accompanied cadences in his opera *The Shepherd's Lottery* (1751) in *MLE* C/iv, 8 and 40; and the "Song from Anacreon" in *Lyra britannica* (*MLE* F/iii, 55).

[85] Quantz, *Versuch*, 272; Reilly trans., 292.

moment. Hence, 3 is more powerful in the delayed structure than in the brief, and in the "4 3" secco realization of the brief (Ex. 5.2b and c) than in the simple dominant triad (Ex. 5.2a).

Concerning melody, the major third is a larger interval than the minor and thus the fall is more spectacular. The feminine ending is less abrupt and gives the singer an additional length of time for expressive purposes. The third degree is most conspicuous, I think, when preceded by a leap (especially from 7 below) or by scale degree 4, which almost forces 3 to sound like an unusual passing tone between 4 and 1. The most effective way to approach 4 is to leap to it from above. Thus the formula 6-4-3-1-(1) contains three descending intervals, two of them leaps, and this, in turn, plunges still further down to the accompaniment's scale degree 7 before resolving back to 1. The longer 3 is delayed, the more accentuation it receives. Thus, once the formula commences, the insertion of rests between the notes of the melody and the repetition of notes (especially scale degree 4 and sometimes 6) act to create suspense before the arrival of the 3.

Lively rhythm can considerably enhance the effect of all elements of the cadence. The melodic formula is strongest when the accented syllable falls on beat 1 or 3 of a measure and the final I chord follows two beats later. The more rests that occur in the accompaniment, the less the instruments will attract attention away from the singer. If harmonic rhythm is slow, with the IV chord sustained for a long time, attention will turn more readily to the voice. A faster change of harmonies, on the other hand, may contribute to a livelier rhythm and hence may also act to make the vocal line more noticeable.

Harmony acts mainly to determine the dissonances within the melodic formula. Most often IV or IV$_6$ precedes V, causing 3 to be conspicuously dissonant. In the brief cadences, the following 1 is also dissonant with the V chord, and the two dissonances in succession create powerful forward momentum. To a certain extent, as discussed above, the voice's final 1's can also sound like a dissonance when V is delayed by a rest, or at least project a powerful sense of incompleteness, which is resolved only by scale degree 7 in the accompaniment moving finally to 1. Therefore, the combined melody formed by the voice and the instruments is strongest when scale degree 7 is at the top of the V chord. In addition, the authentic cadence contains more strength than the deceptive, especially when it concludes a recitative. In this case, the listener has more time to ponder and reflect upon the events of the cadence.

Instruments can also influence the total effect. Events in the vocal line become most conspicuous in the later type of accompanied recitative, in which vigorous rhythmic outbursts in the orchestra contrast with passages for voice alone. Even the sustained-chord type of accompanied recitative adds luster to the voice part. Within secco recitative, the harpsichord projects a sharper sense of rhythm, and the strength of the simultaneously played notes of both the V and I chords contrasts with the gentler arpeggios elsewhere in the accompaniment. When the organ accompanies, however, the voice can be heard more clearly when the chords or bass notes are not held their full value.

*   *   *   *   *

All of these variable musical elements, then, can combine to produce cadences of widely differing effect. It is noteworthy, however, that as the history unfolds, a process of selection causes an evolution toward those elements that reinforce the most conspicuous third degree, the most vigorous downward leap, and the most emphatic impact on the accented 1. Thus, gradually most preferred is the structure with the V chord delayed by a rest, the formula with the major third degree preceded by 4 and the 4 by 6, the delay of 3 by rests or the repetition of 4 or 6, lively rhythms with the accented syllable on beat 1 or 3 and rests in the accompaniment, subdominant harmony against which 3 is dissonant, scale degree 7 on top of the accompaniment's V chord, resolution to a conclusive tonic chord, and, finally, a preference for the accompanied type of recitative in which the unaccompanied solo voice alternates with dramatic rhythms in the instruments. In addition, the cadences tend to become more conspicuous in general because the amount of recitative in a work, as well as the number of cadences within a recitative, both diminish. Furthermore, the falling-third type decreases in frequency in relation to the falling fourth.

Added to these musical variables are the different sounds peculiar to a certain language and the particular combination of letters which form the accented syllable. And all of this, finally, is projected by the many means of delivery available to the singer: the volume, the tone color, the timing, the pronunciation, especially of the consonants in the accented syllable, and the various unpitched sounds of breathing, sighing, gasping, whispering, et cetera.

Consideration of this area suggests the possibility of improvised ornamentation, involving mainly the appoggiatura. This, however, is such a complex matter that it will be treated here in a separate chapter.

Chapter 6

THE APPOGGIATURA

SCALE DEGREE 2 sometimes occurs in recitative cadences as an appoggiatura to the final accented 1. It lies between the two notes that form the falling third and thus acts to destroy this characteristic leap (see the similar effect during the Renaissance in Ex. 3.6e and f). It therefore usually reduces the role of scale degree 3 to a mere passing tone. It may appear in either the brief or delayed structure. It may be added by the singer as a part of improvised performance practice, or notated by the composer.

Ex. 6.1 The appoggiatura between 3 and 1

Ex. 6.1 shows the usual written forms of the vocal cadence in (a) and (f). The appoggiatura in the feminine endings is sometimes notated as in

(*b*) through (*e*) and is performed by replacing the first 1 as in (*c*) or by dividing the first 1, as in (*e*), into two halves.[1] In the masculine cadence (*f*), the appoggiatura in (*g*) imitates the melody of (*c*), but this time with the two concluding notes on a single syllable (*h*), whereas the appoggiatura in (*i*) and (*j*) is of briefer duration.

The earliest notated appoggiatura in a falling-third cadence occurs in J. S. Bach's Cantata No. 61 from 1714.[2] It is first described in a publication by Telemann in 1725–26. Bach seems to employ it for expressive purposes, whereas Telemann uses it as a means of emphasizing certain accented syllables of text.

Telemann and the Prosodic Appoggiatura in the Brief Cadence

In the preface to the cantatas in the *Harmonischer Gottes-Dienst* Telemann states that the singers must not always sing the exact notes in the recitative, but now and then make use of a so-called *Accent*. He writes out the first nine bars of the vocal melody of the first recitative without its text, showing on a staff below that twelve of the written notes are to be altered or ornamented by an *Accent* or appoggiatura.[3] The excerpt includes the two falling-third cadences in Ex. 6.2. Here we see that in (*a*) the first 1 in a feminine cadence on the top staff has been replaced on the staff below by an appoggiatura in the manner of Ex. 6.1c, in order to mark the accented

---

[1] Will Crutchfield refers to this type of appoggiatura as "divided" in "The Prosodic Appoggiatura in the Music of Mozart and His Contemporaries," *JAMS* 42 (1989): 264–7, and in *Performance Practice: Music After 1600*, ed. Howard Mayer Brown and Stanley Sadie (New York: Norton, 1990), 299.

[2] *NBA* I/i, p. 13, m. 9.

[3] *Harmonischer Gottes-Dienst*, i, second and third pages of the unpaged *Vorbericht*: ". . . haben die Sänger in acht zu nemen, dass sie nicht allemal so singen, wie die Noten da stehen, sondern sich hin und wieder eines so genannten Accents bedienen." The musical excerpt comes from pp. 5 and 6 of the first cantata. See *TM* ii, pp. V–VI (with modern German spelling) and 4–5. The *Vorbericht* is printed in Rackwitz (1981), 130–38; the appoggiatura example in Robert Donington's *The Interpretation of Early Music*, New Version (1975), 211, and partially in *NHD*, 45, and in Donington's *A Performer's Guide to Baroque Music* (New York: Charles Scribner's Sons, 1973), 188–9.

syllable of the word *eingefunden*. In Ex. 6.2*b* the accented single 1 in a masculine ending has acquired an appoggiatura like Ex. 6.1*h*.[4]

Ex. 6.2 Brief cantata cadences with appoggiaturas
(Telemann, 1725–26)

Elsewhere in the excerpt a similar technique occurs also at the end or middle of very brief melodic phrases and is sometimes applied to an accented single-syllable word such as *Schatz* in Ex. 6.2*b*. All these appoggiaturas are essentially prosodic in nature, because they emphasize the accented syllable of a word or the accented word in a phrase without regard for the expressive meaning of the text. They are only omitted when, as on *Heil* in Ex. 6.2*a*, they would produce an awkward melodic effect.[5]

---

[4] *Seligkeit* actually has its main accent on the first syllable, with only a secondary one on "*keit*." In the brief cadences, however, such words are ordinarily treated with a masculine ending, since there is not time for the sort of setting which we will see later in the delayed cadences.

[5] Four of the twelve appoggiaturas occur on a masculine ending which is approached once from a descending third (the cadence in Ex. 6.2*b*), twice from the same pitch, and once from a step below, but with an appoggiatura also from below. In the twelve feminine endings the repeated notes are approached once from a descending second, four times from an ascending second, and three times from the descending third (the cadence in Ex. 6.2*a*, as well as two noncadential examples, one at the end of a brief

In Ex. 6.2 I have included the basso continuo for each cadence, and above it the realization from Ex. 5.2*b*, one of those which Telemann felt was appropriate, as we have seen, in cantatas. On one occasion later in the volume, he includes in the score the grace-note appoggiatura shown in Ex. 6.3; here the sixteenth-note value of the grace note may indicate a shorter appoggiatura than the usual eighth-note value notated in Ex. 6.2*b*. Ex. 6.3, however, does point out the special situation that occurs when the V chord is preceded by IV$_6$ instead of the root position of IV shown in Ex. 6.2. In this case there are parallel perfect fifths between the two outer parts: thus between the A in the bass and E in the voice moving to G-sharp and D-sharp. Ordinarily Telemann does not include a grace note when IV$_6$ precedes V, presuming that the singer will supply the usual eighth-note appoggiatura according to the demonstration in the preface. Ex. 6.4 shows such an example, where the outer two staves give Telemann's notation and the middle staff shows the appoggiatura replacing the first 1 as in Ex. 6.2*a*, thereby causing parallel fifths with the notes of the bass.[6]

Ex. 6.3 A notated appoggiatura (Telemann, 1725–26)

Telemann, however, justifies such fifths on several occasions. In his *Singe-, Spiel- und Generalbass-Übungen* of 1733–35, he explains the fifths caused by the realization in Ex. 6.5, even though they could easily have been avoided: "The voice part has G F-sharp with D C-sharp above it [the top voice of the realization, which he writes out]; there are two perfect and

melodic unit followed by a rest, the other in the middle of a phrase). Following this excerpt, Telemann gives a second example to show that an appoggiatura on D-natural can occur simultaneously with a D-sharp in the bass; here a notated falling third appears at the beginning and end of a brief quasi close.

[6] Exx. 6.3 and 6.4 are from *Harmonischer Gottes-Dienst*, i, 302 and 34 (*TM* iii, 259, and ii, 25).

forbidden fifths, which may pass because the F-sharp is to be regarded as only an ornament, and it is really the following E which counts."[7]

Ex. 6.4 An unmarked appoggiatura preceded by IV$_6$
(Telemann, 1725–26)

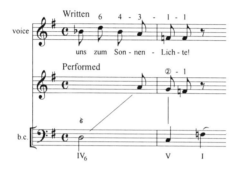

Ex. 6.5 Acceptable fifths between the voice and the realization
(Telemann, 1733–34)

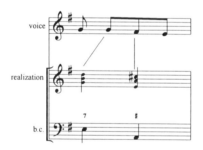

[7] No. 17: "Sein Diener," mm. 16 and 18: "Die Stimme hat g fis und oben ist d cis; sind 2 grosse und verbotene 5ten; sie mögen durchwischen, weil das fis nur als eine Manier anzusehen, und eigentlich das folgende e gilt." I have partly followed the translation by Frank Thomas Arnold in *The Art of Accompaniment from a Thorough-Bass as Practised in the XVIIth and XVIIIth Centuries* (OUP, 1931; repr., New York: Dover, 1965), i, 286.

Ex. 6.6 Acceptable fifths caused by a 4′ stop on the organ
(Telemann, 1744)

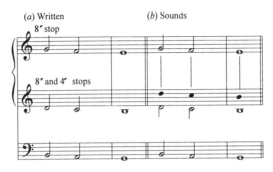

He elaborates even further in the preface to the cantatas in his *Musicalisches Lob Gottes* of 1744, where he gives a list of situations in which inoffensive parallel fifths or octaves are heard but not seen. His first example is the pipe organ's quintadena stop, which has a naturally emphasized second overtone at the interval of a twelfth above the fundamental pitch. Next he mentions using 8′ and 4′ or 4′ and 2′ stops together on the organ: I presume he refers to the situation in Ex. 6.6, where a passage in trio style has a series of notated first-inversion triads (*a*). If the organist uses both an 8′ and 4′ stop for the middle voice, the 4′ stop produces the pitches an octave higher shown by the blackened notes. Parallel perfect fifths then are heard between the blackened notes and the voice on the top staff. The organist does not feel as though he were playing the middle part in octaves, of course, but rather has created with the 8′ and 4′ stops a new sound in which the octave overtone has been enhanced.

Ex. 6.7 Acceptable fifths caused by appoggiaturas (Telemann, 1744)

The next item on his list of acceptable "ear" fifths involves "certain appoggiaturas and so-called ornaments." Here he refers the reader to the musical examples at the end of the preface, some of which are shown in Ex.

6.7. In (*a*) a quarter-note appoggiatura fills in the interval of a falling third much as it would in the cadences of Exx. 6.3 and 6.4. In (*c*) there is another falling third, and in (*b*) this framework has been filled in by a large-note appoggiatura on A. In both (*a*) and (*c*) the appoggiatura is presumably not indicated in the score, but, when added by the performer, causes the consecutive fifths marked by the vertical lines.

He concludes his list with a situation which seems to have precipitated his discussion in the first place: the possibility of substituting a tenor or bass on an alto or soprano part, but an octave lower. If the voices were notated as in Ex. 6.6*a*, and the upper part were sung an octave lower, then fifths would result between the two upper parts. He feels that even these bold fifths "would be justified to some extent."[8]

I have discussed Telemann's attitude toward these "ear" fifths in some detail for several reasons. First of all, it means that the production of parallel perfect fifths by an appoggiatura is not a valid reason for delaying the appearance of V, even though the delayed cadences do, in fact, eliminate such fifths completely. Secondly, J. S. Bach, as we will see in the next section, probably shared Telemann's point of view, at least in regard to fifths caused by appoggiaturas. And thirdly, the parallel fifths in the falling-third recitative cadences are extremely conspicuous. The cadence itself is a conspicuous event, especially its concluding syllables. The appoggiatura then becomes the most noticeable element of all, for it occurs on the

---

[8] Apparently the boys who would sing the alto and soprano parts were less easily available or perhaps less reliable than the men who sang the tenor and bass in these cantatas for two or three solo voices. See the *Musicalisches Lob Gottes, Vorbericht,* his Exx. *a, b* (concerning singing an octave lower), and *h* (appoggiaturas), and the second through the fifth paragraphs of the text. He writes, beginning in the third paragraph:

> Ich wusste wohl, dass die Umkehrung der Noten, wenn nähmlich der Discant in den Tenor verwandelt wird, besonders bey vielen fortschreitenden Sexten, wobey der Alt die Terzien über dem Fundamente ausmachet, eben so viel grosse Quinten verursachen würde, hielt aber auch davor, dass die auf solche Ahrt vorkommende Quinten einigermassen zu verantworten wären.
>
> Es giebt Augen- und Ohren-Quinten, wovon man jene auf dem Papiere siehet, diese aber höret, wann sie schon dort nicht stehen. Die letztern haben bereits das Bürgerrecht, wo nicht gar die Würde, als Schönheiten gewonnen: In den Orgeln bey der Quintadena und dergleichen; bey 4. mit 2., bey 8. mit 4. Fuss etc.; bey gewissen Vorschlägen und so genannten Manieren; bey allerhand täglichen Vorfällen, wo, z.E. in Ermangelung eines Discant- und Altistens, Tenor oder Bass, oder umgekehrt, einer des andern Stelle vertreten muss.

The text of the *Vorbericht* without the examples is in Rackwitz, 225–30 (quotation on 226).

accented syllable, is preceded by a dissonant scale degree 3 on a weak part of the beat, and is itself emphasized by a greater volume and a greater intensity of delivery of both the pitch and the text.   The cadential appoggiatura is thus a bold feature of the cadence, and when IV$_6$ precedes V the fifths produced are equally bold—more like those in Ex. 6.7a than those in Ex. 6.7b. This is equally true, I think, whether the appoggiatura appears in a masculine ending like Ex. 6.3 or a feminine one like Ex. 6.4.

So far we have been concerned with the appoggiatura in Telemann's cantatas. As far as I know, he makes no comment anywhere, however, about appoggiaturas in opera. He does indicate, as noted in the last chapter, that a different realization occurs in operatic recitative. Ex. 6.8 shows the cadence from Ex. 6.2a, but this time accompanied by Telemann's opera realization from Ex. 5.2a. This combination, however, reveals some unusual traits, for now the final vocal 1 is no longer an appoggiatura, but an anticipation.

Ex. 6.8 Cadence of Ex.6.2a with operatic realization

One of the most characteristic elements of the falling-third cadences from the very beginning was the main appoggiatura on scale degree 1, which was followed by the framework's 7 to 1. This appoggiatura was emphasized in the voice part in the unbroken cadences of Ex. 4.3b and c; this emphasis continued in the voice in the broken cadences, even though the succeeding 7 to 1 moved to the continuo realization (Ex. 4.3e and f). As long as the broken cadences had no other appoggiatura added, the voice's single or repeated 1 ensured a strong and vigorous presence of this principal appoggiatura.

Ex. 6.9 Combined melody of accompaniment (upward stems) and voice with appoggiatura (downward stems) in the brief cadence

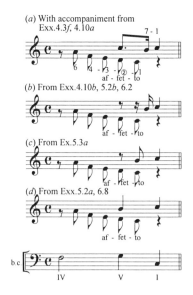

When the voice, however, fills in the falling third with scale degree 2, this creates a secondary appoggiatura which ornaments the principal appoggiatura on 1 or even causes it sometimes to sound, as in Ex. 6.9a and b, more like a passing tone. Ex. 6.9 shows the melodic effect of adding this second appoggiatura in the various types of brief cadence. As in Ex. 5.17 in the preceding chapter, the downward stems indicate the voice part, the upward stems the accompaniment. The parts are shown in different octave levels so they may be distinguished more readily, although they may, of course, actually appear on the same or a different level. On the bottom staff is the bass-line for all the lines above.

When Heinichen's favorite realization (and one that meets Telemann's requirements for the cantata) is applied in (a), the accompaniment continues to sustain scale degree 1 (or pitch C in Ex. 6.9) during the appoggiatura on 2; the latter, in turn, moves on to 1 before the accompaniment's 7-1. In the other cantata realization in (b), 1 is reduced to the eighth note in the voice, but it still occurs before the 7 in the accompaniment (I have added the combined melody also on a separate staff below Ex. 6.2). When the V chord is delayed by an eighth rest as in (c), the eighth-note 1 in the voice occurs simultaneously with the 7. The 1 in this case is apparently still interpreted as an appoggiatura, but one which coincides with its resolution on 7. This sort of simultaneity happens also, as we have seen, when there is no secondary appoggiatura on 2 and when the full V chord enters with the first or single 1 (see Ex. 5.17c).

Such simultaneity, however, pushes to the limit the degree to which the presence of 1 can be diminished. Ex. 6.9d shows Telemann's operatic realization, which produces the combined melody also shown on the separate staff below Ex. 6.8. Here the 1 in the voice occurs after the 7 in the V chord and thus is no longer an appoggiatura to 7. It is now simply an anticipation of the 1 in the final tonic chord. It is difficult to believe that 7 intervenes in any sense between the two 1's on the lowest staff of Ex. 6.8, either in fact (since, as we have seen, the V chord is "abrupt" and staccato rather than sustained its full value) or in imagination. As we move from (a) to (d) in Ex. 6.9, the principal appoggiatura on 1 is progressively weakened until, with (d), it seems to exist no longer at all.

Comparing each of the melody lines in Ex. 6.9 with the bass below, one can see that the added appoggiatura on 2 is itself one of the chord tones in the V chord and hence not dissonant with it in (b), (c), and (d). It is only dissonant when 4 3 appears in the figured bass, as in (a), and it is heard simultaneously with the 1 in the realization. This secondary appoggiatura on 2 is therefore relatively weak in its effect. Although not referring specifically to cadences, Agricola writes in 1757:

> A strong-beat dissonance on a main note that is intended to stand out would be thwarted and its expression weakened by a consonant appoggiatura [*Vorschlag*]. The appoggiatura would be contrary to the intended effect and would achieve the exact opposite result.[9]

In the case of the falling-third cadences, then, the strong dissonance on scale degree 1 is weakened when preceded by an appoggiatura on 2 which is *consonant*.

Although Telemann commented in a footnote of his *Singe-, Spiel- und Generalbass-Übungen* of 1733–35 about different realizations, he actually writes in the song on this page the realization in Ex. 5.2a, which is the one

---

[9] *Anleitung zur Singkunst*, 75; trans. from Baird, 108.

appropriate for opera. He shows no appoggiatura on 2 in the voice, however, and makes no comment about such a possibility. Since this is a book devoted to beginning exercises for singers as well as for keyboard players, one would expect some mention of an appoggiatura if, in fact, it did occur in operas. The strong implication, of course, is that Telemann is telling us that he did not use in his operas the sort of prosodic appoggiatura which he applied so abundantly in his cantatas.

We noted in the last chapter the bass figures which were sometimes marked in the scores themselves. Since Scarlatti as well as other composers before around 1700 usually marked 4 3 over scale degree 5 in the bass, the acceptable melody in Ex. 6.9*a* would result if an appoggiatura on 2 were added by the singer. Yet, at the same time, a far greater number of melodic formulae were employed during this period, with a substantial number ending with the melodic figure 2-3-1. Adding an appoggiatura on 2 following 3, when the same pitch precedes, would seem to me a somewhat uninteresting embellishment. Inserting 2 into 4-3-1 is certainly more meaningful, but considering the long history of this falling-third progression, there was certainly no compelling reason to feel that anything was awkward about it. The cadences were very numerous at that time, and I suspect that composers were more interested in strengthening the principal appoggiatura on 1 with both the voice and the realizing instrument.

If we take the bass figures of later Baroque composers literally, most of them preferred the full dominant chord with the first or single 1 for cadences in operas, oratorios, and secular cantatas. Including a secondary appoggiatura on 2 then produced the effect in Exx. 6.8 and 6.9*d*. We can compare performances of the brief cadence with and without this added appoggiatura in recent recordings of Handel's familiar cadence in Ex. I on "for our God": Hogwood, Pinnock, and Parrott include the appoggiatura on 2, Gardiner does not. They all perform the brief structure as notated.[10]

A number of observations made by Tosi in 1723 and his translators in 1743 and 1757 do seem to suggest the absence of such appoggiaturas in opera. First of all, church recitative, which is more solemn and noble, "requires . . . many appoggiaturas" and "yields more liberty to the singer [for embellishment] . . . particularly in the final cadence." In contrast, he states

---

[10] Christopher Hogwood's recording in 1980 with the Academy of Ancient Music and tenor Paul Elliott appears on L'Oiseau-Lyre's CD 430 488-2 from 1991 as well as the earlier LP D189D3. Trevor Pinnock and tenor Howard Crook record in 1988 on Archive CD 423630-2, Andrew Parrott and tenor Joseph Cornwell on EMI Records CDS7 49801 2 from 1989, John Eliot Gardiner and tenor Anthony Rolfe-Johnson on Philips LP 6769107 from 1983.

that "the theatrical [that is, operatic recitative] leaves it not in our election to make use of this art [of improvised ornamentation], lest we offend in the narrative, which ought to be natural, unless in a soliloquy."[11] Numerous appoggiaturas, such as Telemann wanted in the solo recitatives of his church cantatas, might indeed distract an operatic listener from following carefully the thread of the narrative. In the conversational style, moreover, the transition from one singer to another usually needs to be swift and smooth, especially at the cadence which concludes the first singer's portion. The broken cadences were perhaps designed for this very purpose. Being concise, they already concentrate three important events into a very brief period of time: the accentuated leaning on 1 following the falling third, the framework 7 in the accompaniment, and its resolution finally to 1. Adding still further to this eventful and sensitive moment by including an appoggiatura on 2 would theoretically not take any more time, but it would add complexity at a moment when the listener's attention should be moving quickly to a new character. Presumably Telemann recommended the full dominant triad in the accompaniment in order to contribute to this purpose.

In addition, Tosi describes the performance of the brief cadences more specifically when he refers (as we noted in Chapter 4) to the "tedious chanting that offends the ear, with a thousand broken cadences in every opera." He may be objecting not only to the great number of such cadences, but also to the chant-like effect of the two 1's repeated without an appoggiatura on 2. I cannot think of any other feature in the cadences that would sound like "tedious chanting." The 1's are conspicuous because all other musical elements, especially the leap of the falling third, drive toward them and find completion there. His solution is not to add appoggiaturas to the brief cadences, for that might impede the flow of the narrative, but to substitute for some of them the unbroken type, which does allow the singer more opportunity for embellishment. He may also be referring to the effect of the unornamented brief cadences when he complains elsewhere that "there are some who sing recitative on the stage . . . in a perpetual chanting, which is insufferable." On another page he writes that "it is insufferable to be any longer tormented in the theatres with recitatives sung in the style of a choir of Capuchin friars." Although he is complaining here mainly about

---

[11] Tosi, *Opinioni*, 41–2; quotation from Galliard, *Observations*, 66 and 68. The church recitative to which he refers occurs presumably in Latin motets or possibly even in oratorios; see Hansell in *MQ* 54 (1968): 244 and n. 45.

inexpressive singing, he may also be referring once again to the unadorned repeated notes at the ends of the numerous brief cadences.[12]

Considering Tosi's suggestive remarks, as well as the unsatisfactory melody that results in Exx. 6.8 and 6.9*d* when Telemann's opera realization accompanies the appoggiatura on 2, it is tempting indeed to conclude that this secondary appoggiatura was excluded for very practical reasons from opera, whereas it was, on the other hand, included often in church music. In his chapter on the appoggiatura, Tosi makes fun of composers who actually notate appoggiaturas, but Galliard adds this footnote in 1743: "In all the modern *Italian* compositions the appoggiaturas are marked, supposing the singers to be ignorant where to place them." I cannot find any Italian recitative from this period, however, in which appoggiaturas are marked. Perhaps he refers only to arias or to the downward-fourth recitative cadence in which scale degrees 1-1-5 in the voice are sometimes notated as 1-5-5. In this case, the singer often replaced the penultimate notated 5 with 1, which was sometimes considered at that time to be an appoggiatura resolving by leap.[13]

In any event, it was Telemann who first mentioned the appoggiatura on 2. It is difficult for us, however, to determine whether he was describing an ornament he heard the Italian singers performing, or whether he or perhaps other German composers introduced it as a way of adapting the style of recitative to their own language.

J. S. Bach and the Expressive Appoggiatura in Brief and Delayed Cadences

On three occasions Handel notates a secondary appoggiatura on 2 in a brief cadence. In Ex. 6.10*a* the 2 appears as a large note which affects only the first 1 as in Ex. 6.1*e*. Ex. 6.10*b* shows more complex embellishment, with the trill beginning, as was customary, with an unnotated appoggiatura on its

---

[12] The three quotations are from Tosi, *Opinioni*, 47, 43, and 45; trans. in Galliard, *Observations*, 75, 69, and 72. In the first two quotations Tosi uses the word *cantilena*, which Galliard translates as "chanting" and which my modern Italian dictionary defines as "sing-song" or "monotonous song."

[13] Tosi, *Opinioni*, 22–3; Galliard, *Observations*, 37–40.

upper note or scale degree 2.[14] Following the trill is a sort of mordent or
Nachschlag on 7—all of this preceding the final 1 in the voice.

Ex. 6.10 Appoggiaturas on 2 by Handel

(*a*) Opera *Arminio* (1736–37), *HG* lxxxix, 79

(*b*) Secular solo cantata "Figlio d'alte
speranze" (n.d.), *HG* liiA, 176

(*c*) Oratorio *Joseph* (1744), *HG* xlii, 25

In Ex. 6.10*c*, finally, a small grace note on 2 precedes the single 1 in a
masculine cadence, resulting presumably in two eighth notes sung on a
single syllable as in Ex. 6.1*h*. In each of these cadences the person who
realized the continuo would presumably have noticed that in spite of no
figures for the bass, he would have to play scale degree 7 in his dominant
chord after the voice's last 1 (as in Ex. 5.2*b* or *c*) in order to avoid the
problems of Ex. 6.8. The notated appoggiaturas in these examples, however,
seem to do more than simply emphasize an accented syllable of text. They

---

[14] According to Tosi (*Opinioni*, 28; Galliard, *Observations*, 48) a trill should be
prepared on the note above, especially in a final cadence. All of Galliard's examples on
Plate IV begin with the upper note, even the "short shake" in No. 4.

seem mainly to have an expressive purpose. In (*c*), Joseph, who is in prison, has just been summoned to interpret Pharaoh's dream and responds: "Blest vicissitude! Jehovah . . . once more will deign deliverance to his servant's soul." And in (*a*) the exclamation on *morte* (death) clearly represents a dramatic and emotional moment.

It is J. S. Bach, however, who more frequently notates an appoggiatura on 2 for specifically expressive reasons. He indicates such an appoggiatura with a small grace note on at least forty-two occasions from 1714 to 1747. Five of the cadences are brief, the others delayed. Thirty-one are secco, eleven accompanied; thirty-five are masculine, seven feminine; thirty-four are minor, eight major; and thirty-one of the grace notes are written as eighth notes, eleven as sixteenths. Twenty-six occur in church cantatas, three in secular cantatas, nine in Passions, and four in oratorios. In larger works such as the *St. Matthew Passion*, some of the falling-third cadences have an appoggiatura while others do not.

Ex. 6.11 shows a unique passage in which a brief cadence is followed immediately by a delayed cadence, both with an appoggiatura on 2. The text concerns Peter's third denial (Matthew 26:74): "Then began he to curse and to swear, *I know not the man. And straightway the cock crew*." The brief structure seems appropriate for Peter's abrupt and angry falsehood. The sharp is directly above the continuo's scale degree 5. This was probably performed like Telemann's realization in Ex. 5.2*b* or *c*, by delaying scale degree 7 in the accompaniment until after the voice's final 1. Considering the great care with which Bach ordinarily marks the figures in the bass-line, however, it is possible, I suppose, since he did not write "4 3" in this case, that he intended that the full dominant triad sound simultaneously with the appoggiatura on 2. This would produce, of course, the result in Ex. 6.8, which might match the equally outrageous and false denial by Peter.

Ex. 6.11 Bach, St. Matthew Passion (1727), *NBA* II/v, 178

In addition, Bach's use of the iv₆ chord to precede V causes the parallel perfect fifths we noted in Telemann's cadences in Exx. 6.3 and 6.4. However, Bach agreed with Telemann, I believe, in regard to such fifths caused by ornaments. Bach writes a similar but far more conspicuous example in the Sixth Trio Sonata for organ. When the second section of the second movement is repeated, the first ending precedes the first bar of the repeated section as in Ex. 6.12*a*. This is the same situation Telemann demonstrated in Ex. 6.7*a*. Earlier in Bach's sonata, the notation in (*b*) is most likely performed as in (*c*), with the appoggiatura prolonged for a sixteenth note to fit with the movement of the bass. By the time (*a*) arrives, the rhythm of (*c*) has been well established through both other appoggiaturas and large notes. One is actually thinking past the appoggiatura in (*a*) to the D-sharp, which is part of a V$^4_2$ chord. In this organ trio, however, there is no continuo realization to emphasize the harmonic progression, so that with only two voices, the effect is unusually conspicuous. In Ex. 6.11 Bach could easily have avoided the fifths, if he had found them offensive, by sustaining the iv chord instead of shifting to the first inversion.[15]

Ex. 6.12 Bach, Sixth Trio Sonata for organ, *BWV* 530 (*c.*1727), second movement, *NBA* IV/vii, 82–5

[15] There has been controversy concerning fifths caused by ornaments. Frederick Neumann feels they are unacceptable, Robert Donington disagrees. See *Acta musicologica* 41 (1969): 78 and Ex. 6 in Neumann's article about Couperin, and 42 (1970): 252–4 for two replies; also Donington's *A Performer's Guide to Baroque Music*, 217–18. Neumann discusses fifths in Bach in his *Ornamentation in Baroque and Post-Baroque Music, with Special Emphasis on J. S. Bach* (Princeton University Press, 1978 and 3rd printing with corrections, 1983), 13–15, 101 (his Ex. 14.8*a* and the "questionable fifths" an appoggiatura would create), and 135–8. On p. 136 he prints my Ex. 6.12*a* and recommends pre-beat performance of the appoggiatura to avoid the fifths. See also his "Ornamentation and Forbidden Parallels" in *Festa musicologica: Essays in Honor of George J. Buelow*, ed. Thomas J. Mathiesen and Benito V. Rivera (Stuyvesant, NY: Pendragon Press, 1995), 435–53; and David Fuller's article in *Performance Practice: Music after 1600*, ed. Brown and Sadie (1990), 129–30 and 143 n. 51.

Two of Bach's other brief cadences also have a IV$_6$ chord and the resulting fifths. In these two masculine cadences, however, the figured bass indicates $^6_4$ and $^5_3$ chords, which coincide presumably with an eighth-note appoggiatura followed by an eighth note. This avoids the problem arising in Ex. 6.8 when only a V chord occurs and scale degree 1 becomes an anticipation rather than an appoggiatura.[16] In a brief cadence in the *St. John Passion* the $^6_4$ chord is preceded by a half measure of rest, which follows a diminished seventh chord on the raised fourth degree, a chord which will not cause parallel fifths to occur.[17] So far, all of these cadences have an appoggiatura represented by a small eighth note. A small sixteenth note, however, appears before the first 1 in an accompanied brief cadence in Cantata 51. The V chord is preceded by IV, and the bass figures are $^5_3$ and 3 below the two 1's. In this case, one wonders if Bach is using the sixteenth note to indicate an appoggiatura only to the first 1 as in Ex. 6.1*d* and *e*.[18]

Most of Bach's falling-third cadences have a V chord delayed by a quarter rest as in Exx. 6.13, 6.14, and 6.16. Most of his appoggiaturas also occur in delayed cadences. The delay of V means that no parallel fifths are threatened even if IV$_6$ precedes the rest, and no figures on the bass's 5 can cause the situation in Ex. 6.8. Here also Bach uses two different values for the small-note appoggiaturas. C. P. E. Bach writes in 1753 that "because of their variability, such appoggiaturas have been notated of late in their real length" and shows examples ranging from a whole note to a thirty-second.[19] Agricola agrees and gives his own examples from a half note to a sixteenth in duration.[20] He had been a pupil of J. S. Bach at Leipzig from 1738 to 1741 and after 1741 became acquainted with Quantz, C. P. E. Bach and others in Berlin. He was known as an outstanding organist and singing teacher. Whether these two musicians, both so close to J. S. Bach, were

---

[16] *BWV* 8 (second version, probably 1747) in *NBA* I/xxiii, 218; and *BWV* 248 (the *Christmas Oratorio*, 1734–35), *NBA* II/vi, 227. The latter concludes the text: "When Herod had heard these things, he was troubled, and with him all Jerusalem."

[17] *NBA* II/iv, 38, when the officers and servants made a fire of coals and "warmed themselves" (*wärmeten sich*). The cadence, which is itself in the minor mode, resolves deceptively to a major tonic triad in first inversion.

[18] *NBA* I/xxii, 90. The cadence is printed in *NG* iv, 698, but, unlike *NBA*, with an eighth-note appoggiatura.

[19] *Versuch über die wahre Art das Clavier zu spielen*, i (Berlin, 1753; repr., Leipzig: Breitkopf & Härtel, 1969), 63–4 and Tab. III, Fig. 1; trans. by William J. Mitchell from *Essay on the True Art of Playing Keyboard Instruments* (New York: Norton, 1949), 87–8. See Neumann, *Ornamentation in Baroque and Post-Baroque Music*, 125, 184, and 189.

[20] *Anleitung zur Singkunst*, 61; Baird trans., 93–4.

indeed speaking of a method of notation used by the older composer, we cannot be certain. Bach apparently does not use it in the organ work in Ex. 6.12. He does, however, seem to employ it, and rather consistently, in his falling-third cadences.

Ex. 6.13 Bach, Secular cantata *BWV* 207a (1735), *NBA* I/xxxvii, 51

Ex. 6.14 Bach, Church cantata *BWV* 185, fourth version (1723), *NBA* I/xvii/1, 40

Two values would be especially useful in feminine endings, where a single one cannot indicate whether the first 1 should be divided (Ex. 6.1*d* and *e*) or replaced (*b* and *c*). Six of the thirty-seven delayed cadences with appoggiatura have a feminine ending. In one of them (Ex. 6.13) an eighth-note appoggiatura apparently replaces the first 1. This is from a cantata to celebrate the name day of August III, who loved the hunt and "never paused a moment until *the beautiful animal fell.*" Two examples have a sixteenth grace note to the first 1, probably to indicate the divided performance in Ex. 6.1*e*.[21] Another has the trill marked in Ex. 6.14, somewhat like Handel's cadence in Ex. 6.10*b*, but this time with the opening appoggiatura on the upper note written separately with a sixteenth-note value. This is also a sort of divided type, since the trill and its appoggiatura affect only the first 1.

---

[21] Cantatas *BWV* 60, *NBA* I/xxvii, 24; and *BWV* 157, *NBA* I/xxxiv, 64. Neumann prints the cadence from Cantata 60 in *Ornamentation in Baroque and Post-Baroque Music*, 160, but, unlike either *NBA or BG*, with an eighth-note appoggiatura.

The text concerns the casting out of the beam from one's own eye from the Sermon on the Mount (Matthew 7:3–5); the admonition "correct first your own defects [*Mängel*]" is therefore to be performed with the same vigorous delivery an orator would employ. The appoggiatura and the trill both contribute an expressive quality to the first of the two 1's.

The thirty-one delayed cadences with masculine endings also employ both rhythmic values for the appoggiatura. Twenty-four have an eighth-note value, as in Ex. 6.16 (last measure) or the second full measure of Ex. 6.11. Both are probably performed as in Ex. 6.1*h*. Two appear in the *St. John Passion:* one when Peter answers "I am not" (*Ich bins nicht*) when asked if he were one of the disciples, the other when Jesus utters "It is finished" (*Es ist vollbracht!*).[22] One in the *Christmas Oratorio* accompanies the text "and they were sore afraid."[23] Four others are in the *St. Matthew Passion*: "He is at hand that doth betray me," "smote Him on the head," "called the field of the blood unto this day," and "more bitter is our trial."[24] All of these eighth-note appoggiaturas are slurred to a quarter note and probably take half of its value as in Ex. 6.1*h*.

Seven of the masculine cadences, on the other hand, have a sixteenth-note appoggiatura. The sixteenth note may again indicate in these endings the exact value of the appoggiatura. On one occasion, the main note on 1 is itself only an eighth note which is followed by rests, so that the sixteenth-note appoggiatura slurred to it can again take half its value—this time, however, only the value of a sixteenth note. In this way the word *blind* makes a crisp and jaunty conclusion to the statement that music, unlike love, is not blind. This cadence is followed two measures later by another, but this time with an eighth-note appoggiatura slurred to a quarter note.[25]

The other sixteenth-note appoggiaturas in the masculine endings are attached to quarter notes, so that the performance is probably a sixteenth note followed by a dotted eighth as in Ex. 6.1*j*. In the case of Ex. 6.15 such a rhythm is probably necessary in order for the voice to avoid interfering with the two oboes d'amore on the second half of the first beat of measure 11. The text in this funeral cantata speaks of one who does not fear or tremble when his creator calls (*heisst*) him to depart. In the other five examples there is ample time to perform either Ex. 6.1*h* or *j*. The brisk rhythm of Ex. 6.1*j*, however, would provide a percussive accentuation for

---

[22] *NBA* II/iv, 37–8 and 131.

[23] *BWV* 248, *NBA* II/vi, 65. For another example, see 141.

[24] *BWV* 244, *NBA* II/v, 92, 223, 195, and 225, repectively.

[25] Secular cantata *BWV* 210 (around 1738–41), *NBA* I/xl, 53, mm. 13–14 and 16.

expressive reasons on the last syllable of words such as *verbrannt* (<u>banished</u>, the trifles of this world from my breast), *abgewandt* (<u>turned away</u>, my heart from God), *hält* (God <u>covers</u> thy retreat and opposes thy foes), *giesst* (grace <u>is poured</u> into a pure heart), and *mir* (I [Christ] will take with him the evening supper and he with <u>me</u>).[26]

Ex. 6.15 Bach, *Trauer Ode*, BWV 198 (1727), *NBA* I/xxxviii, 220

Ex. 6.16 Bach, Church cantata *BWV* 135 (1724), *NBA* I/xvi, 219

Considering the sixteenth-note appoggiaturas in Exx. 6.14 and 6.15, as well as the one attached to an eighth note, it is evident that sometimes a short value is required to fit a musical situation. When Bach notates one appoggiatura as a sixteenth note and another two measures later as an eighth, he shows us that he uses the two values deliberately for some specific purpose. Therefore, he presumably intends that the other appoggiaturas in his falling-third cadences should be short or long depending on their grace-note value and that they serve to enhance the expression of passages almost all of which possess an obviously intense emotion. The cadential sixteenth-

---

[26] Church cantatas *BWV* 94, *NBA* I/xix, 61; *BWV* 132, *NBA* I/i, 111; *BWV* 58, *NBA* I/iv, 227; *BWV* 121, *BG* xxvi, 12; and *BWV* 61, *NBA* I/i, 13.

note appoggiatura appears in works dating from 1714 until about 1740, the eighth-note in pieces from 1723 until 1747.

Such expressive appoggiaturas may occur elsewhere in the music, as with the word *alt* in Ex. 6.16 at the end of a quasi close and *Angst* in the middle of a phrase. Both are treated, like the masculine cadential endings, with the appoggiatura and the main note sung to a single syllable. Bach leaves other noncadential masculine endings without an appoggiatura. On the other hand, he does not generally add an appoggiatura, even for expressive purposes, to the repeated 1's in a feminine noncadential situation.[27]

Bach also uses other musical elements for expressive purposes. Most of the cadential appoggiaturas occur in the minor mode. Harmony becomes expressive through diminished seventh chords: the two in succession in Ex. 6.16, or the one on *Tier* in Ex. 6.13. Harmony is sometimes equally expressive by its absence, as in measure 25 of Ex. 6.11. Bach manifests his expressive use of harmony also by the great care with which he figures the bass. The final cadence chords may include, depending upon the expressive effect desired, a simple dominant triad (Ex. 6.14), a dominant seventh (Ex. 6.11, measure 25), or a I$^6_4$ moving to a dominant (Ex. 6.16). The melodic formula in the voice also participates in the expression, with the more placid 4-3-1 in Exx. 6.11 and 6.14 contrasting with those that contain more unusual leaps before scale degree 3: the diminished fourth from E-sharp to A in the 7-3-1 formula of Ex. 6.13, the diminished seventh from D-sharp to C in Ex. 6.16. An expressive melodic clash occurs in two recitative duets when the 2 moving to 1 coincides with the downward fourth's 1 to 5; for an instant the appoggiatura on 2 is heard simultaneously with its note of resolution.[28] Occasionally a brief expressive melisma breaks the usual syllabic style of the recitative, as on the syllable "*man*" at the end of Ex. 6.16.

---

[27] It is possible that Bach expected that the usual half-value appoggiatura would be added by the singer as a prosodic gesture. I have found only three exceptional cases in the cantatas that require notation. A sixteenth-note appoggiatura indicates the divided type in *BWV* 21, *NBA* I/xvi, 150, and in *BWV* 157, *NBA* I/xxxiv, 55. In *BWV* 127, *NBA* I/viii/1, 143, the usual eighth-note appoggiatura must be carefully synchronized with a rhythmic string accompaniment. In addition, *BWV* 155, *NBA* I/v, 182, shows a trill on the first of the two 1's.

[28] *BWV* 130, *NBA* I/xxx, 37: a feminine ending on a text concerning angels watching to destroy Satan's onslaught; and *BWV* 249 (the *Easter Oratorio*), *NBA* II/vii, 47: a masculine ending with a text involved with weeping and yearning. In both cases the appoggiatura has the value of an eighth note, which in the first example presumably replaces the first of two eighth notes, and in the latter takes half the value from a single quarter-note 1.

Rhythm also plays an expressive role, especially in the dotted figures in which scale degree 3 is a sixteenth note (Exx. 6.13, 6.15, and 6.16) or in the pattern of an eighth and two sixteenth notes in measure 24 of Ex. 6.11. Instrumentation is significant when noncontinuo instruments add expressive color, as do the two oboes d'amore in Ex. 6.15. Structure, finally, can be expressive with Bach, for his rare use of the brief cadence in Ex. 6.11 seems a deliberate attempt to portray the nature of Peter's lie. Although Bach ordinarily preferred the delayed cadences and employed them throughout the entire period when he was composing cantatas, he occasionally did use the brief structure along with the appoggiatura in works dating from 1724 to 1734 or 35. I see no reason why the V chord should be delayed in Bach's brief cadences any more than in those of Telemann or any other Baroque composer.

Bach devoted almost all his attention to church music rather than to opera. He seems to have developed a unique approach to the musical expression of impassioned text. In this respect he seems to contrast with almost all of his contemporaries. Instead of a prosodic appoggiatura that recurs on every accented word and syllable and just gives to the recitative a continual undulation, he preferred an expressive appoggiatura which appeared only rarely and at those places where text, plot, and mood all generate a special intensity. Additional appoggiaturas performed at other places would, of course, diminish the expressive effect of those that are notated. Under these conditions, the absence of an appoggiatura at cadence, as in Exx. 5.9–5.11, becomes itself expressive in its own different way. Until evidence to the contrary is discovered, it therefore seems to me safe to assume that in his falling-third cadences Bach wanted appoggiaturas sung only where he notated them, and that they should be performed generally with the rhythmic value he indicated. Scheibe refers in 1737 to Bach's careful and deliberate notation when he states that "all ornaments, all little graces, and everything included in the technique of performance he expresses with actual notes." Although Scheibe does not confine his comment to any particular type of music, he did, as we will see in the next chapter, have a special interest in recitative and wrote extensively about it.[29]

---

[29] Johann Adolph Scheibe, *Der critische Musikus*, i (Hamburg, 1738), 46–7 in the issue for May 14, 1737; also in *Critischer Musikus, vermehrte und besserte Auflage* (Leipzig, 1745), 62—both available on microcard or microfiche from the Sibley Music Library at Eastman School of Music, University of Rochester (UR-55 464-74 and UR-59 180-200). He follows this quotation with the famous comment that Bach thereby "not only takes away from his pieces the beauty of the harmony, but also makes the melody

Ex. 6.17 Boyce, Birthday Ode for George, Prince of Wales,
MLE F/iv, 15ᵛ of No. III (1752)

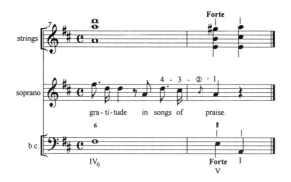

One other composer also seems to use an expressive appoggiatura. William Boyce has falling-third cadences around mid-century that are both brief and delayed. Although those available to me have masculine endings, some, presumably for expressive reasons, include an appoggiatura and some do not. Ex. 6.17 shows one of his accompanied brief cadences in which the strings presumably play the complete dominant chord precisely with the voice's appoggiatura on scale degree 2. This is the unusual situation described above in Ex. 6.8. His three examples of this sort are the only ones I know in which a notated appoggiatura occurs simultaneously with the V chord in an accompanied brief cadence. It is difficult to say whether this is evidence of a wider practice, or whether it is a uniquely English tradition or simply part of Boyce's individual style. Since he also has both secco and accompanied examples of the delayed cadence, it seems unlikely that he wanted V in Ex. 6.17 delayed in the manner later described by Callcott and others.[30]

---

unintelligible throughout." See also *The Bach Reader*, ed. Hans T. David and Arthur Mendel (New York: Norton, 1945), 238.

[30] See also *The Shepherd's Lottery* in *MLE* C/iv, 8 and 40 for cadences with and without an appoggiatura. The many brief secco cadences in his works can be performed, of course, like Telemann's, with the realizations in Ex. 5.2; see *MLE* C/iv, 11, 36, and 46; F/iii, 18, 75, and 106. Maurice Greene, with whom Boyce studied in his youth, has one example of a delayed masculine cadence with an appoggiatura, according to the edition by Frank Dawes (London: Schott & Co., Ltd., 1956) of the oratorio *The Song of Deborah and Barak* (1732), 39. Since there are no other falling-third cadences in the work, it is difficult to say whether the ornament is expressive or prosodic.

The Appoggiatura in Delayed Cadences with Italian Text
1750–1850

Although evidence for the appoggiatura before 1750 is limited, it is clear that two types did emerge in German recitative, especially in the church cantata and other related forms. Telemann expected the singer to include a prosodic appoggiatura to mark the word or phrase accent at almost every falling third, and at other places as well, without regard for the meaning of the text or whether the ending was masculine or feminine, cadential or noncadential. J. S. Bach, on the other hand, carefully notated appoggiaturas for those special falling-third cadences, both masculine and feminine, whose text could be expressed more eloquently thereby. Others he left unembellished. For the noncadential falling thirds, however, he treated only the masculine ones in this expressive manner, leaving the far less frequent feminine ones unmarked.

After 1750 the broken recitative cadences with both the falling third and falling fourth lived on in newly composed music until the 1830s and in isolated cases until around mid-century. Eventually the brief type dies out and only the delayed remains. They now appear in more diverse forms than before: Italian recitative may occur after 1750 in both serious and comic operas by Italian and non-Italian composers; German recitative in operas, oratorios, Passions, church cantatas, and songs; English in oratorios, secular cantatas, and odes. Scores for Italian recitative seldom include notated appoggiaturas, and few German and English scores are available, for much of the music was either written for a single performance at a specific occasion or was in a form that later generations did not consider important.

In spite of these limitations, however, a number of sources of information do exist. First of all, there is a series of writers in Germany from 1757 to 1795 and another in Italy from 1774 to 1847. In addition, there are three types of musical score: the greatest number, in which no appoggiaturas are marked, a few in which the expressive ones are notated, and an even smaller number in which all the appoggiaturas—both prosodic and expressive—are included.

Drawing together all of these diverse sources, it is possible, I think, to arrive at least at a tentative theory of appoggiatura practice during this period: in Italian recitative, with its predominantly feminine endings, the cadential appoggiatura is expressive, the noncadential generally prosodic; the rare masculine endings are expressive in both situations. German and English recitative eventually seems to follow the Italian practice, but, due to the greater number of masculine endings, seems at first to favor prosodic rather than expressive appoggiaturas for both cadential and noncadential masculine endings.

Five different steps are required to reach these conclusions in regard to Italian recitative. First of all, the main feminine cadence becomes the downward-fourth type and its melodic pattern of 1-1-5. This is confirmed by both writers and, as we have seen in Chapter 5, by the composers themselves. In 1762 Marpurg shows four feminine cadences with 1-1-5 and one with 6-4-3-1-1 (without appoggiatura) and explains that "those with the falling fourth are really more usual in the secular style than the one with the repeated 1's."[31] For Scheibe in 1764, 1-1-5 is the proper feminine cadence, whereas 6-4-3-1-1 with the first 1 changed to an appoggiatura on 2 is one of the types which are *verkehrt* or perverted.[32] Other German writers simply present 1-1-5 as the typical feminine cadence without comment: thus Agricola (1757), the author of the article on recitative in Sulzer's *Allgemeine Theorie* (1774), Rellstab (1786), and, finally, Beethoven (in the chapter on recitative in his notes from Albrechtsberger's teachings in 1794–95).[33] Ex. 6.18 shows in (*a*) the way this cadence was usually written and in (*b*) the usual method of performance.[34]

---

[31] *Kritische Briefe*, ii (1763), 351–2: "Unter diesen Cadenzen sind die mit der fallenden Quarte . . . im weltlichen Styl am Ende gebräuchlicher, als die mit dem wiederhohlten Einklange . . ."

[32] Johann Adolph Scheibe, "Abhandlung über das Recitativ" in *Bibliothek der schönen Wissenschaften und der freyen Künste*, xi (Leipzig, 1764), 263.

[33] Agricola, *Anleitung zur Singkunst*, 151 and 162 (Baird trans., 172 and 181); Sulzer's *Allgemeine Theorie*, ii, 950–51; and Johann Carl Friedrich Rellstab, *Versuch über die Vereinigung der musikalischen und oratorischen Declamation* (Berlin), copy at the Library of Congress, 46. For Beethoven's work, see Ignaz Ritter von Seyfried, *Ludwig van Beethoven's Studien in Generalbass, Contrapunkt und in der Compositionslehre aus dessen handschriftlichem Nachlasse*, 2nd edn. by Henry Hugo Pierson (Leipzig and New York: J. Schuberth & Co., [1852]), 322: under the title "Cadenzen zu weibliche Ausgängen" appears (*a*) from my Ex. 6.18, which "muss so gesungen werden" as in my (*b*). In the English version of Pierson's edition (J. Schuberth, 1853), the words for masculine and feminine are deleted and not translated.

[34] Occasionally Ex. 6.18a was performed by changing the first 5 to 6 instead of 1. See Agricola, *Anleitung zur Singkunst*, 152 (Baird trans., 172–3); Johann Adam Hiller, *Anweisung zum musikalisch-zierlichen Gesange* (Leipzig, 1780; repr., Leipzig: Edition Peters, 1976), 102 (Beicken trans., 116); and Peter Urbani, *A New Edition of The Singer's Guide* (Dublin, c.1816), 13 and 14 (see my note 91). From a survey of the works in *IOB*, *IOG*, *ERO*, and *IOR*, it appears that before 1700 most of the downward-fourth cadences were notated as 1-5-5, whereas between 1700 and 1750 both 1-5-5 and 1-1-5 occur; from 1750 to 1800 most are 1-1-5, and after 1800 almost all are 1-1-5. Somewhat surprising is

Ex. 6.18 Main cadences after 1750

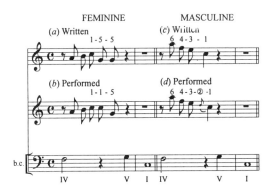

Although the falling thirds become gradually less frequent at cadence, they remain, however, as numerous as ever at the ends of smaller, noncadential phrases. The second step on the way to our theory involves the appoggiatura added by the singer to the noncadential downward third in the feminine endings of Italian recitative. I use the word "noncadential" here to refer to any ending different from the falling-third or falling-fourth cadences; see Ex. 6.30*a*, *b*, and *c* for some of these noncadential types, which can be compared to the falling-third cadence in (*d*). In 1757 Agricola depicts such noncadential descending thirds which have a divided type of appoggiatura and a trill "for tender places" and a replacing type "for places without feeling."[35] Succeeding writers, however, define a specifically prosodic rather than expressive appoggiatura and, since most endings in Italian are feminine, frame the rule in terms of repeated notes rather than

the number of works which include both 1-5-5 and 1-1-5, sometimes on a single page: see, for example, Pietro Bencini's oratorio *Il sacrificio di Abramo* (1708) in *IOR* xv, 57ᵛ; Georg Christoph Wagenseil's opera *Euridice* (1750) in *IOB* lxxv, 81; and Gluck's *Semiramide riconosciuta* (1748) in *IOB* lxxiv, 281. Except for being considerably less dissonant than a falling-third cadence (with or without an appoggiatura), the falling-fourth cadence acts in a similar fashion: with the same harmonies, in either mode, masculine or feminine, brief or delayed, and presumably with an appoggiatura on 1 usually replacing or dividing the first 5 in 1-5-5 or taking half the value from a notated single 5. Perhaps scholars will some day study these cadences and discover why there seems to be a contradiction between the theorists' insistence on a 1-1-5 performance and the seemingly different implications in some of the notated scores.

[35] *Anleitung zur Singkunst*, 154–5; Baird trans., 174–5. He also shows a grace note and trill on a single note following a descending third, thus on a masculine ending, which is rare with an Italian text.

intervals. Thus the popular Italian bass singer Luigi Lablache writes in 1829 in his singing method:

> The Italians long ago introduced the custom of frequently making appoggiatura notes, or rather substitutions of notes, in certain places of the recitative; this gives indeed more elegance, and destroys a little of the monotony resulting from the frequent repetition of the same sounds.
>
> It is impossible to determine, beforehand, all the places where this substitution of note is practicable; but, in general, wherever the strong part of a beginning or an end of a phrase of a recitative is formed of two equal notes, a note one degree higher may be put in place of the first of the two notes.[36]

According to Manuel García around mid-century, the appoggiatura replacing this first note is not an ornament but a raising of the voice to mark the long syllable as a prosodic accent.[37] Many other writers, both Italian and non-Italian, describe the same practice, some preferring the divided method and some referring to both aria and recitative, but all of the falling thirds in their examples, as far as I can tell, are exclusively noncadential in nature.[38]

[36] The practice thus applies not only to the numerous falling thirds, but also to other intervals both descending and ascending. The quotation comes from *Lablache's Complete Method of Singing . . . translated from the French* (Boston: Oliver Ditson & Company, [after 1857]), copy in the Mary M. Vial Library, Oberlin College, Conservatory of Music, 99–100. He gives examples from Rossini's opera *Mosè in Egitto*. According to Dennis Libby in *NG* ix, 49, the original *Méthode de chant* dates from 1829.

[37] *García's New Treatise on the Art of Singing* (London, [1857]), copy in the British Library, 58–9 and 71–2. See also the original *Traité complet de l'art du chant*, ii (Paris, 1847; repr. Minkoff, 1985), 40 and 63–4; and the trans. by Donald V. Paschke in *A Complete Treatise on the Art of Singing*, ii: *The Editions of 1847 and 1872* (published by the translator, 1972; repr., New York: Da Capo, 1975), 117 (with incorrect translation of *piani* and *sdruccioli*, which should refer to a penultimate and antepenultimate accent, respectively) and 180. García presents the same ideas in his later *Hints on Singing* (London, [1894]), repr. ed. by Byron Cantrell (Canoga Park, CA: Summit Publishing Co., 1970), 66–7 and 73.

[38] See, for example, Domenico Corri, *A Select Collection of the Most Admired Songs, Duetts . . . from Operas . . . and from Other Works*, i (Edinburgh, c.1779; repr., Rome Bardi, 1993; and New York: Garland, 1993), p. 2 of the Introduction; and *The Singers Preceptor* (London: Chappell & Co., 1810), repr. in *MOS* iii: *The Porpora Tradition*, ed. Edward Foreman (1968) and in *A Select Collection*, iii (repr., Garland, 1995), p. 70. See also Giacomo Gotifredo Ferrari, *A Concise Treatise on Italian Singing* (London, preface dated 1825), copy at UCLA Music Library, 6 (the work was first published in 1818); Pietro Lichtenthal, *Dizionario e bibliografia della musica*, ii (Milan,

This, along with the preference for the downward fourth at cadence, suggests that these writers are not speaking of cadences and that their prosodic appoggiatura is applied only in noncadential phrases such as those shown in their examples. The next step confirms that the few falling thirds that remain in cadences are treated differently in some musical scores from those that are noncadential. Two major composers—Haydn and Rossini—mark a significant number of appoggiaturas in falling-third cadences. A few are notated in works by other composers. In almost all these cases, the cadential thirds are treated in a manner different from the noncadential. With Haydn and Rossini, very few noncadential thirds have notated appoggiaturas, since they presumably relied upon the singer to add them, if desired, for prosodic reasons. These noncadential appoggiaturas are only notated with grace notes when further information is required by the singer: when a divided rather than replacing type of performance is desired;[39] when an accidental is required on the appoggiatura;[40] when the appoggiatura occurs within rather than at the end of a phrase, especially when there is a series of more than two repeated notes;[41] when the word involved has an accent on the antepenultimate syllable;[42] or when the recitative is accompanied by noncontinuo instruments, especially when the strings

1826), 149; and Nicola Vaccai, *Metodo pratico di canto italiano* (London, 1832), trans. by John Glenn Paton as *Practical Method of Italian Singing* (New York: G. Schirmer, 1975), Lesson XIV, pp. 34–6. Also see the other sources mentioned by Mackerras, Smith, Neumann, and Crutchfield in the articles cited below. Crutchfield and Mackerras emphasize the prosodic function of the noncadential appoggiatura and feel that it should always be added regardless of the emotion involved. Smith and Neumann, on the other hand, feel that the singer should consider the expressive effect when deciding whether or not to include it. All of these authors present their point of view eloquently and persuasively, and it is not my intent to support one above the others. For my purposes it is sufficient to show that the falling third is treated in two quite different ways, depending upon whether it is at the cadence or not. In spite of the singer's possible consideration of expressive effect, I will refer here to an appoggiatura in a noncadential feminine ending during this period as "prosodic" simply because almost all of the contemporary writers emphasize this aspect.

[39] See, for example, Rossini's *La gazza ladra* (1817) in *RE* I/xxi, 156, 374, 376, 473, and 475, where a sixteenth grace note is slurred to the first of the two 1's. At that time the sixteenth grace note was often written like an eighth with a slash through it.

[40] Haydn, *Orlando paladino* (1782), *HW* xxv/11, 263; or *La fedeltà premiata* (1780) in *HW* xxv/10, 364.

[41] Haydn, *Orlando paladino*, 379; or *Armida* (1783), *HW* xxv/12, 21.

[42] Rossini, *La gazza ladra*, 470.

sustain the note of resolution simultaneously with the appoggiatura.[43] Most noncadential appoggiaturas are not notated, however, and the few that are do not seem to have a specifically expressive purpose.

The absence or presence of a cadential appoggiatura, on the other hand, does seem to be primarily an expressive matter, and in some cases the method of notation is different from the noncadential. In a total of fifty-five falling-third cadences in works with Italian or Latin texts, Haydn notates an appoggiatura on eleven: ten with a grace note, one with a large note. Thirteen of the cadences without an appoggiatura occur in works in which others do have one. Half of the sixty falling-third cadences of Rossini that I have located have an appoggiatura, with twenty-three notated as a large note to indicate the replacing type and seven with a grace note half the value of the first 1 to show the divided type. Seventeen of his cadences that do not have an appoggiatura occur in the same operas with others that do.[44]

Ex. 6.19 Haydn, Latin oratorio *Applausus* (1768),
HW xxvii/2, 67 and 97

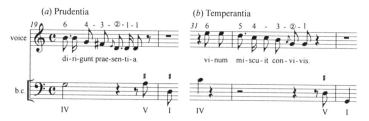

Six of Haydn's cadential appoggiaturas occur in his Latin oratorio *Applausus* of 1768. Three are on the antepenultimate syllable (Ex. 6.19*a*), three on the penultimate (Ex. 6.19*b*). In a letter Haydn explains that the appoggiatura is to replace the following large note (Ex. 6.1*c*) rather than divide it (Ex. 6.1*e*), so he shows both with the same general rhythmic value. Thus in Ex. 6.19*b*, the eighth-note grace replaces the first of the two 1's, and in (*a*) the grace note, even though undotted, apparently replaces the first of the three 1's.[45]

---

[43] Haydn, *L'anima del filosofo ossia Orfeo ed Euridice*, *HW* xxv/13, 19 and 116; and Rossini, *Le siège de Corinthe*, *ERO* xiv, 421, and *Guillaume Tell*, *RE* I/xxxix, 189. Rossini uses the same notation in both his Italian and French works.

[44] The number of appoggiaturas will no doubt increase as more of the works of Rossini become available in the complete works.

[45] H. C. Robbins Landon, *The Collected Correspondence and London Notebooks of Joseph Haydn* (London: Barrie & Rockliff, 1959), 10; original German in *HW* xxvii/2,

Text expression is apparent in Haydn's Italian opera *La vera costanza* (1785) when the count, while testing his wife's fidelity, says, "and yet I feel a certain emotion in my heart"; a replacing appoggiatura accompanies the feminine ending of *petto*. Twenty measures earlier, on the other hand, he had said, "I want to enjoy my liberty" and emphasizes the text by expressively omitting an appoggiatura on *godere* in the falling-third cadence.[46] In *La fedeltà premiata* (1780), Amaranta, learning of her lover's infidelity, sings, "Evil fate! I shall die." Following the appoggiatura to *morta*, she faints. This appoggiatura occurs late in the opera and bears special expressive weight because of the twenty-six other falling-third cadences in the same opera which have no appoggiatura.[47] Ex. 5.14 from *Lo speziale* also has no appoggiatura—this time, I think, simply because the text is matter-of-fact and not emotionally expressive at all: at the beginning of the opera the apothecary's assistant describes his boring and unskilled job in which he dispenses medicine to the sick now from one jar, then from another—*a caso* (at random).[48]

Two other expressive examples occur with an appoggiatura to a single

1. In the oratorio *Il ritorno di Tobia* the phrase "*morto è Tobia*" leads to a masculine ending with an appoggiatura. Haydn also treats the name *Tobia* elsewhere in the work as a two-syllable word accented on the last syllable.[49] In the Italian opera *L'incontro improvviso* of 1775 the word *mia* occurs in the phrase "*languisce l'alma mia*" (my soul languishes) as a single syllable which concludes a masculine cadence with appoggiatura.[50]

2. Haydn shows a noncadential phrase which ends with an ascending-fourth leap to a quarter-note appoggiatura followed by two quarter-note repeated pitches. Considering this example, it seems logical to expect the appoggiaturas in the cadences to have the same value as the following large note, as indeed is suggested in *HW* xxvii/2 (edited by Heinrich Wiens with the assistance of Irmgard Becker-Glauch in 1969). Curiously, in the piano/vocal "Erstdruck" edited by Robbins Landon in *Diletto musicale* 500 (Vienna, Munich: Doblinger, 1969) some of the appoggiaturas have only half the value of the succeeding note and some are omitted, although above the score they are usually shown replacing the following note.

[46] *HW* xxv/8 (second version), 118–19 (mm. 4 and 23) in Act I, sc. ix.

[47] *HW* xxv/10, 403 (in Act II, sc. xiii).

[48] None of the seven falling-third cadences in this opera has an appoggiatura on 2.

[49] *HW* xxviii/1, 99 (in the Recitativo No. 4a in the *Parte prima*). See also the word *Tobia* on pp. 97 and 101, for example.

[50] *HW* xxv/6, 106 (in Act I, sc. vi). See also the appoggiatura in the feminine cadence on p. 115. Mozart also writes an appoggiatura to a single quarter note on the word *Dio* in the phrase "*oh Dio!*"; see the noncadential phrases in *La finta giardiniera* (1775), *NMA* II:5/viii, 290 (descending second) and 309 (descending third), and in *Il re pastore* (1775), *NMA* II:5/ix, 201 (another descending second). Singers probably actually

Haydn does not add as many other expressive elements as J. S. Bach did. Four of the passages are in the minor mode, and four are accompanied. "*Languisce l'alma mia*" does have more active string accompaniment, with *languisce* separated by a quarter rest from "*l'alma mia*," which is preceded by the bass on a raised fourth degree and followed by a brief cadence in which an eighth-beat V^7 is delayed by an eighth rest (similar to Ex. 4.7*b*). Several other examples use a similar rhythm, and in another, scale degrees 4 and 3 are on sixteenth notes.   Otherwise, harmony is simple and as predictable as the melodic notes in the pattern 6-4-3 or sometimes 6-5-4-3 that precedes the appoggiatura.   Only once does Haydn use a large note instead of a grace note, probably to make clear the coordination with a second singer in *Le pescatrici* (1769). Curiously, this is also on the word *mia*, but this time as a two-syllable word with a feminine ending.[51]

Lablache mentions that "the appoggiatura notes are often written in ordinary large notes, with their determined value."   He encourages all composers to adopt this method in order to avoid being misinterpreted by "performers of imperfect musical sentiment." He makes clear, however, that "the manner in which the appoggiatura is written makes no change in the color which it should have."[52]

Rossini, unlike Haydn, prefers this notation for his usual replacing type of appoggiatura. He shows his diversity of approach, however, in the opera *La scala di seta*, where he treats the falling-third cadences in four different ways. First is the usual replacement appoggiatura, shown by the large note for scale degree 2 in Ex. 6.20*b*. Here Giulia, who is secretly married to Dorvil, is attaching the silken ladder to the balcony in preparation for his later appearance: "attachiamo la nostra scala sul *balcone e andiamo*." The final word thus expresses her anticipation and excitement. Earlier in the opera, however, another type of appoggiatura occurs in Ex. 6.20*a*, written this time as a grace note half the value of the following large note. This

---

sing such words with two syllables rather than prolonging the "*o*" in *Dio* or the "*a*" in *mia* or *Tobia* through both the appoggiatura and its note of resolution. Curiously, all these examples by both Haydn and Mozart date from 1775. Vincenzo Manfredini, in the second edition of his *Regole armoniche* (Venice, 1797), 65, does mention that composers sometimes set words such as *mai* and *dei* to a single note because the poet treated them as one-syllable words. In this case, "the singer must nevertheless always treat them as disyllables and sing them with an appoggiatura from above . . ."; trans. in Charles Mackerras, "Sense About the Appoggiatura," *Opera* 14 (1963): 672, and *NG* ix, 47.

[51] *HW* xxv/4, 9 (in Act I, sc. i). With 6-4-3-2-1 the second voice sings 4-2-1-7-1 rather than a melody ending with 1-1-5, as happened earlier in recitative duets.

[52] *Method of Singing*, 52 n. and 54.

happens when Dorvil, after spending the night, must leave *quickly* ("*tosto andate*"). The urgency and haste seem to me to be expressed by the divided appoggiatura, which embellishes the first 1 before moving on to the second. This same opera also shows two types of situation in which the appoggiatura is omitted: first of all, when the text is essentially inexpressive (one character hopes that someone will sign his marriage contract tomorrow: "*Doman sia fatto*"), and secondly, when the leap of the falling third is itself expressive (when another character has to quickly find a place to hide and darts inside a door on the word *prestamente*).[53] Rossini thus incorporated two types of appoggiatura: the replaced and the divided, and two types of falling third: the expressive and the inexpressive.

Ex. 6.20 Rossini, *La scala di seta* (1812), *RE* I/vi, 97 and 292

Other expressive elements are even less frequent with Rossini than with Haydn. All his appoggiatura cadences are feminine. Only four are in the minor mode. Harmony is always very simple. Most are secco before 1817, but accompanied thereafter. Only rhythm occasionally plays a role. The 3 is sometimes on a sixteenth note, thus pushing the momentum rapidly toward the appoggiatura. This occurs in *L'italiana in Algeri* when a character utters an astonished exclamation to herself: "If there is an equally bad churl anywhere, may I fall on my nose!" (*caschi il naso*).[54] This can be compared to Ex. 5.16 from the same opera, where the matter-of-fact comment that "we will conclude our undertaking" (*impresa*) is simply set to a cadence with the last four pitches on eighth notes without an appoggiatura. In *La donna del lago*, 4 and 3 on quarter notes to emphasize the word *tenebroso* (darkness) lead to 2 and 1 on eighth notes when two lovers pledge that their love will remain true "either wed or in the kingdom of darkness."[55]

---

[53] For these two cadences without appoggiaturas, see *RE* I/vi, 154 and 390.
[54] *RE* I/xi, 178.
[55] *RE* I/xxix, 344.

Often in accompanied recitative the concluding vocal phrase is completely unaccompanied, as in his tragédie lyrique *Le siège de Corinthe* (1826), with a divided appoggiatura on the first syllable of *fête*,[56] for example, or in the opéra comique *Le Comte Ory* (1828), with a large-note replacing appoggiatura on *madame* (when the countess greets the count disguised as a woman) and a grace-note divided one on *admire*.[57] Rossini thus applies the cadential techniques from his Italian works also to those in French.[58] Whether the appoggiatura is dividing, replacing, or absent, a wide range of expressive color is added, of course, by the manner of vocal delivery, including the tone of voice, the dynamics, and the intensity with which consonants are pronounced.   Rossini became alarmed in 1814, according to Stendhal, about the extravagant embellishments added by singers: "My mind is made up: I will not leave them room for a single appoggiatura. These ornaments . . . shall form an integral part of my song, and shall be all written down in my score."[59] Two years earlier, as we have just seen, he does notate the expressive cadential appoggiaturas in the recitative of *La scala di seta*.

Other composers show similar treatment of the cadential appoggiatura.   In the Italian version of *Alceste* for Vienna in 1767 Gluck includes a sixteenth grace to the first of two eighth notes in the feminine ending on *consiglio* to express the sense of mourning and danger following the death of the king.[60]   Gian Francesco de Majo has appoggiaturas on two cadences in *Adriano in Siria* (1769), each notated as an eighth grace to the first of two eighth notes.[61]   The same notation occurs in Giovanni Pacini's *Il*

[56] *ERO* xiv, 264.

[57] *ERO* xvi, 324 and 431; other appoggiatura cadences are on 93 and 143.

[58] For cadential appoggiaturas in other works by Rossini, see the following Italian operas: *L'equivoco stravagante* (1811), ed. Vito Frazzi (Florence: Edizioni Musicali Otos, n.d.), 50, 155, 174, 183–4, 299, and 353; *Tancredi* (1813) in *RE* I/x, 104 and 705; *Il turco in Italia* (1814), *RE* I/xiii, 363, 540, 542, 638, 724; *Otello* (1816), *RE* I/xix, 128; *La gazza ladra* (1817), *RE* I/xxi, 375; and *Ricciardo e Zoraide* (1818), *ERO* x, 228. See also the cantata *Le nozze di Teti, e di Peleo* (1816), *RE* II/iii, 120; and the incidental music *Edipo Coloneo*, *RE* II/i, 47.

[59] Henri Beyle (Stendhal), *Vie de Rossini* (Paris, 1824), passage trans. by Richard Mackenzie Bacon in *Elements of Vocal Science* (London, dedication dated 1824), new edn. with notes and introduction by Edward Foreman in *MOS* i (1966), 57–8 n. See also Richard N. Coe's translation in *Life of Rossini* (New York: Criterion Books, 1957), 329–31.

[60] *C. W. Gluck: Sämtliche Werke* (Bärenreiter, 1951–), I/iiia, 33 (Act I, sc. i).

[61] *IOB* xlix, Act II, p. 72 in sc. v and p. 95 in sc. x.

Barone di Dolsheim of 1818 on *"mio dolore."*[62] In his *L'ultimo giorno di Pompei* of 1825, however, there are large-note appoggiaturas for *"core ingruto"* and *"cor feroce,"* but an eighth grace to a quarter note in the feminine ending of *"dover rammenta"* and *"sua pena."*[63] Bellini uses grace notes of the same value as the first 1 in *Il pirata* of 1827, and with half the value in *La straniera* of 1829.[64]

Ex. 6.21 Ricci, *Un'avventura di Scaramuccia* (1834), *IOG* xliv, 184

In spite of some diversity of notation by other composers, however, Rossini always seems to differentiate conspicuously between the cadential and noncadential appoggiatura when it replaces the first 1. In this case the cadential 2 is written as a large note, whereas the noncadential, in the few cases when it is notated to give necessary information, occurs as a grace note preceding and with the same value as the first of the two repeated 1's.

As the fourth and penultimate step in developing a theory of the cadential appoggiatura in Italian works, there are operas by Luigi Ricci in which all appoggiaturas, prosodic as well as expressive, are included in the notation. One of them, *Un'avventura di Scaramuccia* (1834), contains three falling-third cadences. One of these appears in Ex. 6.21, where the appoggiatura on 2 (on the syllable *"al"* of *altro*) is a large note. Differing visually from this is the noncadential falling third on *Sandrina*, where the syllable *"dri"* is sung on an appoggiatura written this time as a grace note which presumably replaces the first of the repeated F-sharps.[65] This sort of notation implies that the cadences play a role in the music quite different

---

[62] *IOG* xxix, 46; and see p. 54 for a cadence without appoggiatura.

[63] *IOG* xxxii, 109, 166, 190, and 191.

[64] *ERO* i, 45ʳ and 113ᵛ of Act II; and *ERO* ii, 67.

[65] For the other two cadences, see *IOG* xliv, 70 and 206. Each page of score is filled with notated prosodic appoggiaturas. Most have the same value as the following large note—usually an eighth or sixteenth note. Occasionally a sixteenth precedes a large eighth, or, curiously, an eighth sometimes stands before a sixteenth.

from the noncadential endings, and that they should therefore be treated in a different manner. Rossini's late cantata from 1847 in honor of Pope Pius IX also includes all appoggiaturas, but its only falling-third cadence shows the divided type with an eighth grace slurred to a quarter note. The noncadential falling thirds almost all show an eighth grace preceding two large eighth notes.[66]

Domenico Corri also notates everything to be performed, this time for the benefit of English singers, in his collections of music by other composers published during the 1790s. In this case, the appoggiaturas in all feminine endings—whether cadential or not—appear as large notes, whereas those in masculine endings (and other places where both the appoggiatura and its note of resolution are sung to a single syllable) are written as grace notes. Three feminine falling-third cadences have appoggiaturas either notated by the original composer or added by Corri.   Their expressive nature is emphasized by tempo markings—one is *lento*, another *lento con espressione*—and in two cases by a fermata on scale degree 6 in the 6-4-3-2-1 melody.[67]

The fifth and last step, finally, in understanding the Italian appoggiatura, concerns the masculine ending. This is so rare in Italian that most writers do not even mention it. Ferrari, however, writes in 1818 that appoggiaturas never occur on such endings unless the text is particularly expressive.   He illustrates with a grace-note appoggiatura filling in the falling third on words such as *amor* and *desir*.[68] Both Haydn and Rossini notate such expressive appoggiaturas as grace notes in noncadential endings, usually an eighth grace preceding a large quarter note.[69] Occasionally the appoggiatura has even briefer value in relation to the large note.[70] When the

---

[66] The cadence is in *RE* II/vi, 248.

[67] *Select Collection*, iv (Edinburgh, 1790s; repr., Rome: Bardi, 1993; and New York: Garland, 1995), 3 (*La dolce compagna* by Sarti), 12 (*Caro bene* by Kozeluch), and 24 (*Ti lascio al ben che adoro* of Sarti).

[68] *A Concise Treatise on Italian Singing*, edition of 1825, pp. 6–7; the chart is given by Crutchfield in *JAMS* 42 (1989): 261, from the first edition of 1818.

[69] See, for example, Haydn's *Armida* (1783), *HW* xxv/12, 103 on *cor*; or *L'anima del filosofo ossia Orfeo ed Euridice* (1791), *HW* xxv/13, 48 on *amor*. See also Rossini's *Tancredi* (1813), *RE* I/x, 103 on *Signor* (to be sung "*incerta*" or hesitantly); or *La Donna del lago* (1819), *RE* I/xxix, 797 on *valor*.

[70] In Haydn's *La vera costanza* (1785), *HW* xxv/8, 273, an eighth grace precedes a half note; and in Rossini's *Otello* (1816), *RE* I/xix, 297, a sixteenth leads to a quarter.

text is not expressive, of course, the appoggiatura is absent.[71] If masculine endings are rare in noncadential situations, they are rarer still in cadences. I have located only the two examples mentioned above in which Haydn sets the usually feminine words *Tobia* and *mia*. In both cases, as we have seen, the text is intensely emotional.

It appears, then, that both cadential and noncadential appoggiaturas are *expressive* in masculine endings, as they also are, as we have seen from the evidence in the steps above, in feminine cadences. It is apparently only in noncadential feminine endings that the appoggiatura is generally *prosodic*. In most works, however, even the expressive appoggiaturas are not marked. Therefore one must assume that it was up to the singer, in such cases, to determine which masculine endings and which feminine cadences could be enhanced by an expressive appoggiatura. Mozart, for example, notates very few appoggiaturas in recitative, in some operas none at all. In a few cases, most notably in *Idomeneo*, he does include a few grace notes to noncadential masculine endings on falling thirds, both on expressive words of one syllable and on a single syllable of longer words.[72] I have found only one example in this opera of an appoggiatura to a noncadential feminine ending, and in this case a sixteenth grace to a quarter note presumably indicates a divided performance.[73]

Ex. 6.22 Mozart, *La finta semplice* (1768), *NMA* II:5/ii, 82 and 194

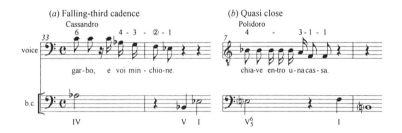

---

[71] See, for example, Haydn's *Ritorno di Tobia* (1775) in *HW* xxviii/1, 99: the falling third from "*za*" to "*ria*" in *Azaria* has no appoggiatura. This occurs two bars before the cadential appoggiatura on *Tobia* mentioned above.

[72] *NMA* II:5/xi, p. 69, m. 59 on *duol'*; and p. 23, m. 33 on the syllable "*di*" of *gratitudine*, and m. 36 on "*tor*" of *genitor*. For an example of an appoggiatura in a two-syllable word with the accent on the second syllable, see the setting of *pietà* in *Il re pastore*, *NMA* II:5/ix, p. 219, m. 33.

[73] *NMA* II:5/xi, p. 432, m. 51 on *lorde*, with this preceded in m. 50 by a masculine type on the second syllable of *sangue*.

Only six of the one hundred and fifty-five falling-third cadences by Mozart, however, have a notated appoggiatura. These six all appear in the first act of *La finta semplice*, composed in 1768 when he was twelve years old. The appoggiaturas in this case are written out in large notes as shown in Ex. 6.22*a*. Six more falling-third cadences occur in Acts II and III of the same opera, but without appoggiaturas. Since this is the earliest work by Mozart that includes falling-third cadences, it is tempting to conclude that he was learning about them for the first time and was demonstrating in Act I how the singer might sing the cadences even when he wrote only the customary repeated notes in Acts II and III. If this is indeed a training exercise, then we need not look in the text for any serious expressive intent in the appoggiatura of Ex. 6.22*a*; here Cassandro says to his brother, "I'm a man of elegance and you're a dolt." Curiously, Mozart does not ordinarily add such an appoggiatura for similar noncadential endings anywhere in the opera.[74] Ex. 6.22*b* shows an unusual example of a quasi close like those in Ex. 4.1, but with the concluding chord delayed to create the same rhythmic structure as the cadence in Ex. 6.22*a*. Presumably Mozart expected the singer to add a prosodic appoggiatura in Ex. 6.22*b* as a matter of course. As we have noted in some other sources, there is a deliberate distinction here between the cadential and noncadential endings, with the implication that each should be treated in a different manner.

In spite of its notated cadential appoggiaturas, however, *La finta semplice* does not act as a guide to their use. When preparing to perform the falling-third cadences in *Idomeneo*, for example, the singer must decide which of four categories each represents: expressive without an appoggiatura or with a replacing or dividing one, or inexpressive without appoggiatura. A particular singer might decide, for example, that the falling-third cadence on the word *celebrar* ("let the court prepare to *celebrate* this day") was matter-of-fact and not in need of an expressive appoggiatura. Perhaps the cadence on *stesso* ("I will break the bonds of the prisoners, but why can I not do as much *for myself!*") and *resisto* ("I can *bear* it no more!") can best be strengthened expressively by the leap of the unembellished downward third. The replacing type of appoggiatura, however, seems effective for "*non posso*" ("I *cannot* deny him my tears"), "*afflitto core*" (afflicted heart), and "*pianto eterno*" (endless lamenting). The divided type, which adds a trembling sound to the voice, might best express *tormenti* ("grant me respite

---

[74] For a rare exception, see *NMA* II:5/ii, p. 95, m. 15 on the first syllable of "*io*." On the same page, however, are numerous noncadential phrases ending with two repeated notes. Downward thirds occur in mm. 6 and 16.

from my *torments!*") or *orrori* (horror).[75] Four of the expressive passages have a diminished seventh chord before the rest and the V chord. Two have dramatic accompaniments which add to the expressive effect.

The sensitive and conscientious singer will react to these musical surroundings and will study the plot, the character, and the situation. The decision about an appoggiatura may change several times before the final production, or change from one performance to another, as the expressive content becomes more clearly defined. In addition, if many noncadential endings are provided with appoggiaturas, the singer might feel that the cadences would contrast more conspicuously for expressive or structural reasons by preserving their downward-third leap. In any event, I do not think that singers at Mozart's time felt that the falling third was in any sense strange and in need of an appoggiatura solely to correct its unusual melodic shape.

The Appoggiatura with German and English Texts
1750–1850

German and English words, as we have noted before, have far more masculine endings than Italian. Thus these endings became a special concern of German writers during the second half of the eighteenth century. They describe them in both a cadential and noncadential role. The earliest sources deal with cadences. For both the downward-fourth and falling-third cadences there is a masculine version that corresponds to the feminine and uses the same melody notes. When the appoggiatura in Bach's cadence in Ex. 6.16 takes half the value from the following large note, it produces the same melody and rhythm as the replacing type of appoggiatura in Ex. 6.13. In the feminine ending both the appoggiatura and its note of resolution receive a separate syllable of text; in the masculine, they are both sung to a single syllable. Similarly, in the masculine version of the downward-fourth cadence, the last two notes in Ex. 6.18b occur on only one syllable rather than two.[76]

---

[75] *NMA* II:5/xi, 34 (m. 3), 53 (m. 5), 69 (m. 64), 66 (m. 20), 351 (m. 10), 476 (m. 27), 33 (m. 121), and 106 (mm. 14–15), respectively.

[76] Bach writes the feminine downward-fourth cadence in large notes as it is to be sung (as in Ex. 6.18b); see Cantata *BWV* 130, for example, in *NBA* I/xxx, 37. He handles the masculine version in three different ways: either without appoggiatura (*St. John*

Hiller in 1780 gives only the falling fourth for both masculine and feminine cadences.[77]   Other writers, however, increasingly confine the downward fourth to the feminine and prefer the falling third in Ex. 6.18*d* for the masculine.   Marpurg shows masculine cadences with both intervals, but says that the falling third is the best.[78]   The author of the article in Sulzer's encyclopedia states in 1774 that the masculine cadence is that in Ex. 6.18*c*, to which the singer adds an appoggiatura as in Ex. 6.18*d*.   He feels furthermore that one should never write a falling fourth for a masculine cadence, even though some composers sometimes do; in this case the singer will add an appoggiatura on 1 and produce the melody of Ex. 6.18*b*, which is "very tedious" (or "dragged out," referring presumably to the two 1's) and "unpleasant."[79]   Lasser adds in 1798 that "the whole expression would be made *matt* [dull, flat, or feeble]."[80]   Beethoven writes that the masculine cadences are written like Ex. 6.18*c*, but are performed like Ex. 6.18*d* (except that he shows a sixteenth grace to a large quarter note).[81]   According to Rellstab in 1786, young composers sometimes write the appoggiatura on scale degree 2 with a large note, but he feels that a grace note would be understood more easily by the singer.   He refers to noncadential as well as cadential masculine endings in which the appoggiatura is notated so that the work will be "well performed."   If this implies that the singer might omit the appoggiatura if not notated, then he is perhaps describing an optional rather than a prosodic type.[82]

Several German writers also discuss the noncadential falling third, including not only the feminine ending which the Italians describe, but now also the masculine.   Hiller writes in 1774 that "at all descending thirds the intervening note can be bound with the following note as an appoggiatura." His examples with German text show grace-note appoggiaturas on both

---

Passion in *NBA* II/iv, 37), or with an appoggiatura written as a large note (*NBA* II/iv, 43) or a grace note (Cantata *BWV* 210 in *NBA* I/xl, 53). Here again, the appoggiatura seems to occur at those moments when the text is especially expressive.

[77] *Anweisung zum musikalisch-zierlichen Gesange*, 101 (Beicken trans., 116-18).

[78] *Kritische Briefe*, ii, 352; the falling-third version is shown by Crutchfield in *JAMS* 42 (1989): 258.

[79] *Allgemeine Theorie der schönen Künste*, ii, 950–51: "höchst schleppend und wiedrig."

[80] Johann Baptist Lasser, *Vollständige Anleitung zur Singkunst* (Munich, 1798); identical 2nd edn. (Munich, 1805), copy at the Music Library, University of Michigan, 161 (concerning Figs. 15 and 16 on p. 165): "so würde hiedurch der ganze Ausdruck matt gemacht."

[81] Seyfried, *Beethoven's Studien*, 322.

[82] *Versuch*, 48–9.

masculine and feminine noncadential endings.[83] He adds in his later book
from 1780 that "for accentuation in recitative [that is, for prosodic purposes],
one uses not only appoggiaturas [referring to the divided type of feminine
ending], but one also often raises a note a whole step [the replacing type]."[84]
Lasser also gives examples of appoggiaturas on noncadential endings, both
masculine and feminine. According to him, one uses the divided type when
a word has two different and separable consonants in the middle, such as
sendet or *würdig*.[85]

Both Hiller and Lasser speak of the falling third, thus including both
masculine and feminine endings. This contrasts with the Italian writers, who
refer to two repeated notes, thus limiting their statements to the feminine.
Rellstab seems to follow the latter when he describes feminine noncadential
endings: "In recitative almost all appoggiaturas are written neither with little
notes nor with large ones, but rather one doubles the main note and divides
the note values and leaves the appoggiatura up to the singer." "Leaving it
up to the singer," however, might mean that it was expected, but it might
also mean that it was optional, since, as we have seen, it is left, when not
notated, to the singer's "discretion." He seems to confirm the latter when he
interrupts the discussion to say that "at the theatre the singer, if he knows
what action is, makes generally few or no appoggiaturas, and in the church
and chamber, where recitative is sung more slowly and with more noble
ornamentation for the sake of solemnity, I would rather hear the plain
performance" [without any appoggiatura] than the replacing type of
appoggiatura. He then concludes that if one wants to notate his preferred
divided type, one should precede the two quarter-note 1's with an eighth
grace note.[86]

---

[83] *Anweisung zum musikalisch-richtigen Gesange* (Leipzig, 1774), 202; 2nd edn.
(Leipzig, 1798), copy at the Music Department of the Haags Gemeentemuseum, 201.
See Crutchfield in *JAMS* 42 (1989): 232–4.
[84] *Anweisung zum musikalisch-zierlichen Gesange*, 102 (Beicken trans., 117).
Johann Friedrich Schubert, in his *Neue Singe-Schule oder gründliche und vollständige
Anweisung zur Singkunst* (Leipzig, 1804), seems to agree with Hiller; see Crutchfield in
JAMS 42 (1989): 266.
[85] *Vollständige Anleitung zur Singkunst*, 160–63. His Fig. 1 shows masculine
endings, Fig. 2 the replacing type of feminine, Fig. 3 the divided type, and Fig. 4 both
replacing and divided. See Crutchfield, *JAMS* 42 (1989): 234–5 and 265–6.
[86] *Versuch*, 46–8; see Crutchfield, *JAMS* 42 (1989): 259 (German in note 23).
The bass notes included in the examples make clear that Rellstab deals first with the
downward-fourth feminine cadence, then with the noncadential falling-third feminine
ending, and finally with both cadential and noncadential falling-third masculine endings.

His remark about few appoggiaturas in theatrical music echoes similar comments by Tosi ("lest we offend in the narrative"), Agricola, Marpurg, and Hiller ("so as not to spoil the speech-like character").[87]   These remarkable comments span almost the entire century. In addition, Rellstab strongly implies that he is referring not just to elaborate embellishment, but to the simple appoggiatura that fills in the interval of the falling third. None of the German writers, however, mentions any expressive purpose. It is only Rellstab who may be hinting that the appoggiatura is optional or, in the opera, perhaps even forbidden in noncadential feminine endings.

English sources present a variety of views about the appoggiatura in recitative.   Callcott ignores it completely in Ex. 5.4, even though his example is obviously instructional in nature. August Kollmann, with whom he corresponded, writes, in fact, that the last note in the "clauses with which the vocal part ends its different periods or strains . . . must neither be suspended by the preceding [that is, delayed in a masculine downward-fourth cadence by repeating the preceding note], nor graced by an appoggiatura; and even the progression by one diatonic degree to the last note is seldom found in recitatives by great authors." He may, of course, be referring only to the score itself, but he makes no mention of an embellishment by the singer.[88]

Several other English writers, however, do discuss the appoggiatura. In 1810 Domenico Corri follows Italian practice by describing the feminine ending: "When a bar, or the half of a bar begins with two similar notes, the first of the two is often sung a note higher." He also shows an example in which one masculine noncadential ending has an appoggiatura and another does not. Here also he agrees with the Italian composers.[89] Like Corri, Bacon also refers to feminine noncadential endings when he states in 1824 that "when the same note is repeated in recitative . . . the first is almost invariably to be taken one note higher." Such appoggiaturas are prosodic in function, since "they are applied under the influence of every emotion or passion indiscriminately." Both of his examples are noncadential and show only ascending intervals.[90]

---

[87] Tosi, *Opinioni*, 42; Galliard, *Observations*, 68; Agricola, *Anleitung*, 152–4 (Baird trans., 173–4); Marpurg, *Kritische Briefe*, ii, 263 (section 13); and Hiller (1780), 100 (Beicken trans., 116).

[88] Augustus Frederic Christopher Kollmann, *An Essay on Practical Musical Composition* (London, 1799; repr., New York: Da Capo, 1973), 80.

[89] *The Singers Preceptor*, 70. See also his *Select Collection*, i (c.1780), 2, for a similar comment.

[90] *Elements of Vocal Science*, new edn. in *MOS* i, 104–5 and footnote.

Peter Urbani makes a more systematic presentation of recitative.   In his *Singer's Guide* from around 1800 he identifies four moods: sacred, serious, plaintive, and comic; and two instrumental accompaniments: *speaking* (that is, secco) and *accompanied*. He illustrates with examples in both Italian and English (see the excerpts in Ex. 6.23). Following all the musical examples, he states: "In the various recitatives, when two, three or more [repeated] notes close a period [thus not a masculine ending], the first of them must always be sung a tone or semi-tone above, according to the modulation of the music."

He also adds, referring now to masculine endings: "Where a single note closes the period, then it is sung with an appoggiatura," as he shows in

Ex. 6.23 Urbani, Sacred recitative (*c*.1800)

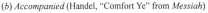

the opening measure of Ex. 6.23*a* on the word *Lord* and in four brief noncadential examples with Italian text, three of which have a downward-third interval. He also mentions, however, that in accompanied recitative "the singer may ornament with graces, but must be careful to use [those] suitable to the subject; for instance, *dear, lovely, my soul*, etc. require soft expressive graces, whereas *tyrant, traitor, death, horror*, etc. must be sung bold, firm, and resolute, without adding any graces."[91]

It appears that all three of these English writers are referring principally to noncadential endings. Bacon makes this clear in two brief examples with an antepenultimate accent, and Urbani does the same in four masculine examples. At the same time both Corri and Urbani also include in their longer examples some falling-third cadences which do have appoggiaturas. Urbani concludes his excerpt from Handel's *Messiah* in Ex. 6.23*b* with an appoggiatura to a masculine cadence, which we can compare with Handel's version in Ex. I in the Introduction. The final instrumental chords are delayed by Urbani as in Ex. 5.4 and there is some alteration of rhythm in the melody. As we have seen, however, German writers had already depicted the falling-third masculine cadence with an appoggiatura since at least 1762.

The feminine version of the cadence, on the other hand, was not ever shown with an appoggiatura, as far as I know, by either German or Italian theorists. The Germans did not even recognize a feminine falling-third cadence, as we have noted, and composers setting Italian texts (Haydn, Rossini, and others, as we have seen) considered an appoggiatura in this case to be expressive rather than prosodic. The only possible didactic examples of an appoggiatura in a feminine falling-third cadence with Italian text are those in the 1790s by Corri mentioned above, and in this case they seem to appear in an expressive context and may have even been notated by the original composers. It is thus conspicuous when such examples occur in instructional works connected with recitative in any language. This does

<hr/>

[91] *The Singer's Guide* was first published in Edinburgh. A film of *A New Edition* (Dublin: I. Willis) was available to me from the Harvard University Library. The latter edition states that Mr. Willis purchased the copyright from Urbani "before the expiration of the first 14 years," and that Urbani had just recently died (in 1816). Therefore, the original publication must have been around 1800, thus allowing for its sale before 1814 and the subsequent new edition in or shortly after 1816. Ex. 6.23 comes from pp. 12 and 13, the quotations from pp. 14 and 12, respectively. For a facs. of Ex. 6.23*b* presumably from the original edition, see Nancy Phelan, *Charles Mackerras: A Musicians' Musician* (London, 1987), 262, and Mackerras's "Appoggiaturas Unlimited?" in *Records and Recording* 8/5 (Feb 1965): 15 (and see p. 16 for another example from Urbani's book).

happen with English texts in the works of both Corri and Urbani. The latter places it at the end of the passage in Ex. 6.23*a* and writes the appoggiatura as a large note, thus making clear that it completely replaces the first of the two final 1's.   It is also distinguished thereby from the grace-note appoggiaturas to the masculine endings in the opening measure of Ex. 6.23*a* and at the cadence of Ex. 6.23*b*.

In 1810 Corri quotes the vocal part from a recitative in Handel's oratorio *Theodora* and on a separate staff below shows how a singer would add ornaments and change the rhythm. The emotional text leads to a 4-3-1-1 cadence in which Corri changes the penultimate 1 to a large-note appoggiatura on 2. In addition, the two final eighth notes on the word *mercy* have been changed to a quarter and a half note to illustrate his instruction that "particular care must be taken in the utterance of the last note concluding a passage, phrase, or period, which note must always be made longer than it is written, giving it a sudden cres. or dim." Although he does not include the continuo part, one assumes that at this date the delayed structure was again substituted for the brief.[92] It is difficult to assess the function of the appoggiaturas in these two feminine cadences of Corri and Urbani. The texts themselves could justify the expressive type. Neither author, however, mentions that the repeated notes at the end of a cadence are treated any differently from those that conclude a noncadential phrase.

Turning, then, to the composers themselves, we generally find a somewhat different situation.   Unfortunately, there are few available examples with German text and even fewer in English. Two earlier sources show appoggiaturas on all cadences. In his brief tales and fables of 1759 Herbing marks an eighth-note grace before the first of the two eighth notes in all feminine endings and before the quarter note at the end of all masculine endings in both cadential and noncadential situations.[93] In his Passion oratorio from 1764 Johann Ernst Bach shows a large-note appoggiatura on every falling-third cadence, but on only some of the noncadential masculine endings.[94]

---

[92] *The Singers Preceptor*, 70. For Handel's original score from 1750, see *HG* viii, 61, where Theodora sings: "Oh worse than death indeed! Lead me, ye guards, lead me, or to the rack, or to the flames, I'll thank your gracious mercy!"

[93] August Bernhard Valentin Herbing, *Musikalischer Versuch* (1759), modern edn. in *DDT* xlii: see p. 41, for example, for cadences on *haben* and *nicht* and noncadential endings on *Gaben* and *spricht*.

[94] *O Seele, deren Sehnen*, modern edn. in *DDT* xlviii: on p. 8, for example, there are appoggiaturas on *nieder* and *trinkt* at cadence, and on the noncadential *gerinnt* but not

Ex. 6.24 Pasquali, Cantata *Pastora* (1757), Plate XXIV

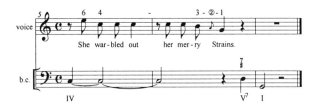

More commonly, however, German and English composers seem to follow Italian practice. For both cadential and noncadential masculine endings, this means that an appoggiatura appears only for expressive purposes. This becomes most evident when a composer includes masculine endings both with and without appoggiaturas within the same work. Pasquali's brief cantata in his thorough-bass book of 1757 includes the masculine cadence in Ex. 6.24 with an appoggiatura on the word *strains*. In a later edition from 1763, however, this appoggiatura has been deleted, perhaps so that this happy moment would contrast with a sad masculine cadence with appoggiatura which accompanies Pastora's rejection of a young man. Similarly, three noncadential falling-third masculine endings occur in the four measures before Ex. 6.24, with appoggiaturas on *plains* and *sing*, but not on *Spring*.[95] Similar examples occur with German texts in works by Scheibe,[96] Johann Christoph Friedrich Bach,[97] and Johann Heinrich Rolle. Ex. 6.25 shows a cadence from the latter's oratorio *Lazarus*

on *Ruh*. The V-I chords that follow the two cadential eighth notes in the voice are themselves each an eighth note in duration.

[95] Nicolo Pasquali, *Thorough-Bass Made Easy* (Edinburgh, 1757); facs. of Plate XXIV in *OAS* viii: *Tigrane*, ed. Michael Collins (1983), 19. See the reprint of the 1763 edition of Pasquali's work with introduction by John Churchill (OUP, 1974), Plate XXVII, for the appoggiatura on the second syllable of *away* in the sentence "He rose and walk'd away."

[96] *Bibliothek der schönen Wissenschaften und der freyen Künste*, xi (Leipzig, 1764) contains an excerpt from his cantata *Die Auferstehung und Himmelfahrt Jesu*: for a masculine cadence with appoggiatura, see pp. 249–50 (printed also in Sulzer's *Allgemeine Theorie*, ii, as Ex. VII following p. 947); for two without appoggiatura, see pp. 256 and 260. The excerpt also includes a number of noncadential masculine endings without appoggiaturas.

[97] In his cantata *Der Tod Jesu* from 1769, modern edn. by Hermann Salzwedel (Bückeburg: Hans Neschen, 1964), see pp. 108 and 134 for cadential and noncadential masculine endings both with and without appoggiaturas. The appoggiaturas are written as large notes.

(1779). Preceding this excerpt, the brother of Lazarus says to a young man: "Sing a song of death," and in Ex. 6.25 says to Jemina (who herself had been raised from the dead by Jesus): "*You* [sing] *a song of resurrection.*" The impassioned nature of the exhortation is thus emphasized by the appoggiatura. In the same work there are three other masculine and two feminine falling-third cadences without appoggiaturas, as well as noncadential masculine endings both with and without an appoggiatura.[98]

Ex. 6.25 Rolle, *Lazarus* (1779), 46

In view of this sensitive use of the appoggiatura by the composers mentioned above, one is tempted to assume expressive purpose even when no masculine cadences occur in the same work without an appoggiatura for comparison. Schulz, for example, includes one falling-third masculine cadence in a song from 1782, and it does have an appoggiatura.[99]

Many songs of Zumsteeg, Loewe, and Schubert also contain brief passages marked "Recit.," and noncadential masculine falling thirds may or may not have an appoggiatura. Such sections seldom have complete cadences, but Schubert does have four with feminine endings. One of these has an appoggiatura (Ex. 6.26), and one of those without occurs in the same song. Although the text in Ex. 6.26 does seem expressive ("and he will triumph"), the grace note would have been required even if the appoggiatura were prosodic in order to show the accidental or possibly to indicate the divided method of performance. Almost all of Schubert's grace-note

---

[98] *Lazarus oder Die Feyer der Auferstehung* (Leipzig: Johann Gottlob Immanuel Breitkopf), copy in the Special Collections of the UCLA Music Library. For falling-third cadences without appoggiaturas, see pp. 8, 12, and 89 for masculine endings, 15 and 34 for feminine.

[99] "Serenata, im Walde zu singen" from *Lieder im Volkston*, i (Berlin, 1782), modern edn. in Max Friedländer's *Das deutsche Lied im 18. Jahrhundert* (Stuttgart and Berlin, 1902), i/2: *Musikbeispiele*, 283.

Ex. 6.26 Schubert, *Lodas Gespenst* (1816), *NSA* IV/vii, 113

appoggiaturas are half the value of the following large note, usually a sixteenth grace to an eighth note or an eighth grace to a quarter.[100]

Cadences with both German and English texts occur, finally, in two oratorios by Haydn and two by Mendelssohn. Haydn, whose Italian works were so valuable for the study of the appoggiatura, seems to employ the same approach in *The Creation* and *The Seasons*. The former, which was written from 1796 to 1798, was first published in 1800 with both the German text to which Haydn composed the music and the original English from which Baron van Swieten made the translation.[101] *The Seasons*, composed in 1799–1800, was published in 1802 in two versions, one with German and English, the other with German and French.[102] The cadence in Ex. 6.27 shows how the endings in the two languages can sometimes differ, in this case with an antepenultimate accent in German and a masculine one in English. This marks the end of the sentence sung by the angel Uriel: "And God said, Let the earth bring forth . . . beasts of the earth after their kind" (Genesis 1:24); this is followed by an accompanied recitative in which the animals appear one by one. The appoggiatura in Ex. 6.27 thus seems to add expressive emphasis to God's command. Also in *The Creation* is another expressive appoggiatura on the last word of the sentence: "Then let our [the angels'] voices ring, united with their [Adam and Eve's] song [of

[100] For Schubert's falling-third cadences without appoggiaturas, see *NSA* IV/vii, 107 (*Lodas gespenst*), IV/ii, 153 (*Der Liedler*), and IV/vi, 139 (*Der Taucher*, second version).

[101] See *Franz Joseph Haydn, Die Schöpfung (The Creation)*, vocal score ed. by A. Peter Brown with Julie Schnepel (OUP, 1991), p. v of *Preface*.

[102] H. C. Robbins Landon, *Haydn: Chronicle and Works*, v (Bloomington, IN: Indiana University Press, 1977), 123.

praise to God]." In this case *Lied* and *song* both provide a masculine ending in which a quarter grace precedes a large half note.[103]

Ex. 6.27 Haydn, *Die Schöpfung* (The Creation) (1796–98),
Part 2, sc. 2, No. 20

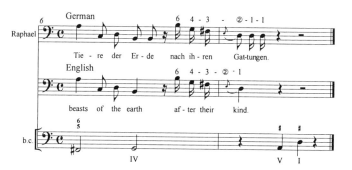

There is somewhat more variety in *The Seasons*. Three falling-third cadences have an antepenultimate accent in both languages, with the appoggiatura written as a large dotted eighth note followed by a sixteenth and a quarter. Two of these occur in the section on Autumn: when Jane (or Hanne, the farmer's daughter) describes the plentiful harvest "to glad the husbandman," and when Simon (the farmer) tells of the boy climbing in the hazelnut tree who mischievously throws a nut at his girlfriend ("the rolling nut he flings"). The third one is in the final section on Winter, when the group rests after a session of spinning in order to hear a story "that bonny Jane is now to tell." All three cadences might have expressive significance: the joy of a good harvest, the exuberance of young love, and the expectation of a relaxing story. In the first of them, the orchestra's V chord coincides with the final note in the voice; in the second, the continuo's V is an eighth note later, and in the third, a dotted quarter later.

Two other cadences seem expressive by omitting an appoggiatura: Jane says during the jolly process of wine making, "Hear the exulting cries from every part resound" (masculine ending in English, feminine in German), and Simon complains when Winter "extends o'er nature all his gloomy reign" (masculine in both languages). When the vapors of Spring, however, pour out "the pride and wealth of nature fair" (again, masculine in both languages), the cadence seems to simply omit the appoggiatura because

[103] The two cadences appear in Brown's vocal score, 85 and 118 (Part 3, sc. 1, No. 27); and in the full score also ed. by A. Peter Brown (OUP, 1995), 172 and 239.

there is no particular expressive element to emphasize. My own interpretation of the expressive nature of these passages is, of course, purely subjective. The important fact is that Haydn deliberately notated some of these falling-third cadences with appoggiaturas and others without, and hence seems to have had some expressive purpose in mind.[104]

In regard to the noncadential endings, the feminine ones seem to be without a notated appoggiatura except when an accidental is required or the grace note has half the value of the following large note.[105] Masculine endings are likewise either with or without an appoggiatura, but in this case some of the appoggiaturas are not required for information, but seem to be mainly expressive.[106] If, in fact, Haydn is indeed following Italian practice, then the feminine ending on *Erde* at the beginning of the top staff in Ex. 6.27 is without an appoggiatura because the singer is expected to add one for prosodic reasons. The masculine ending on *earth* on the second line, on the other hand, apparently has no appoggiatura because Haydn felt it was more appropriate to sing it that way.

Mendelssohn's oratorios, like those of Haydn, were popular in both England and Germany. *St. Paul* (Paulus) was completed, first performed, and published in 1836 with both German and English texts.[107] *Elijah* (Elias) was finished in 1846, first performed the same year, and published in 1847 with both German text and English translation.[108] Thus like Haydn,

---

[104] These cadences appear in the full score of *Die Jahreszeiten* (Leipzig: C. F. Peters, n.d.), repr. as *The Seasons* (New York: Dover, 1986), on pp. 161, 181, and 277 (those with an appoggiatura) and pp. 226, 285, and 51, respectively (those without). According to Robbins Landon in *Haydn: Chronicle and Works*, v, 124, this edition was based on the original German-English edition of 1802, presumably using the same English translation.

[105] See *The Seasons* (New York: Dover, 1986), 24, where the middle syllable of *erheitert* or "and clear-ed" has both a flat and a sixteenth grace preceding two eighth notes.

[106] *The Creation,* full score, 237, for example, on the second syllable of *geweckt* and *appears*, or on *Klang* and *wak'd*; or *The Seasons*, full score, 51, on the last syllable of *erwärmt*.

[107] In 1836 the piano/vocal score appeared, one version with German text (which had been prepared by Julius Schubring from Biblical sources) and another with English (adapted by Wm Ball). The full score followed in 1837 with both German and English texts. These were published by N. Simrock in Bonn and J. Alfred Novello in London. See Arntrud Kurzhals-Reuter, *Die Oratorien Felix Mendelssohn Bartholdys* in *Mainzer Studien zur Musikwissenschaft*, xii (Tutzing: Hans Schneider, 1978), 28–9, 236–7.

[108] Published in 1847 were a piano/vocal score with German text (again by Schubring), an English version by William Bartholomew, a revision of the latter by the composer after the first performance, and the full score with both languages (Bonn: N.

Mendelssohn composed his works to a German text, but approved an
English version that was included in the original publications which he
himself could proofread. By this time, however, there were even fewer
falling-third cadences, so that conclusions are more difficult to draw. Each
of Mendelssohn's oratorios contains two such cadences. In *St. Paul* they
both occur in the same recitative in which a narrator reports what happened
when Paul preached at Antioch. First, the Holy Spirit speaks to the
congregation: "Set ye apart Barnabas and Paul, for the work where unto I
have called them" (Acts 13:2–3). Here the falling third of the cadence is
filled in with an appoggiatura on the first syllable of *habe*. In English,
however, scale degree 2 occurs as a passing tone on the second syllable of
cal-led, with this followed by a masculine ending on 1 without an
appoggiatura for *them*. The text then continues: "And when they [the
congregation] had fasted and prayed . . . , they sent them [Barnabas and
Paul] *away*," ending with another cadence, this time with a large-note
appoggiatura on the first syllable of *gehen* in a feminine ending; in English
the first syllable of *away* is on scale degree 3, the second on 1 as a masculine
ending without appoggiatura.[109]

Ex. 6.28 Mendelssohn, *Elias* (Elijah) (1846), *MW* xiii/2, 54

Simrock; London: Ewer & Cie.). See Kurzhals-Reuter, *Die Oratorien*, 240 and the
Bemerkungen on 241.
  [109] See the full score in *MW*, ed. by Julius Rietz as No. 85 in Series 13 (1878), p.
207 in No. 23. Presumably the English translation is the same one appearing in the
original publication.

Both falling-third cadences in *Elijah* end as in Ex. 6.28 with a feminine German and masculine English ending, and with an appoggiatura for both. In the first case (Ex. 6.28) Elijah had just told the evil King Ahab that there would be no rain, so an angel told him to hide at a certain place "according unto his [God's] word" (I Kings 17:3–6). Three years later God commanded Elijah to return to Ahab and tell him that "the Lord will then send rain again upon the earth" (I Kings 18:1). Here the appoggiatura falls on *Erden* and *earth*.[110]

In regard to the cadences with English text, Mendelssohn has two masculine examples such as Ex. 6.28 in *Elijah* with an appoggiatura and one in *St. Paul* without. One might therefore conclude that the appoggiatura in this case is expressive rather than prosodic. One cannot reach any conclusions, however, concerning the other cadences, for there are no feminine examples in English nor masculine examples in German, and the feminine ones in German all have appoggiaturas. The noncadential endings are also too few to assess.[111] One suspects that at this late date in the history of the falling third, Mendelssohn simply wrote out, as Ricci did in his opera (Ex. 6.21) and Rossini in his cantata from 1847, exactly what he wanted sung. His use of a large note to indicate the replacing type of appoggiatura in the feminine cadence certainly had precedent: we have seen it with Rossini (Ex. 6.20*b*), in later works by Pacini and Ricci (Ex. 6.21), and in the instructional books of Corri and Urbani (Ex. 6.23*a*).

In summary, then, a definite practice concerning the appoggiatura between the two notes of the falling third in recitative with Italian text was suggested, as we have seen, by the limited but somewhat diverse sources available to us. For feminine endings a prosodic appoggiatura is expected on internal, noncadential phrases, but is included or excluded for expressive reasons from the far less frequent but structurally more significant cadences themselves. The rare masculine endings, both cadential and noncadential, also include an appoggiatura if justified by expression. Although German writers seem to imply that the appoggiaturas in masculine cadences or in all noncadential endings are prosodic, German and English composers seem rather to follow Italian practice by considering them expressive in all

---

[110] The full score in *MW*, ed. by Rietz as No. 86 in Series 13 (1878; repr., New York: Dover, 1995), with German text by Julius Schubring and English trans. by William Bartholomew, 54 (in No. 6) and 89 (in No. 10).

[111] In German none of the noncadential masculine endings has an appoggiatura, but all of the feminine ones do, whereas in English some of the endings, both masculine and feminine, do and some do not. See *St. Paul*, 45, 207, and 279, and *Elijah*, 89, 222, and 246.

masculine endings. Even though German and English examples in musical works are more limited in number than the Italian, there are few cases, as far as I know, in which Italian practice is actually contradicted.

Therefore, it appears to me that in the delayed cadence from around 1750 to 1850, and with German and English as well as with Italian texts, the appoggiatura in both masculine and feminine cadences is usually present or absent for expressive purposes. The prosodic appoggiatura seems confined to the far more frequently occurring noncadential feminine endings, where it is apparently, though not described by theorists as expressive, sometimes added or not at the discretion of the singer. Famous performers no doubt sang whatever they pleased. In spite of this, however, and until new evidence proves otherwise, these rules seem to have generally governed the use of the appoggiatura in recitative after 1750.

The Appoggiatura after 1850

The history of the falling-third cadences in newly composed works does not extend, for the most part, past mid-century. Mendelssohn's *Elijah* of 1846 and Rossini's cantata of 1847 contain very late examples. Both the cadences and the possibility of an appoggiatura do continue, however, in performances of older works. Since there was still greatest interest in the production of new works, the older ones that survived were few in number and contained very few falling-third cadences. Those with Italian texts include Mozart's *Nozze di Figaro* with seven feminine cadences and *Don Giovanni* with six, and Rossini's *Barbiere di Siviglia* and *Guillaume Tell* with none at all.[112] English texts occur in Handel oratorios, especially *Messiah* with one masculine cadence (Ex. I) and to a lesser extent *Israel in Egypt*, also with one. German appears in the four masculine examples in Graun's *Der Tod Jesu* as well as in Bach's *St. Matthew Passion*, which includes five masculine cadences with grace-note appoggiaturas and sixteen others (eight masculine, eight feminine) without. Both English and German occur, finally, in Haydn's *Creation* and Mendelssohn's *Elijah*.[113]

---

[112] Concerning the production of these operas in England, see Herman Klein, *The Golden Age of Opera* (London: George Routledge & Sons, Ltd., 1933). For some Mozart performances in Vienna and Paris, see *NG* xix, 724 and 727, and *NG* vi, 429.

[113] Concerning these oratorios, see *NG* xi, 210 (the Handel Festival), and *NG* xiii, 674–5. On Graun's Passion, see *NG* vi, 157, and *NG* vii, 646.

Among these few large-scale works that survive, some include no appoggiaturas by the composer: the Mozart operas, the Handel oratorios, and the Graun Passion. Notated appoggiaturas occur in the works by Bach, Haydn, and Mendelssohn. *The Creation* and *Elijah*, however, contain no examples without an appoggiatura for comparison. The operas of Haydn and Rossini which, like the works of Bach, show cadences both with and without appoggiaturas, are not among the works that continue to be performed. Furthermore, feminine cadences continue only in the thirteen examples from the two Mozart operas and in the eight German examples by Bach and the two in *Elijah*. One ending with an antepenultimate accent remains in *The Creation*.

The number of appoggiaturas actually sung and heard in falling-third cadences during the second half of the nineteenth century was therefore very small indeed. In addition, the number that were *seen* was even smaller, for during this period two important sets of complete works appeared which included no editorial appoggiaturas at all. The first was the Handel *Werke* edited by Chrysander from 1858 to 1894. Although he carefully shifted the V chord in the brief cadences, as we have seen, he adds no appoggiaturas and, as far as I can determine, never mentions the subject in the prefaces or in any of his writings. The Mozart *Werke* from 1877 to 1910 followed the same policy, influenced perhaps by Julius Rietz, who contributed to both editions.

In spite of all this, however, the Mozart tradition seems to have been preserved until the end of the century by the singers themselves and by the singing teachers. Evidence comes from various writings and, beginning around 1889, from recordings. Herman Klein (1856–1934) was an English music critic who studied voice for four years with Manuel García. In *The Bel Canto* from 1923 Klein describes the famous singers who performed in *Don Giovanni* in London in 1872 and in *Le Nozze* around 1875: "Their manner of interpreting Mozart's operas tallied more or less exactly with the general rules laid down by García."[114] In 1847 the latter had described the

[114] *The Bel Canto: with Particular Reference to the Singing of Mozart* was published in London by OUP; it is reprinted in *Herman Klein and The Gramophone*, ed. William R. Moran (Portland, OR: Amadeus Press, 1990). The quotation comes from p. 19. Klein, who helped García prepare his *Hints on Singing* for the press, quotes him on pp. 53–4. The only falling thirds in the examples of García and Klein are noncadential. Jean-Baptiste Faure, who sang the title role in the 1872 production of *Don Giovanni* mentioned by Klein (see his *Golden Age of Opera*, 20–25), writes in *La voix et le chant* (Paris: Henri Heugel, date on portrait 1886), copy at the University of North Carolina, Chapel Hill, NC, p. 169, that since it is impossible to determine precisely which note

noncadential prosodic appoggiatura, which he illustrated with examples from recitatives in *Don Giovanni*.[115] Will Crutchfield writes that recordings of excerpts from this same opera by Peter Schram in 1889 display "appoggiaturas and ornaments that correspond closely to practices observable in Mozart's own day."[116] In 1889 William Smith Rockstro writes in the article on recitative in the first edition of Grove's *Dictionary* that "in phrases ending with two or more reiterated notes, it has been long the custom to sing the first as an appoggiatura, a note higher than the rest." His examples are all noncadential.[117]

Ex. 6.29 Appoggiaturas in Mozart's *Marriage of Figaro*
according to Shakespeare (1899)

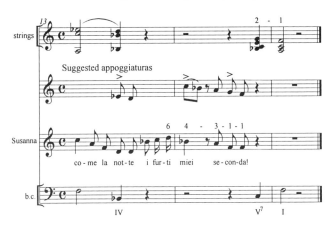

Several sources from this period, however, state or seem to imply that this rule should be extended to include also the cadences. Franklin Taylor, in the article on the appoggiatura in the first edition of Grove's, adds that the appoggiatura "is more appropriate at the close of the whole recitative than after its component phrases, and is especially so when the melody descends

ought to receive an appoggiatura, it is up to the singer to decide (compare the comments of Lablache quoted above).

[115] *Traité complet de l'art du chant*, ii, 63–4; Paschke's trans., 178–81; and *García's New Treatise*, 71.

[116] *Performance Practice: Music After 1600*, ed. Brown and Sadie (1990), 453.

[117] *A Dictionary of Music and Musicians (A.D. 1450–1889)*, ed. George Grove, iii (London: Macmillan, 1889), 83.

a third or a fourth."[118] In 1899 William Shakespeare (1849–1931) gives "examples of the traditional addition of the appoggiature in the recitative 'Giunse alfin il momento' from Mozart's opera, *Le Nozze di Figaro*" (which precedes the aria "Deh! vieni, non tardar"). The inner two staves of Ex. 6.29 show the last three bars of his example, to which I have added the instrumental accompaniment. Here he has included an appoggiatura not only to the noncadential endings on *notte* and *miei* (the first feminine, the second masculine), but also to the falling-third cadence on *seconda*.[119] In addition, Adolf Beyschlag quotes Telemann's examples in his book of 1908, but says that the appoggiaturas on masculine endings (including the cadence in my Ex. 6.2*b*) are almost obsolete ("bald veraltet"), while those on feminine endings (such as my Ex. 6.2*a*) appear in the works of most of the composers from Handel to the middle of the nineteenth century.[120]

After around 1900, however, the singers who had preserved the Mozart style finally disappeared and the tradition of the appoggiatura was almost lost for about fifty years. Klein documents this state of affairs in his reviews in *The Gramophone* and elsewhere. In *The Bel Canto* of 1923 he explains in the chapter on the appoggiatura that "Rossini . . . found himself better served by supplying his own ornaments," but that for earlier music "composers left the choice of ornaments and graces to the artists who sang their music." He complains about "those who imagine that every note written by the old masters, in recitative or elsewhere, should be literally sung as it appears on the printed page; who imagine that because Bach does not require—nor should he indeed receive—the usual Italian interpretation of the appoggiatura, the same strict law must perforce apply to Mozart."[121] In a review from 1932 of a performance of "Deh! vieni, non tardar" and its preceding recitative (Ex. 6.29) he writes with considerable passion:

[118] Ibid., i (1890), 78. His Ex. 36, entitled "Bach, 'Passionsmusik',," has an appoggiatura on a feminine falling-third ending for the word *nothing* in the phrase "They answered nothing." In the *St. Matthew Passion* (*NBA* II/v, p. 196, m. 24), however, the phrase "antwortete er nichts" ends with a masculine falling-third cadence without appoggiatura.

[119] *The Art of Singing*, ii (London: Metzler; Boston: Oliver Ditson, 1899), 115, with this page identical in the one-volume editions by Ditson in 1910 and 1921. The accompaniment in Ex. 6.29 comes from *NMA* II:5/xvi, 509 in Act IV, sc. x.

[120] *Die Ornamentik der Musik* (Leipzig: Breitkopf & Härtel, 1908; 2nd edn., apparently a reprint, 1953), 105: "diese Rezitativformeln und Gesangsmanieren [finden] ihre Anwendung auf die Werke sämtlicher Komponisten von Händel bis zu Berlioz und Mendelssohn (beide exclusive) und in Italien sogar bis zu Verdi, mit alleiniger Ausnahme von J. S. Bach und Spohr."

[121] *The Bel Canto*, 53.

This is the worst example of suppression of the *appoggiatura* that has yet reached this country.   One by one have Mozart's ornaments been eliminated until not a single example remains.   I can positively declare that I failed to recognize the recitative when it began, and only a little of it when it had ended. . . . It seems to me sheer vandalism, and the more barbaric because the German endings to the words, where the higher penultimate note was intended, suffer from its omission quite as badly as would the Italian to which the music was written. . . . I would again remind them [the conductor and his colleagues] that Mozart is not Sebastian Bach; that there is no justification whatever for treating their vocal writing on identical lines.[122]

On several occasions he emphasizes the difference between Mozart and Bach. The former marked none of the appoggiaturas in the recitatives of *Le Nozze* and *Don Giovanni*, whereas Bach, as we have seen, did include some of them in the *St. Matthew Passion*, with the implication that they were not to be performed unless notated. According to Klein's reviews of "Deh! vieni" from 1925, one singer "gives us the recitative but not the *appoggiature*," while another sings it "minus a single *appoggiatura*."[123] Concerning still another, he exclaims, "And lo! She sings not one solitary *appoggiatura*, but apparently makes a virtue of never raising the penultimate note, as if *Deh vieni* were from Bach's *Passion*."[124]

In 1963 Charles Mackerras asks, "Why . . . are performances with unwritten appoggiaturas so rare today?" He blames conductors for the situation and their misguided reverence for the written score. He even mentions performances in which "some singers perform the unwritten appoggiaturas and others do not." "Conductors," he explains, "anxious to expunge all the excessive ornamentation in which nineteenth-century singers indulged, threw out the baby with the bath-water and got rid of the appoggiaturas as well, forgetting that the appoggiatura is not just an optional embellishment but forms an essential part of the melodic style of all vocal music of the eighteenth and early nineteenth centuries, particularly the

---

[122] *Herman Klein and The Gramophone*, 544, concerning the soprano Adele Kern and the conductor Julius Prüwer.

[123] Ibid., 126, about Claire Dux, and 389 about Fritzi Joki.

[124] Ibid., 88, on a recording by Graziella Pareto. He complains also of the lack of appoggiaturas in arias: see p. 485 on Elisabeth Rethberg's recording of "Porgi amor" from *Le Nozze*, which is "minus appoggiaturas, of course (as is the modern fashion)," and p. 423 on Master E. Lough's rendition of Handel's "I know that My Redeemer Liveth" from *Messiah*, where "the omission of the *appoggiatura* is quite indefensible."

recitatives."[125]   As late as 1982 Frederick Neumann could write that "until recently most recitative formulas were sung as written."[126]

During the 1950s and 60s, however, the situation began to change when several writers discovered the prosodic appoggiatura. Bernhard Paumgartner describes it in an article first published in 1953 in which he quotes Tosi, Telemann, Lichtenthal, Mancini, Quantz, C. P. E. Bach, and others.[127]   Luigi Ferdinando Tagliavini, who edited some of the first dramatic works for the *Neue Mozart Ausgabe*, discusses it in a series of prefaces written between 1956 and 1966. He emphasizes García's statement that the recitative appoggiatura was not an ornament but a prosodic accent. He shows numerous examples in small notes above the voice part.[128]   The same point of view is explored historically by Charles Mackerras in a series of articles between 1963 and 1965.[129]   Although his ideas were challenged by Erik Smith writing in 1964 and 1965 about the expressive appoggiatura,[130] the prosodic concept was generally accepted until around 1972 for the noncadential feminine endings and until about 1980 for the cadential. Thus the Mozart volumes appearing up to 1972 included editorial

[125] "Sense About the Appoggiatura," *Opera* 14/10 (Oct 1963): 677, 678, and 669.

[126] "The Appoggiatura in Mozart's Recitatives," *JAMS* 35 (1982): 116.

[127] "Von der sogenannten 'Appoggiatur' in der älteren Gesangsmusik und der Notwendigkeit ihrer Anwendung in der heutigen Aufführungspraxis," *Jahresbericht der Akademie für Musik und darstellende Kunst "Mozarteum," Salzburg*, 1954–55, copy in The Library of Congress, 7–21; first published, according to Tagliavini on p. 179 of the article from 1992 cited below in note 128, in *Schweizer pädagogische Blätter* 14 (Jan 1953): 1–15.

[128] *NMA* II:5/v: *Ascanio in Alba* (1956), pp. X–XI; I:4/ii: *Betulia liberata* (1960), p. IX; and II:5/iv: *Mitridate* (1966), p. XIV. See also his article "'Sposa! Euridice!': Prosodischer und musikalischer Akzent," in *De editione musices: Festschrift Gerhard Croll zum 65. Geburtstag*, ed. Wolfgang Gratzer and Andrea Lindmayr (Laaber: Laaber-Verlag, 1992), 177–202.

[129] "Sense About the Appoggiatura," *Opera* 14/10 (Oct 1963): 669–78; Correspondence in *The Gramophone* 42/498 (Nov 1964): 265; "Appoggiaturas Unlimited?" *Records and Recording* 8/5 (Feb 1965): 14–17. See also *Charles Mackerras: A Musicians' Musician*, ed. Nancy Phelan (London: Victor Gollancz, 1987), 255–74.

[130] "The Appoggiatura and Its Use for 'Suitable Expression'," booklet with recording of Rossini's *L'italiana in Algeri* conducted by Silvio Varviso and issued in several releases including London OSA 1375, A 4375 (London: Decca Record Company Limited, 1964); Correspondence "Appoggiatura," *The Gramophone* 42/496 (Sept 1964): 128; and "The Use and the Abuse of the Appoggiatura," *Records and Recording* 8/4 (Jan 1965): 16–19.

appoggiaturas in many noncadential endings and in all falling-third cadences.[131]

In the edition of *Idomeneo* in 1972, however, Daniel Heartz introduced a new approach in which the cadential appoggiaturas remained prosodic, but the noncadential endings were treated as expressive (just the opposite, that is, of the conclusions I have reached). He explains his method in an analysis of a passage of recitative which contains two falling-third cadences. He describes the first as "the classic case in which the interval of a third is filled in melodically by a descending-second appoggiatura." The other one is preceded six measures earlier by a phrase which he terminates with an upward appoggiatura in order to throw the downward appoggiatura in the cadence "better into relief."[132] This new approach was then followed by a few succeeding editors.[133] The idea that the falling-third cadences, both masculine and feminine, should include an appoggiatura on scale degree 2 regardless of any expressive purpose was shared unanimously by all scholars of the period—and these include those who were exploring the brief cadences from 1962 to at least 1987,[134] and also all the editors of the Scarlatti operas in Grout's series.[135] The cadential appoggiatura was simply taken for granted without question.

---

[131] See *NMA* II:7/i (1967), p. XIX, where Stefan Kunze quotes extensively from García.

[132] *NMA* II:5/xi, pp. XXVIII–XXX, concerning the cadences on *rivale* on p. 24 and *core* on p. 26.

[133] See *NMA* II:5/xvi: *Le Nozze di Figaro* (1973), ed. Ludwig Finscher, p. XVI: "In den Rezitativen . . . wurden Appoggiaturen-Vorschläge verhältnismässig reichlich angebracht, und zwar sowohl bei den stereotypen Schlussformeln als auch—mit etwas grösserer Zurückhaltung—dort, wo eine Appoggiatur zur Pointierung des Ausdrucks dienen könnte."

[134] Westrup, "The Cadence in Baroque Recitative" (1962), 250: "the usual appoggiatura"; Hansell, *MQ* 54 (1968): 236–7; Dean, *ML* 58 (1977): 400; Westrup, *NG* xv, 644; Donington, *NG* xiii, 833; Collins, "Cadential Structures" (1984), 212: "the use of the appoggiatura is too well known to warrant discussion here"; Dale E. Monson, "The Last Word: The Cadence in *Recitativo semplice* of Italian Opera Seria" in *Pergolesi Studies* 1 (1986): 93: "an appoggiatura was always substituted on the supertonic"; and Winton Dean and J. Merrill Knapp, *Handel's Operas, 1704–1726* (OUP, 1987), 32: "the vocal appoggiatura was obligatory at recitative cadences."

[135] Grout established the model for this set in *OAS* i: *Eraclea* (1974), 11–12. Musical examples showing very clearly how the music is written and how the appoggiatura is sung are included in this volume and also in *OAS* ii, 18; iii, 10; vi, 21; and vii, 22. Collins writes in *OAS* viii: *Tigrane* (1983), 13: "ornamentation in recitatives should be restricted to cadential appoggiaturas."

The most influential work on the expressive appoggiatura, however, was Neumann's article in 1982 on "The Appoggiatura in Mozart's Recitative." Although he speaks mostly about noncadential endings, he does state that "the need for an inserted appoggiatura will normally be greatest for the falling third at the cadence, because there, a stepwise descent, along with the prosodic accent, would reflect the gradual tapering of a falling speech melody better than a downward leap to the accented syllable."[136]   He illustrates this by quoting part of "Giunse alfin il momento" from *Le Nozze* and showing, as Shakespeare does in my Ex. 6.29, a cadential appoggiatura on *seconda*. He does not include the two noncadential appoggiaturas shown in Ex. 6.29.[137]   He felt that earlier volumes of the *Neue Mozart Ausgabe* included too many editorial appoggiaturas, and his article hastened the trend, already in progress, toward decreasing their number.

Several subsequent prefaces cite his article and contain a statement saying that the suggested appoggiaturas are optional, to be determined finally by the singer.[138]   This attitude apparently extended at times to the cadences themselves, since at least one volume, *Lucio Silla* edited in 1986 by Kathleen Kuzmick Hansell, contains falling-third cadences both with and without editorial appoggiaturas.   Ten of them (all feminine) have appoggiaturas, three (two masculine and one feminine) do not. She includes appoggiaturas when the emotion is tender or melancholy, but omits them for a matter-of-fact statement or when the expression of anger or determination

[136] *JAMS* 35 (1982): 115–37 (quotation on 117).   The article is reprinted in Neumann's *Essays in Performance Practice* (Ann Arbor, MI: UMI Research Press, 1982), 251–71, and appeared in German in *Mozart-Jahrbuch* (1980–83): 363–84 .
[137] This example appears only on pp. 194–5 (his Ex. 12.18e) of *Ornamentation and Improvisation in Mozart* (Princeton, NJ: Princeton University Press, 1986), where Chapter 12: "The Appoggiatura in Recitative" (pp. 184–203) is an expanded version of the *JAMS* article.   See also his reply to Crutchfield's article in "A New Look at Mozart's Prosodic Appoggiatura," *Perspectives on Mozart Performance*, ed. R. Larry Todd and Peter Williams (Cambridge University Press, 1991), 92–116.
[138] See, for example, *NMA* II:5/ii: *La finta semplice*, ed. Rudolph Angermüller and Wolfgang Rehm (1983), p. XXII: "Diese Vorschläge sind nicht verbindlich, sondern wollen die eigenschöpferische Improvisation der Sänger anregen." The same statement recurs in *NMA* II:5/ix: *Il re pastore* (1985), p. XVI, and in *NMA* II:5/xviii: *Così fan tutte* (1991), p. XIX, where the editors add: "mit dem Hinweis allerdings, dass in dieser Frage ein Konsens gefunden werden sollte!"   See also Neumann's article "Improper Appoggiaturas in the *Neue Mozart Ausgabe*," *The Journal of Musicology* 10 (1992): 505–21, which deals mostly with the ascending appoggiatura in questions.

would thereby be weakened.[139] This is the same method I applied above in my discussion of the cadences in *Idomeneo*.

Just as the *Neue Mozart Ausgabe* was settling into the new idea of an expressive appoggiatura, however, along came Will Crutchfield in 1989 vigorously advocating a return to the prosodic type. He discusses the prosodic appoggiatura in Mozart arias as well as recitatives, but, like Neumann, speaks almost exclusively about noncadential endings. Unlike Neumann, he feels that the *Neue Mozart Ausgabe* suggests too few appoggiaturas. None of his Mozart examples contains the type of cadence we are concerned with, and many do not even include the bass-line.[140]

It was too late for the *Mozart Ausgabe* to react to this latest change of direction, for the final opera was published in 1991. Two other complete works, however, seem to have responded, for both the *Hallische Händel-Ausgabe* and the *Sämtliche Werke* of Fux, which from 1958 to 1976 had included editorial appoggiaturas, suddenly left them out completely in editions beginning around 1991. This change coincided, for the most part, with the practice of printing the V chord in the brief cadences as the composer notated it.[141] Hopefully, future volumes of complete works will

---

[139] *NMA* II:5/vii, p. XXXVII: see the cadences without an editorial appoggiatura on pp. 292, 296, and 372, and those with on pp. 95, 183, 204, 294, 374, 415, 418 (two of them), 445, and 448. Two of the fourteen feminine falling-third cadences in *Così fan tutte* also lack editorial appoggiaturas, but this may be due to the fact that both are duets with a downward-fourth cadence in a second voice; see *NMA* II:5/xviii, p. 84, m. 17, and p. 182, m. 42.

[140] "The Prosodic Appoggiatura in the Music of Mozart and His Contemporaries," *JAMS* 42 (1989): 229–74. On pp. 247–8 he includes in a list of appoggiaturas sometimes omitted in transcriptions "the most obvious and final-sounding kind that fills in a concluding fall of a third"; his example in note 15, however, refers to the quasi close in *Don Giovanni*, *NMA* II:5/xvii, 47, which has the chord progression (V$_6$-I) of my Ex. 4.1*a* with the melody (4-3-1-1) of Ex. 4.1*b*. See also the section entitled "The Prosodic Appoggiatura" from his chapter on voices in the Classical era in *Performance Practice: Music After 1600*, ed. Brown and Sadie (1990), 298–300.

[141] For Handel volumes with editorial appoggiaturas, see, for example, *HHA* II/xxxix: *Serse* (1958), II/viii: *Amadigi* (1971), and I/ix: *Acis and Galatea* (1991); for those without, see II/xiii: *Flavio* (1993), II/iv: *Rinaldo* (two versions, 1993 and 1996), and II/ix: *Radamisto* (1997). Two volumes with English texts include examples of both: I/xiii: *Saul* (1962), which has six falling-third cadences with editorial appoggiaturas (both masculine and feminine) and one masculine without; and I/xxviii: *Susanna* (1967), which has fifteen with and nine without, all masculine. In the Fux *Sämtliche Werke*, early volumes with editorial appoggiaturas are IV/i: *La fede sacrilega . . .* (1959), V/i: *Julo Ascanio, Re d'Alba* (1962), and V/ii: *Pulcheria* (1967); recent volumes without are IV/iii: *Il trionfo della fede* (1991), V/iii: *Gli ossequi della notte* (1994), and V/v: *La decima*

be strictly "critical" and not "performance" editions and will follow the composer's score in regard to both the cadential structure and the presence or absence of an appoggiatura. This would allow the singer to see what the composer wanted him to see. It would also remove from the editor the impossible task of reflecting the constantly changing attitudes of scholars as they seek laboriously to discover the truth. As I submit now my own new and different concepts, I can thus feel somewhat relieved that if anyone finds them of merit, then at least the latest editions will not have to change in order to accommodate them.

Summary of Appoggiatura Practice 1714 to the Present

Figure 6 is an attempt to summarize the various ways in which the appoggiatura on scale degree 2 occurs in the falling-third cadences of recitative. The first line concerns notation and indicates whether none, some, or all of the appoggiaturas are marked. The second line describes performance, showing when none, some, or all appoggiaturas are sung. The bottom line identifies the appoggiatura in each category or time period as prosodic or expressive. Up to around 1850 recitative occurs mostly in newly composed works. In this case the first line represents the composer's score, the second line the vocal practice as described by writers of the time. After 1850, on the other hand, Fig. 6 refers to the few previously composed works that continue to be performed. Therefore, the first line indicates in this case the additions and suggestions of editors, the second the appoggiatura practice deemed correct at the time by conductors, singers, and scholars. Fig. 6 represents only the cadential endings, not the noncadential.

Concerning the expressive appoggiatura, we have seen it carefully notated in the works of several composers before 1850: in the cantatas and Passions of J. S. Bach from 1714 to 1747 (Exx. 6.11, 6.13–6.16), in the Latin oratorio and Italian operas of Haydn from 1768 to 1785 (Ex. 6.19) and in his German and English oratorios from 1798 to 1800 (Ex. 6.27), in Rossini's operas from 1812 to 1828 (Ex. 6.20) and his later cantata of 1847, and in Mendelssohn's oratorios of 1836 and 1846 (Ex. 6.28). These composers may then act, in the absence of information to the contrary, as a

---

fatica d'Ercole (1996). One earlier edition without appoggiaturas is IV/ii: *La donna forte* (1976).

Fig. 6 Performance of the cadential appoggiatura
(Chart does not apply to the noncadential appoggiatura)

	Before 1750			1750–1900 old works after 1850		1900–1955	1956–80	1981–90	1991–98
	German sacred		opera						
	J. S. Bach	Telemann							
Written	some notated	almost none marked	none marked	sometimes notated (Haydn, Rossini)	usually not marked	none added by editor	all marked	some marked	none added by editor
Performed	sung as notated	all sung	none sung	sung as notated	sung if expressive	usually none sung	all to be sung	sung as desired	all sung
Type	*EXPRESSIVE*	PROSODIC		*EXPRESSIVE*			PROSODIC	*EXPRESSIVE*	PROSODIC

guide to the use of the appoggiatura in works, such as most of those by Mozart, in which none is notated.

Fig. 6 therefore shows the expressive appoggiatura with J. S. Bach, with Haydn, Rossini, and others who notate it when wanted, with composers from 1750 to 1850 who let the singers decide when to provide it, and with performers who continue to use it from 1850 to 1900 in older works that survive. I would include here examples from 1750 to 1800 in the German language, since the composers seem to treat the appoggiatura in masculine cadences as expressive even though many theorists do not. The expressive appoggiatura is also seen emerging again briefly during the 1980s.

Fig. 6 also shows the prosodic appoggiatura, beginning with the cantatas of Telemann (Ex. 6.2). This concept seems to reappear in cadences during later periods when scholars rediscover the prosodic appoggiatura in noncadential endings and extend it, incorrectly in my view, also to cadences: thus from around 1956 to 1980 and again during the 1990s and extending probably to the present day. There seems to be a tenacious persistence to the idea that the cadence itself is even more deserving of an appoggiatura than the structurally less important internal phrases. This concept may extend well back into English history, for we saw it implied in examples by Urbani around 1800 (Ex. 6.23) and by Shakespeare in 1899 (Ex. 6.29), and stated clearly by Taylor in 1883 in Grove's *Dictionary*.

Also on Fig. 6 are two columns which show no appoggiaturas at all on cadences: the later period from 1900 to about 1955 when the old singing style had been forgotten, and another concerning opera before 1750. The latter is perhaps surprising. We must remember, however, that it is the brief structure which is involved, a structure probably designed specifically for the rapid and functional declamation of narration or conversation, and a structure that I feel is meant to be performed exactly as notated. We have noted Tosi's description of the chanting effect of the repeated notes in the feminine endings of these numerous broken cadences and the opinion of several writers that ornaments are not appropriate in the theater. We have also noted that the continuo realization recommended by Telemann for the opera produces bad results when accompanying an appoggiatura (Exx. 5.2*a* and 6.8). In addition, I think it strange that none of the many instruction books in thorough-bass ever, to my knowledge, mentions the possibility of an appoggiatura in recitative. In the aria the continuo player simply kept strict time so that the singer, when moved to express passion, could use the tempo rubato.[142]   But the recitative was to be sung with considerable rhythmic flexibility, presumably requiring the accompanist to follow the vocal score carefully in order to follow the singer. Yet I have never seen in any of the instruction books, even the most elementary ones for beginners, the warning that the accompanist might, at least on some occasions, actually hear vocal notes different from those notated.

After 1750 a series of writers, beginning with Agricola in 1757, do indicate in books on singing how the two repeated notes in a feminine ending represent an appoggiatura.   As we have seen, they are referring, however, to noncadential rather than cadential endings.   Since this distinction is so important in understanding the appoggiatura, I show in Ex. 6.30 a comparison between the typical delayed cadence and some of the noncadential types.   The examples come from Mozart's *Idomeneo* and all show scale degrees 4-3-1-1 in the voice. In (a) this melodic fragment occurs over a sustained note in the bass. (b) shows the typical quasi close as we defined it in Ex. 4.1.   The two chords of a quasi close relate as V to I, and usually, in order to enhance the sense of forward movement, one or both are in inversion. Thus the progression may be V_2 to I_6, V_6 to I_6 or I, or V to I_6. Less often both chords are in root position as in (c), which in some other context would constitute an authentic cadence; it does not function this way, however, in recitative.   The recitative cadences, of course, are the broken ones with a falling third or fourth, and (d) shows the delayed form of the falling-third cadence for comparison.

One crucial difference between the noncadential endings in (a), (b), and (c) and the cadential one in (d) is the way the V and I fit with the 1-1 in the voice. In the quasi closes of (b) and (c) the first 1 coincides exactly with the I, and the V precedes it. In the cadence of (d), on the other hand, both V and I follow after both 1's, which are preceded not by V but by IV_6. This means that while the voice sings 1-1 in the noncadential endings of (a), (b), and (c), the harmonic progression has reached its resolution, and the two syllables can be sung in a relatively relaxed manner. When the voice sings 1-1 in the cadence of (d), on the contrary, there is a powerful feeling that the music is unfinished and that the harmonic progression must be quickly but conspicuously completed by the following V and I chords played by the instruments, which thus act to provide the melodic cadential framework on scale degrees 7 and 1.

---

[142] See my book *Stolen Time: The History of Tempo Rubato* (OUP, 1994; paperback, 1997), 42.

Now, a dividing or replacing type of appoggiatura may on occasion be added by the composer or the singer to any of the lines of Ex. 6.30. As we might expect, such an appoggiatura in the first three lines creates an effect quite different from that in the cadence. In (*a*), (*b*), and (*c*) an appoggiatura on scale degree 2 is conspicuously dissonant with both the root and third of the tonic chord with which it is sung. It resolves onto the second 1 while the tonic chord is still sustained or, in the case of (*c*), still in effect during the rest. Thus it acts like the traditional appoggiatura which leans upon the

Ex. 6.30 Noncadential 4-3-1-1 endings compared to the falling-third cadence in Mozart's *Idomeneo*, *NMA* II:5/xi

chord below, is sung more loudly and forcibly, and resolves finally onto the softer, weaker final 1 or 1's. In the case of (b) and (c) the 3 which precedes 1-1 is itself dissonant with notes of the V chord.

In the cadence in (d), 3 is also dissonant, this time with notes of the IV$_6$ with which it sounds. When we reach 1-1, however, there is a question about what chord the listener imagines during the rest in the accompaniment. If IV$_6$ continues to be felt at this moment, then an appoggiatura on 2 is not very dissonant, since it forms with the IV$_6$ the second inversion of a ii^7 chord. In this case, the IV$_6$ chord seems to simply be sustained until it reaches the V and forms with it the familiar IV$_6$-V-I cadence. On the other hand, the listener might, as we have discussed above, imagine a I$^6_4$ chord during 1-1. This might be induced by the predominant presence in the same music of the downward-fourth cadence, or, indeed, the falling third may itself have some power to suggest I$^6_4$. In this case, the appoggiatura on 2 would be dissonant with notes of the imagined I$^6_4$ chord, which, in turn, causes the voice's scale degree 1 to sound itself like an appoggiatura that finds resolution in the scale degree 7 of the accompaniment's V chord. This is what happens more obviously in the brief cadences, as we have seen, where V sounds with the appoggiatura and a realization is required (Ex. 5.2b or c) in which scale degree 7 appears only after the resolution to 1. In either the brief or delayed cadence, however, adding a louder, stronger appoggiatura on 2 inevitably weakens the effect of the succeeding 1. Perhaps the ambiguity of chord during the rest in the delayed cadence of Ex. 6.30d adds a sense of mystery to that sensitive moment when the voice completes its phrase alone, but leaves the music sounding urgently in need of further resolution.

One final comparison might be useful. Ex. 6.31 shows a typical cadence from an aria in the same opera. Like most aria cadences it has a melodic framework of scale degree 2 moving to 1, with the 2 extended in length and ornamented; the chords provide the usual authentic cadence in which the final I coincides with 1 in the voice. The cadence in Ex. 6.30d, on the other hand, has a melodic framework of 7-1, which is provided finally by the accompaniment, so that an appoggiatura in the voice does not create a 2-1 cadence structurally. Thus scale degree 2 can play quite different roles: in the recitative cadence of Ex. 6.30d it would be, as an appoggiatura, part of the approach that precedes the framework pitches; in the aria cadence of Ex. 6.31, on the other hand, 2 is itself the penultimate structural note; and in the noncadential phrases of Ex. 6.30a–c, 2 would be an appoggiatura leaning on a passing chord which is part of a larger harmonic progression leading to some distant cadence.

Ex. 6.31 Aria cadence from Mozart's *Idomeneo,*
NMA II:5/xi, 33
(transposed from G minor)

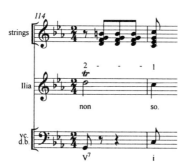

It must be emphasized that Fig. 6 applies only to the cadential appoggiatura and not to the noncadential. If one were to create a similar chart to show the performance of the noncadential appoggiatura, one would begin, of course, with Telemann's sacred cantatas, where both masculine and feminine endings are prosodic. Two problem areas remain, however, before 1750: feminine endings with Bach, who seems ordinarily to notate exactly what he wants, but who does not generally notate appoggiaturas in this case; and opera, which may omit the appoggiaturas from noncadential as well as cadential endings, although I do not think the same compelling reasons would apply in the former case. During the period 1750 to 1900 the feminine noncadential appoggiaturas which the writers describe so often are generally prosodic, the masculine expressive. From 1900 to 1955 there are usually none sung. The feminine appoggiaturas are treated by later editors as prosodic from around 1956 to 1971 and from 1991 on, but as expressive from 1972 to 1990. Thus both cadential and noncadential appoggiaturas in feminine endings are prosodic in Telemann's cantatas and in works performed from 1956 to 1971 and 1991 to 1998. From 1750 to 1900, however, appoggiaturas in noncadential feminine endings seem to be mainly prosodic, while those in cadences are expressive. The comparison in Ex. 6.30 explains, I think, how these two categories can be treated at times in quite different ways

*   *   *   *   *

One of the most important considerations concerning the appoggiatura, it seems to me, is its manner of vocal delivery—that is, the innumerable factors of tone quality, articulation, volume, force, and pronunciation deemed by the singer to be faithful to the sense of the music, the text, the character, the mood, and the plot. Recitative was meant to be declaimed in a voice half sung, half spoken, so that it might be whispered or might be shouted, as the occasion required. It might exaggerate the duration or intensity of unpitched consonant noises such as the hiss of an *s*, the roll of an *r*, or the click of a *k*.

Cadences were those structurally significant places where important sentences, thoughts, or conversations came to a conclusion on sensitive and often emotional words. They thus tended to carry more expressive weight than other parts of the music. Moved by the force of great passions, singers no doubt rendered such cadences with various combinations of the speaking and singing voice—sometimes, perhaps, almost completely spoken. It may well have been the case that on occasion a listener could not even determine whether those final two 1's were sung or spoken, whether there was an appoggiatura or not, or whether an appoggiatura divided or replaced the first 1.

Study of the appoggiatura in the falling-third cadences is confusing for the historian, for he must constantly keep in mind the distinction between the cadential and the noncadential, the feminine and the masculine, the divided and the replaced, the falling third and the falling fourth, and the distinction, finally, between the priorities of prosody and expression.

THE

CONCLUSIONS

Chapter 7

THE 4-3-1 FIGURE IN HISTORY

IT IS THE FALLING-THIRD interval preceded by scale degree 4 which endures the longest in history. Although it may seem at first to be the most awkward of all the configurations, it occurs in the most diverse situations from the time of chant up to the present day. Its popularity and longevity may be due to the fact that it belongs to a number of different melodic families.

First of all, it begins in Gregorian chant as part of a series of downward-third cadences in which scale degree 3 is preceded by a number of different pitches. The melody of chant is usually stepwise, and the usual cadence descends from 2 to 1. In this restrained environment, a leap is conspicuous, especially a leap that is approached from the same direction, and even more especially a leap at the end of a chant. Therefore it is somewhat surprising that 4-3-1 should become one of the favored cadence patterns.

Secondly, the melodic shape of 4-3-1 may appear also on other scale degrees in chant. It is mainly in polyphonic music from the late thirteenth through the early sixteenth centuries, however, that 4-3-1 appears as a distinctive element of style along with the other members of this family of figures, consisting of a descending second followed by a descending third. They all occur, either subtly or boldly, both at cadence and internally. Since it ends on 1, however, it is 4-3-1 that is most useful at cadence. It is only late in the sixteenth century, at the time of Palestrina, that regulations are finally imposed: when 3 in 4-3-1 (or the corresponding note in the other figures) is dissonant, then 1 must be followed by scale degree 2, so that it sounds as though 3 is resolving ultimately to 2. At the same time there is a general trend away from the angular leaps of earlier music and toward a smoother, more stepwise flow, so that the descending thirds in figures such as 4-3-1 are increasingly filled in by inserting scale degree 2 to form 4-3-2-1 (Ex. 3.6e and f).

In Baroque recitative the entire family of 3-1 figures is reborn, this time with even greater diversity in the note which precedes 3, and this time for a variety of purposes: for a momentary phrase over a single chord, for a quasi close, or for a concluding cadence (see Ex. 6.30). It is only late in the eighteenth century, after a long evolution, that 4-3-1 is finally preferred, especially at cadence, where 4 is usually preceded by 6, adding still another descending interval to the two in 4-3-1. Beginning early in the eighteenth century, there is occasionally the desire, as there was at the time of Palestrina, to soften the striking effect of the falling third by inserting 2 between 3 and 1, this time as an appoggiatura. This was also a way of avoiding the monotony of two repeated 1's in a feminine ending.

4-3-1 is also a partner in another recitative group, one which includes the falling fourths. The latter parallel the history of the falling thirds. They originated late in the seventeenth century when the broken cadences or *cadenze tronche* were created (Ex. 4.3d), and occasionally acted as quasi closes (Ex. 4.1c). As cadences, they also made the transition to the delayed type (Ex. 5.1c and d), could be masculine or feminine, and could have an appoggiatura. They competed with the falling-third cadences and finally won out, almost completely superseding them by the nineteenth century.

The 4-3-1 figure also participates in a group of cadences throughout the entire history in which scale degrees 7 and 1 are added as the main structural framework. Ex. 7.1 shows 4-3-1-7-1 cadences excerpted from examples given earlier and extending from the time before polyphony to the Classic-Romantic period. The continued performance of the Mozart opera in (*f*) brings this cadence, of course, up to our own time. Although a cadence ending with 4-3-1 is more common in chant, (*a*) shows an unusual example in which 7-1 is added at the end. (*b*) is the upper part from a three-voiced piece. Although coming from quite different types of composition, (*a*) and (*b*) present 4-3-1-7-1 very clearly in a single voice. On the other hand, (*c*), the soprano, tenor, and bass parts from a four-voiced vocal work, shows the progression broken into two parts, with 4-3-1 in the tenor, 7-1 on the top. This becomes the usual arrangement later in the Renaissance.

A similar transition occurs later in recitative. First the complete progression occurs in the voice part of (*d*), then is broken so that in (*e*) 4-3-1 remains in the voice and 7-1 moves to the continuo realization. This *cadenza tronca* ("broken cadence") in (*e*) continues to use almost exactly the same rhythm as (*d*). Later this brief structure is modified by shifting the two concluding instrumental chords a quarter beat later, usually by placing a rest below the voice's final two notes as shown in (*f*).

In chant the 4-3-1 cadences act as a conspicuous contrast to the
stepwise movement elsewhere in the melody. In medieval and Renaissance
polyphony the same figure blends in as part of the contrapuntal flow,

Ex. 7.1 4-3-1 + 7-1 as a melodic cadence in history

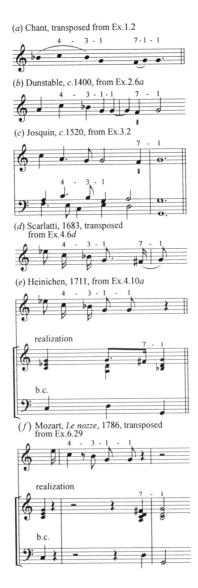

(*a*) Chant, transposed from Ex.1.2

(*b*) Dunstable, *c*.1400, from Ex.2.6*a*

(*c*) Josquin, *c*.1520, from Ex.3.2

(*d*) Scarlatti, 1683, transposed
from Ex.4.6*d*

(*e*) Heinichen, 1711, from Ex.4.10*a*

realization

b.c.

(*f*) Mozart, *Le nozze*, 1786, transposed
from Ex.6.29

realization

b.c.

especially immediately preceding or following the framework notes at cadence. In recitative the figure joins others in the formation of special types of cadence which are completely unique to the form—types that are not heard elsewhere, especially in the aria. The closest that other kinds of music come, as far as I know, is in a cadence somewhat like the quasi close in Ex. 6.30c, but with scale degree 4 replaced sometimes by 2 or 5. In this type of falling-third cadence, which becomes increasingly frequent in homophonic music during the nineteenth century, 3 is a free dissonance over a V^7 chord, is left by leap from 3 to 1 (2 is not involved), and is sometimes approached by leap (especially from 5 up to 3). Sometimes, as in chant, 3-1 seems to become in this case the main cadential framework, especially in the figures 4-3-1 or 5-3-1. Scale degree 3 is sometimes repeated, accentuated, or prolonged to achieve an effect of powerful yearning.[1] Examples occur also in the blues of the early twentieth century.[2]

In spite of startling similarities between the lines of Ex. 7.1, there seem to be actually two distinct and separate developments: the first leading from chant to the late sixteenth-century polyphony of Palestrina, the other, perhaps also originating with chant, spanning the history of recitative from 1600 to around 1850. In the first development the 4-3-1 figures and cadences pose fewer problems for performers today, since, except for *musica ficta*, the sources generally show exactly the pitches and rhythm to be performed. In recitative, on the other hand, two serious problems have troubled performers for a very long time: one concerning structure, the other, the appoggiatura. In the first case, a problem arose originally because of changing tastes, so that by the late eighteenth century Handel's brief cadences were being performed delayed. In the second case, problems arose

---

[1] See, for example, the 4-3-1 cadence in mm. 43–4 of Chopin's *Andante spianato*, Op. 22; the 2-3-1 cadence in mm. 8–9 of the first movement of Schumann's piano quintet, Op. 44; and the 5-3-1 conclusion of the "Valse noble" in his *Carnaval*. Deryck Cooke, in *The Language of Music* (OUP, 1959; repr. 1981), 71, speaks of "that well-known romantic stand-by, the 'dominant thirteenth,' the 'yearning' effect of which is notorious." See also the examples given by E. Markham Lee in "Cadences and Closes," *Proceedings of the Musical Association* 31 (1904–5): 74.

[2] See *A Treasury of the Blues*, ed. W. C. Handy, with an historical and critical text by Abbe Niles (New York: Charles Boni, 1949), for 4-3-1 on pp. 144–5 in mm. 14–15 of Handy's "Basement Blues" (1924), 2-3-1 (G-sharp A F) on p. 206 in his "John Henry Blues" (1922), 1-3-1 (C E-flat C at the end of a section in C major) on p. 41 in the spiritual "Let Us Cheer the Weary Traveller," and 1-3-1 on p. 42 at the end of "Somebody's Wrong About dis Bible," the last two arranged by Handy. A number of pieces in this book show characteristics strikingly similar to Gregorian chant.

because composers did not always notate what they wanted performed. And by our own time, both problems had become far more confused by the misinterpretation of explanations given by earlier writers.

Regarding the matter of structure, we have seen above that Telemann's remarks do not refer to the alteration of the continuo rhythm, but to realizations which occur above the continuo part when played as notated. Thus it is never necessary, or permitted, in my opinion, to change the notated bass-line written by the composer, even in the case of the brief cadence. This simply means that before 1750 the brief structure was generally preferred and that after 1750 taste gradually turned to the delayed type. Modern performers may choose, of course, whether to follow the original intention of a composer such as Handel, or, because of our modern taste, to match a later method of performance. Fig. 4 in Chapter 5 summarizes the history of this structural problem and our modern attempts to resolve it.

A similar summary in Fig. 6 in Chapter 6 depicts the even more complex history of the appoggiatura. The problem first arises in sacred German music early in the eighteenth century when J. S. Bach selectively notates expressive cadential appoggiaturas starting in 1714, while Telemann requests in 1725–26 a prosodic one on almost every ending, cadential or not. Furthermore, Telemann's realizations indicate, along with other evidence, that the appoggiatura was excluded altogether from the brief secco cadences in opera, as it was also in any accompanied recitative when the full V chord was heard with the first or single 1. Numerous writers from 1757 until late in the nineteenth century faithfully transmit the rule that an appoggiatura is intended when the composer writes an ending with two repeated notes. The expressive cadential appoggiaturas of composers such as Haydn and Rossini suggest, however, that during this period when the frequency of falling-third cadences was rapidly diminishing, these writers were all referring, as shown in their examples, only to noncadential endings and not to the cadences themselves. Reaction after 1900 to this bewildering state of affairs is also shown in Fig. 6: first a long period when no appoggiaturas are sung at all at cadence, then periods in which the prosodic and expressive alternate.

Both the structure and the appoggiatura have been considered so important that an attempt at their solution has been included in numerous complete works—works which were otherwise, for the most part, critical rather than performing editions. It is astonishing how much scholarly time and effort have been devoted to these problems of structure and appoggiatura. Yet, because of the great frequency of their occurrence in recitative and because of their conspicuous position at cadence, they affect the resulting sound in very substantial ways. In addition to this, both of the problems involve some of the most beloved works of Western civilization: the cantatas and Passions of Bach, the oratorios and operas of Handel, the operas of Mozart.

It is my hope that this book may provide at least one more step along the way. From the time of Gregorian chant until our own days, the falling thirds have appeared in diverse situations and types of music in order to serve various purposes. It is a curious and unexpected fact of this history that the seemingly unmanageable 4-3-1 pattern should have played such a conspicuous role and survived, finally, far longer than all the rest. It even occurs in 1951 in *The Rake's Progress* by Stravinsky.[3] And it still exists today, of course, every time we see the score of the *St. Matthew Passion*, *Messiah*, or *Le nozze di Figaro*, and every time we hear the examples in these works performed without an appoggiatura. In a musical history in which melodic cadences are ordinarily dominated by stepwise movement from 2 or 7 to 1, it is remarkable, I think, that the falling third played any role at all—let alone such varied and enduring roles that extend from the beginnings of Western music until the present day.

---

[3] Three internal recitative phrases end somewhat like the quasi closes in Ex. 4.1*b* and Ex. 6.30*b* and *c*: see the full and piano/vocal scores (Boosey & Hawkes, 1951), Act I, sc. i, 11 and 12 mm. after the bar marked rehearsal no. 26, 1 and 2 mm. following no. 50, and 5 mm. after no. 55. In the composer's recording with the Royal Philharmonic Orchestra, each of the falling thirds is sung, as one would expect, without an appoggiatura. See *Igor Stravinsky: The Recorded Legacy*, CBS Records GM31/LXX 36940 (1981), xii, side 1.

BIBLIOGRAPHY

Agricola, Johann Friedrich, *Anleitung zur Singkunst* (Berlin, 1757), repr. ed. by Erwin R. Jacobi (Celle: Hermann Moeck, 1966), trans. by Julianne C. Baird as *Introduction to the Art of Singing* (Cambridge University Press, 1995). See also Tosi.

Alençon, J., *Korte aanmerkingen over de zangkonst, getrokken uit een italiaansch boek, betyteld Osservazioni sopra il canto figurato di Pier Francesco Tosi* (Leyden, 1731). See also Tosi.

Bacon, Richard Mackenzie, *Elements of Vocal Science*: *Being a Philosophical Enquiry into Some of the Principles of Singing* (London, 1824), new edn. by Edward Foreman in *MOS* i (1966).

Beethoven, Ludwig van, *Studien in Generalbass, Contrapunkt und in der Compositionslehre aus dessen handschriftlichem Nachlasse*, ed. Ignaz Ritter von Seyfried, 2nd edn. by Henry Hugo Pierson (Leipzig and New York: J. Schuberth & Co., [1852]).

Beyschlag, Adolf, *Die Ornamentik der Musik*, 2nd edn. (Leipzig: Breitkopf & Härtel, 1953).

Buelow, George, J., *Thorough-Bass Accompaniment According to Johann David Heinichen*, rev. edn. in *SM* 84 (1986).

Callcott, John Wall, *Explanation of the Notes, Marks, Words, &c Used in Music* (London, preface dated 1792), repr. on microfiche in *Musical Dictionaries*, Series I (Washington, DC: Brookhaven Press, 1976).

Collins, Michael, "Cadential Structures and Accompanimental Practices in Eighteenth-Century Italian Recitative," *Opera and Vivaldi*, ed. Michael Collins and Elise K. Kirk (Austin: University of Texas Press, 1984), 211–32.

Corri, Domenico (ed.), *A Select Collection of the Most Admired Songs, Duetts . . . from Operas . . . and from Other Works*, i (Edinburgh, c.1779; repr., Rome: Bardi, 1993; and New York: Garland, 1993) and iv (Edinburgh, 1790s; repr., Rome: Bardi, 1993; and New York: Garland, 1995).

Corri, Domenico, *The Singers Preceptor* (London: Chappell & Co., 1810), repr. in *MOS* iii: *The Porpora Tradition*, ed. Edward Foreman (1968).

Crocker, Richard L., *An Introduction to Gregorian Chant* (New Haven and London: Yale University Press, 2000).

Crutchfield, Will, "The Prosodic Appoggiatura in the Music of Mozart and His Contemporaries," *JAMS* 42 (1989): 229–74.

_____, "The Prosodic Appoggiatura," in *Performance Practice: Music After 1600*, ed. Howard Mayer Brown and Stanley Sadie (New York: Norton, 1990), 298–300.

Dean, Winton, "The Performance of Recitative in Late Baroque Opera," *ML* 58 (1977): 389–402.

Dean, Winton, and J. Merrill Knapp, *Handel's Operas, 1704–1726* (OUP, 1987).

Donington, Robert, *A Performer's Guide to Baroque Music* (New York: Charles Scribner's Sons, 1973).

_____, *The Interpretation of Early Music*, New Version (London: Faber and Faber, 1975).

_____, "Ornaments, II: Appoggiaturas," *NG* xiii, 828–37.

Downes, Edward O. D., "Secco Recitative in Early Classical Opera Seria," *JAMS* 14 (1961): 50–69.

Ferrari, Giacomo Gotifredo, *A Concise Treatise on Italian Singing* (London, 1818; later edn., preface dated 1825).

Fux, Johann Joseph, *Gradus ad Parnassum* (Vienna, 1725), repr. in *Monuments of Music and Music Literature in Facsimile*, Ser. 2, xxiv (New York: Broude Brothers, 1966).

Galliard, John Ernest, *Observations on the Florid Song*, 2nd edn. (London: J. Wilcox, 1743; modern edn., London: William Reeves, 1926). See also Tosi.

García, Manuel Patricio Rodriguez, *Traité complet de l'art du chant*, ii (Paris, 1847; repr., Minkoff, 1985), trans. by Donald V. Paschke in *A Complete Treatise on the Art of Singing*, ii: *The Editions of 1847 and 1872* (published by Paschke, 1972; repr., New York: Da Capo, 1975).

_____, *García's New Treatise on the Art of Singing* (London, [1857]).

_____, *Hints on Singing* (London, [1894]), repr. ed. by Byron Cantrell (Canoga Park, CA: Summit Publishing Co., 1970).

Gasparini, Francesco, *L'armonico pratico al cimbalo* (Venice, 1708), repr. in *Monuments of Music and Music Literature in Facsimile*, Ser. 2, xiv (New York: Broude Brothers, 1967); trans. by Frank S. Stillings and ed. by David L. Burrows as *The Practical Harmonist at the Harpsichord* (New Haven, CT: Yale School of Music, 1963).

Hahn, Georg Joachim Joseph, *Der wohl unterwiesene General-Bass Schüler* (Augsburg, 1751).

Hansell, Sven Hostrup, "The Cadence in 18th-Century Recitative," *MQ* 54 (1968): 228–48.

Heinichen, Johann David, *Neu erfundene und gründliche Anweisung . . . zu vollkommener Erlernung des General-Bassus* (Hamburg, 1711), facs.

in *DM* xl (2000) and on Microcard No. UR-56 203-9 from the copy at Sibley Music Library, Eastman School of Music (University of Rochester Press).

_____, *Der General-Bass in der Composition, oder: Neue und gründliche Anweisung* (Dresden, 1728; repr., Hildesheim: Georg Olms Verlag, 1969).

Hiller, Johann Adam, *Anweisung zum musikalisch-zierlichen Gesange* (Leipzig, 1780; repr., Leipzig: Edition Peters, 1976), trans. by Suzanne J. Beicken as *Treatise on Vocal Performance and Ornamentation by Johann Adam Hiller* (Cambridge University Press, 2001).

_____, *Anweiswung zum musikalisch-richtigen Gesange* (Leipzig, 1774; 2nd edn., 1798).

Homan, Frederic W., "Final and Internal Cadential Patterns in Gregorian Chant," *JAMS* 17 (1964): 66–77.

Kaye, Philip R., *The "Contenance Angloise" in Perspective: A Study of Consonance and Dissonance in Continental Music, c.1380–1440* (Garland, 1989).

Kellner, David, *Treulicher Unterricht im General-Bass* (Hamburg, 1732), copy in Sibley Music Library, Eastman School of Music, repr. on Microcard UR-56 127-9 (University of Rochester Press); 2nd edn. with *Vorrede* by G. P. Telemann (Hamburg, 1737; repr., Michaelstein, n.d.).

Klein, Herman, *The Bel Canto: with Particular Reference to the Singing of Mozart* (London: OUP, 1923), repr. in *Herman Klein and The Gramophone*.

_____, *The Golden Age of Opera* (London: George Routledge & Sons, Ltd., 1933).

_____, *Herman Klein and The Gramophone*, ed. William R. Moran (Portland, OR: Amadeus Press, 1990).

Kollmann, Augustus Frederic Christopher, *An Essay on Practical Musical Composition* (London, 1799; repr., New York: Da Capo, 1973).

Lablache, Louis, *Lablache's Complete Method of Singing . . . translated from the French* (Boston: Oliver Ditson & Company, [after 1857]).

Lasser, Johann Baptist, *Vollständige Anleitung zur Singkunst* (Munich, 1798; 2nd edn., 1805).

Lichtenthal, Pietro, *Dizionario e bibliografia della musica* (Milan, 1826).

Mackerras, Charles, "Sense About the Appoggiatura," *Opera* 14/10 (Oct 1963): 669–78.

_____, Correspondence in *The Gramophone* 42/498 (Nov 1964): 265.

_____, "Appoggiaturas Unlimited?" *Records and Recording* 8/5 (Feb 1965): 14–17.

_____, *Charles Mackerras: A Musicians' Musician*, ed. Nancy Phelan (London: Victor Gollancz, 1987).

Marpurg, Friedrich Wilhelm, *Kritische Briefe über die Tonkunst*, ii (Berlin, 1763; repr., Hildesheim: Georg Olms Verlag, 1974).

Mattheson, Johann, *Kern melodischer Wissenschafft* (Hamburg, 1737; repr., Hildesheim: Georg Olms Verlag, 1976).

_____, *Der vollkommene Capellmeister* (Hamburg, 1739), repr. in *DM* v (1954), trans. by Ernest C. Harriss in *SM* 21 (1981).

Monson, Dale E., "The Last Word: The Cadence in *Recitativo semplice* of Italian Opera Seria," *Pergolesi Studies* 1 (1986): 89–105.

Neumann, Frederick, *Ornamentation in Baroque and Post-Baroque Music, with Special Emphasis on J. S. Bach* (Princeton, NJ: Princeton University Press, 1978; 3rd printing with corrections, 1983).

_____, "The Appoggiatura in Mozart's Recitative," *JAMS* 35 (1982): 115–37; in German in *Mozart-Jahrbuch* (1980–83): 363–84.

_____, *Essays in Performance Practice* (Ann Arbor, MI: UMI Research Press, 1982).

_____, *Ornamentation and Improvisation in Mozart* (Princeton, NJ: Princeton University Press, 1986).

_____, "A New Look at Mozart's Prosodic Appoggiatura," in *Perspectives on Mozart Performance*, ed. R. Larry Todd and Peter Williams (Cambridge University Press, 1991), 92–116.

_____, "Improper Appoggiaturas in the *Neue Mozart Ausgabe*," *Journal of Musicology* 10 (1992): 505–21.

Pasquali, Nicolo, *Thorough-Bass Made Easy* (Edinburgh, 1757); 2nd edn. (London, 1763; repr. with introduction by John Churchill, OUP, 1974).

Paumgartner, Bernhard, "Von der sogenannten 'Appoggiatur' in der älteren Gesangsmusik und der Notwendigkeit ihrer Anwendung in der heutigen Aufführungspraxis," *Jahresbericht der Akademie für Musik und darstellende Kunst "Mozarteum," Salzburg*, 1954–55: 7–21; also in *Schweizer pädagogische Blätter* 14 (Jan 1953): 1–15.

Rellstab, Johann Carl Friedrich, *Versuch über die Vereinigung der musikalischen und oratorischen Declamation* (Berlin, 1786).

Scheibe, Johann Adolph, "Abhandlung über das Recitativ," *Bibliothek der schönen Wissenschaften und der freyen Künste*, xi (Leipzig, 1764), 209–68; and xii (Leipzig, 1765), 1–41 and 217–66.

Shakespeare, William, *The Art of Singing*, ii (London: Metzler; Boston: Oliver Ditson, 1899).

Skapski, George Joseph, "The Recitative in Johann Adolph Scheibe's Literary and Musical Work," Ph.D. diss. (University of Texas, 1963; UM 64-3,814).

Smith, Erik, "The Appoggiatura and Its Use for 'Suitable Expression'," booklet with recording of Rossini's *L'italiana in Algeri* conducted by Silvio Varviso; among other releases, London OSA 1375, A 4375 (London: Decca Record Company Limited, 1964).

_____, "Appoggiatura," correspondence in *The Gramophone* 42/496 (Sept 1964): 128.

_____, "The Use and the Abuse of the Appoggiatura," *Records and Recording* 8/4 (Jan 1965): 16–19.

Stölzel, Gottfried Heinrich, *Abhandlung vom Recitativ*, manuscript at Vienna, Gesellschaft der Musikfreunde.

Sulzer, Johann Georg, *Allgemeine Theorie der schönen Künste*, ii (Leipzig, 1774), article "Recitativ," 942–53.

Tagliavini, Luigi Ferdinando, "'Sposa! Euridice!' Prosodischer und musikalischer Akzent," *De editione musices: Festschrift Gerhard Croll zum 65. Geburtstag*, ed. Wolfgang Gratzer and Andrea Lindmayr (Laaber: Laaber Verlag, 1992), 177–202.

Taylor, Franklin, "Appoggiatura," *A Dictionary of Music and Musicians (A.D. 1450–1889)*, ed. George Grove, i (London: Macmillan, 1890), 75–9.

Telemann, Georg Philipp, *Harmonischer Gottes-Dienst* (Hamburg, 1725–26).

_____, *Singe-, Spiel- und General-Bass-Übungen* (Hamburg, 1733–34; repr., Leipzig: Zentralantiquariat der Deutschen Demokratischen Republik, 1983); modern edn. by Max Seiffert (Berlin, 1914).

_____, *Musicalisches Lob Gottes in der Gemeine des Herrn* (Nuremberg: Balthasar Schmid, 1744).

Torres y Martínez Bravo, Joseph de, *Reglas generales de acompañar* (Madrid, 1736; repr., Madrid: Arte Tripharia, 1983); modern edn. and trans. by Paul Murphy as *José de Torres's Treatise of 1736* (Bloomington and Indianapolis: Indiana University Press, 2000).

Tosi, Pier Francesco, *Opinioni de' cantori antichi e moderni, o sieno Osservazioni sopra il canto figurato* (Bologna, 1723); for trans., see Agricola (German), Alençon (Dutch), and Galliard (English).

Türk, Daniel Gottlob, *Kurze Anweisung zum Generalbassspielen* (Halle and Leipzig, 1791), repr. on Microcard UR-59 201-6 from the copy at

Sibley Music Library, Eastman School of Music (University of Rochester Press).

_____, *Anweisung zum Generalbassspielen*, 2nd edn. (Halle and Leipzig, 1800; repr., Amsterdam: Frits Knuf, 1971); *neue verbesserte* edn. (Vienna: S. A. Steiner, 1822).

Urbani, Peter, *The Singer's Guide* (Edinburgh, *c.*1800).

_____, *A New Edition of The Singer's Guide* (Dublin: I. Willis, *c.*1816).

Vaccai, Nicola, *Metodo pratico di canto italiano* (London, 1832), trans. by John Glenn Paton as *Practical Method of Italian Singing* (New York: G. Schirmer, 1975).

Westrup, Jack Allan, "The Cadence in Baroque Recitative," *Natalicia musicologica Knud Jeppesen septuagenario*, ed. Bjørn Hjelmborg and Søren Sørensen (Copenhagen: Wilhelm Hansen, 1962), 243–52.

_____, "Rezitativ," *MGG* xi (1963), 355–65.

_____, "Alessandro Scarlatti's *Il Mitridate Eupatore* (1707)," in *New Looks at Italian Opera: Essays in Honor of Donald J. Grout*, ed. William W. Austin (Ithaca, NY: Cornell University Press, 1968), 133–50.

_____, "Recitative," *NG* xv (1980), 643–8.

INDEX

1-3-1-(1):
blues 186 n. 2
chant 11–12, Ex. 1.7
recitative 43, 45
1-7-5-(5) 25–6, 28–9, 32–3, 35 n. 8,
Exx. 2.8, 2.9, 3.1*a*, *e*, 3.5*a*, *c*
2-3-1-(1):
blues 186 n. 2
chant 10–11, Exx. 1.4–1.6
French 63 n. 1
homophony 186 n. 1
polyphony 15, 24, 28–9, 37–8,
Exx. 2.7, 3.1*e*
recitative 42, 44–6, 51, 61, 90, 123,
Exx. 4.1*a*, 4.3*b*, *e*, 4.6*b*, *c*, Fig. 1
see also échappée
4-3-1-(1) xi–xiii
blues 186 n. 2
chant 5–8, 11–13, Exx. 1.1–1.3
homophony 186 n. 1
polyphony 15, 17–24, 26, 27–33, 35–
8, Exx. 2.2, 2.6, 3.1–3.8
quasi close 42–3, 49, 60–62, 90,
148–9, 172 n. 140, 176–8, 188 n. 3,
Exx. 4.1*b*, 6.22*b*, 6.30*b*, *c*, Fig. 1
recitative cadence xii–xiii, 64, Ex. P*h*,
Fig. 2; 17th century 44–62 *passim*,
Exx. 4.3*c*, *f*, 4.4, 4.5, 4.6*d*, *e*, 4.7*a*,
4.8, 4.10, 4.11, Fig. 1; later 1, 64,
66, 68–9, 74 n. 15, 76, 93–8, 103,
110–11, Exx. I, 5.1–5.10, 5.12–
5.17; with appoggiatura 113, 115–
17, 120–21, 123, 126–7, 130, 132–3,
135, 137–8, 141–4, 146, 148, 154,
157–60, 162, 166, 176–7, 183–8,
Exx. 6.1–6.4, 6.8–6.11, 6.14–6.30,
7.1
see also passing tone, leaping
5-3-1-(1):
chant 12, Ex. 1.8
French 63 n. 1

homophony 186
polyphony 25, 31–2, 37–8, Ex. 2.8
recitative 43, 45, 50, 57
7-3-1-(1) 43, 45, 50, 52, 97, 130, 132,
Exx. 4.7*b*, 5.11, 6.13

Abbatini, Antonio Maria 48 n. 16
accent, textual and/or musical xii
antepenultimate xii, 62, 75 n. 17, 115
n. 4, 139 n. 37, 140, 141, 159–60,
165, Exx. 6.19*a*, 6.27
appoggiatura 114–15, 124, 126, 131–
2, 142, 148 nn. 72 & 73, 149 n. 74
chant 7–8, 12–13
masculine xii, 66, 68, 93–5, 113–15,
120, 126–7, 129, 131–3, 135, 136,
142, 147–8, 150–64, 167, 170–71,
172 n. 141, 175, 179, 180, Exx. 5.1,
6.1, 6.18
parola tronca 54–5
polyphony 23, 26, 34
recitative 42–7, 60–62, 110–11,
Exx. 4.4, 5.1, Figs. 1, 4
accompanied recitative 75 n. 17, 104–5,
109, 110–11, 140–41, 133 n. 27, 159
brief cadence with appoggiatura:
Boyce 135, Ex. 6.17; eighth-rest
delay 143
brief cadence without appoggiatura
187; eighth-rest delay 52, 103,
Exx. 4.7*b*, 5.17*g;* Handel 1, 75–9,
86, 87 n. 53, Ex. I, *see also* Handel
(*Messiah*); Scarlatti 52, 84,
Ex. 4.7
delayed cadence with appoggiatura:
Bach, J.S. 131–2, Ex. 6.15;
Handel/Urbani 154–5, Ex. 6.23*b*;
Haydn 159–60; Mendelssohn 162–
3, Ex. 6.28; Mozart 150;
Mozart/Shakespeare 166–7,
Ex. 6.29; Rossini 144

accompanied recitative (*cont.*):
  delayed cadence without appoggiatura:
    Haydn 94–100 *passim*, 142,
    Ex. 5.14; Mozart 104–5; Rossini
    94–100 *passim*, 144, Ex. 5.16
  see also instruments
Agricola, Johann Friedrich 43 n. 9, 54
  appoggiatura: **1-6-5** 137 n.34;
    absence in theater 153; consonant
    122; grace-note value 129;
    noncadential 138, 176
  authentic cadence 88, 91–2
  deceptive (broken) cadence 54, 67, 88,
    91
  feminine **1-1-5** 137
  see also Galliard; Tosi
Alençon, J. 54
antepenultimate accent, *see* accent,
  textual and/or musical
anticipation xii, 30, 35–6, 102, 120–22,
  129, Exx. P*g*, 3.6, 6.8, 6.9*d*
appoggiatura xii–xiii, 89, 104, 113–80,
  186–8, Ex. P*h*
  absence of 141, 148, 163–4, 174–5,
    179, 187; Bach, J.S. 127, 133, 134;
    before 1750 120–23, 179, 187;
    Haydn 141–2, 148 n. 71, 161;
    Mendelssohn 162; Mozart
    148–50, 168; Rossini 141, 144–5;
    Stravinsky 188; Telemann 115
  divided or replaced first 1 113–14,
    139, 146, 150, 152–9 *passim*, 177,
    180, Ex. 6.1*c*, *e*; Bach, J.S. 130–34;
    Haydn 141–2, 161; Hiller 152;
    Lasser 152; Mendelssohn 163;
    Mozart 148–50; Rossini 141, 143–
    5, 163
  expressive 114, 125–35, 136–7, 140–
    50, 157–64, 169–72, 173–5, 179–80,
    187, Fig. 6; noncadential 136, 147–
    8, 169–70, 179–80
  grace-note value 116, 140 n. 39, 143,
    148, 152, 158–61, 161 n. 105;
    see also Bach, J.S.
  noncadential (general) 138–41, 146–8,

150–64 *passim*, 165–6 n. 114, 175,
    176–80, 187; *see also* Bach, J.S.;
    Haydn; Mozart; Rossini; Telemann
  parallel perfect fifths, *see* Bach, J.S.;
    Telemann
  prosodic 114–25, 134, 152–55, 173–5,
    179–80, 187, Fig. 6; noncadential
    138–41, 151–2, 156, 165–6, 169–70,
    175–8, 187
  to single note on "*bia*" 142, 148
  see also accompanied recitative;
    Bach, J.S.; Gluck; Handel; Haydn;
    Mozart; Rossini; Telemann
aria 41 n. 1, 50, 62, 63 n. 1, 125, 139,
  168 n. 124, 172, 175–6, 178–9, 186,
  Ex. 6.31
authentic cadence 64, 66–7, 88, 91,
  99, 110, 176–9, Fig. 2

Bach, Carl Philipp Emanuel 108, 129,
  169
Bach, Johann Christian 63, 93, 95, 100,
  101
Bach, Johann Christoph Friedrich 157
Bach, Johann Ernst 156
Bach, Johann Sebastian 63, 72, 83, 93–
  102 *passim*, 179
  appoggiatura 127–36, 150, 168, 173–
    4, 187, Fig. 6; grace-note value 127,
    129–33; noncadential 133, 136, 179;
    parallel fifths 119, 127–9
  cantatas 70, 83 n. 37, 87, 91, 93–102
    passim, 107–8, 114, 127, 129–34,
    150 n. 76, 173, Exx. 5.9–5.11, 6.13–
    6.16
  oratorios 131, 133 n. 28
  Passions 127, 165; *St. John* 129, 131,
    150–51 n. 76; *St. Matthew* 2, 127–8,
    131, 133–4, 164, 167 n. 118, 168,
    188, Ex. 6.11
Bacon, Richard Mackenzie 145 n. 59,
  153, 155
Banner, Giannantonio 67, 88
basso continuo 41, 43, 75–6, 82, 101
  bass figures xi, 57, 82–8, 123;

Bach, J.S. 127–9
see also brief cadence; deceptive
   cadence; delayed cadence; harmony;
   harpsichord; instruments; keyboard;
   organ
Beethoven, Ludwig van 137, 151
Bellini, Vincenzo 146
Bencini, Pietro Paolo 86 n. 49, 138
   n. 34
Bernabei, Giuseppe Antonio 85 n. 44
Beyschlag, Adolf 167
blues xi, 186
Bononcini, Antonio Maria 86 n. 48
Bononcini, Giovanni 83 n. 37, 85 n. 47,
   86 n. 48
Boretti, Giovanni Antonio 48 n. 16
Boyce, William 109, 135, Ex. 6.17
brief cadence 45, 58, 64–7, 67 n. 5, 71,
   136, 187, Exx. 4.3*d–f*, 5.1*e*, Fig. 2
   appoggiatura 114–29, 178, Ex. 6-9;
      Bach, J.S. 87 n. 57, 127–9, 134,
      Ex. 6.11; Boyce 135, Ex. 6.17;
      Handel 123, 125–7, 154–5, Ex.
      6.23*b*; Haydn 143; Telemann 71,
      114–25, 187, Exx. 6.2–6.4, 6.8
   bass figures 82–8, 103
   combined melody 103–4, 120–23
   eighth-rest delay 52, 84, Ex. 4.7*b*
   function 89–91
   instruments 107–8
   performance of structure 56–8, 68–82,
      175, 184; Callcott 76, 79 n. 30, 80,
      135, Ex. 5.4; change to delayed V
      75–82, 156, Fig. 4; Hahn 69–72,
      Ex. 5.3; Handel 76–9, 186, 187;
      Heinichen 56–8, 69, 71, Exx. 4.10,
      4.11, Fig. 3; Kellner 68, 70–71,
      Fig. 3; Marpurg 74–5; Telemann
      68–74, Ex. 5.2, Fig. 3; Torres 59;
      Türk 75, 80
   rhythm 95, 99–101, Fig. 5
   Tosi 123–5, 175
   see also accompanied recitative;
      downward fourth
broken cadence 188–9

French 63 n. 1
polyphony 17–20, 25–6, 36–7,
   Exx. 2.2*b*, 2.3–2.5, 2.8, 7.1*c*
recitative 45–62, 64–7, 88–90, 103,
   120–21, 124, 136, 176, Exx. 4.3*d–f*,
   4.4*b*, *c*, 4.6*c*, *e*, 4.7, 4.9*a*, 4.10, 4.11,
   7.1*e*, *f*, Figs. 1, 2
Brollo, Bartolomeus 20–21, Ex. 2.6*b*

cadence:
   starting point 30 n. 5
   structure around 1400 16–17
   see also authentic cadence; brief
      cadence; broken cadence; deceptive
      cadence; delayed cadence; double
      cadence; downward fourth; final
      cadence; Landini cadence; repeated-
      3 cadence; unbroken cadence
cadenza tronca 53–5, 79 n. 30, 90, 92,
   184
   see also Fux; Tosi
Callcott, John Wall 76, 79 n. 30, 80,
   135, 153, Ex. 5.4
cambiata xii, 17, 35, Ex. P*e*
cantata 1, 41, 82, 85, 123, 136
   Bach, J.C.F. 157
   French 63 n. 1
   Graupner 93–6, 100, Ex. 5.8
   Heinichen 56–9, 89; *see also*
      Heinichen
   key signature 83 n. 37
   Pasquali 157, Ex. 6.24
   Scheibe 92 n. 69, 157 n. 96
   see also Bach, J.S.; chamber style;
      church cantata; church style; Handel;
      Rossini; Scarlatti; secular cantata;
      Telemann
Carissimi, Giacomo 48–9, Ex. 4.5
Cavalli, Francesco 43 n. 6, 45 n. 10,
   46 n. 11, 49 nn. 17 & 18, 52–3,
   Ex. 4.8
Cesti, Antonio 46 nn. 11–13, 48 n. 15
chamber style 88–9, 105, 152
   see also cantata; secular cantata
chant xi, 1, 5–13, 38, 183–6,

chant (*cont.*):
  Exx. 1.1–1.8, 7.1*a*
  borrowed 18 20, Exx. 2.4, 2.5
  influence on monody & recitative 41,
    186
  similarity to blues 186 n. 2
  Tosi 124–5
chords, *see* harmony
Chrysander, Friedrich 76 n. 20, 77–8,
  86 n. 51, 165
church cantata 136
  Bach, J.C.F. 157 n. 97
  Bach, J.S. 93–102 *passim*, 107–8,
    127, 129–34 *passim*, Exx. 5.9–5.11,
    6.14, 6.16
  Graupner 93–102 *passim*, Ex. 5.8
  Scheibe 92 n. 69, 157 n. 96
  see also cantata; church style;
    Telemann
church style 41, 88–9, 105, 136, 152
  Bach, J.S. 107–8, 127, 134
  Tosi 123–5
  Urbani 154–5, Ex. 6.23
  see also cantata; church cantata;
    oratorio; Passion
Clarke-Whitfeld (Clarke), John 77
clausul, clausula 58–9, 89–90
Collins, Michael 55 n. 26, 60 n. 36, 67
  n. 4, 70 n. 9, 157 n. 95, 170 nn. 134
  & 135
Colonna, Giovanni Paolo 85 n. 45
continuo, *see* basso continuo
Corelli clash 53
Corri, Domenico 139 n. 38, 147, 153,
  155–6, 163
Crutchfield, Will xiii, 55 n. 27, 114 n. 1,
  140 n. 38, 147 n. 68, 151 n. 78, 152
  nn. 83, 84 & 86, 166, 171 n. 137,
  172

Damett, Thomas 20–21, Ex. 2.6*c*
Dean, Winton xiii, 55 n. 26, 70 n. 9, 73
  n. 12, 82, 170 n. 134
deceptive cadence 32, 66–7, 74, 91–2,
  92 n. 69, 99–100, 110, Fig. 2

to I₆ 66, 86, 87 n. 53, 129 n. 17
to V₆ of V 66, 80
to V₆ of vi 66; Rossini Exx. 5.16,
  6.20*a*
to VI 66, 86, 87 n. 53; Mozart 98,
  100, 102, 106, Ex. 5.15; Ricci
  146, Ex. 6.21; Rossini Ex. 6.20*b*
see also downward fourth
delayed cadence 58, 64, 66–7, 87, 88,
  109–11, 115 n. 4, 176, 184,
  Ex. 5.1*f*, Fig. 2
  appoggiatura 113, 127, 129–34, 178;
    after 1850 164–73; English &
    German 1750–1850 150–64; Italian
    1750–1850 136–50
  changing notated brief cadence 75–82,
    154–6, 187, Exx. 5.4, 6.23*b*, Fig. 4
  combined melody 103–5, Ex. 5.17
  function 88–92
  instruments 107–8
  methods of delaying V 47–9, 67, 72–
    3, 75, 90, 97, 101, 132, Exx. 4.4,
    4.11, 5.12*a*, 6.15
  rhythm 95, 99–101, Fig. 5
  see also accompanied recitative;
    downward fourth
dissonant 3:
  homophony 186
  polyphony 15, 17–22, 25, 29–30, 32–
    7, 183
  recitative 43–4, 50–51, 60–62, 102,
    110–11, 178, Fig. 1
divided first 1, *see* appoggiatura
Donington, Robert 55 n. 26, 70 n. 9, 114
  n. 3, 128 n. 15, 170 n. 134
double cadence 36, Ex. 3.7
double leading-tone 16–17, 20, 26,
  Ex. 2.1*h*
downward fourth 91, 93, 104, 111, 125,
  136–8, 180, 184
  brief cadence 45–6, 62, 66, 137–8,
    Exx. 4.3*d*, 5.1*c* and *d* with *e*;
    Agricola 67 n. 5; delayed by eighth
    rest 84 n. 42; Galliard 54, Ex.
    4.9*a*; Hahn 69, Ex. 5.3*b*; Handel

86–7; Heinichen 57–8; Kellner 68;
  Marpurg 74; Mozart 79; Scarlatti
  50 n. 20; Stölzel 90; Torres 59;
  Türk 75
deceptive cadence: brief 74 n. 15;
  delayed 54 n. 24, 92 n. 69
delayed cadence 66, 137–8, 150–51,
  153, 178, Exx. 5.1c and d with f,
  6.18a, b; Agricola 91; Fux 90–91,
  54 n. 25; main feminine type after
  1750 137, 140; Marpurg 93 n. 70;
  Mattheson 90; Pasquali 106;
  Rellstab 152 n. 86; Sulzer 92 n. 69;
  Torres 59; Türk 75
  duet with falling-third cadence 84
    n. 42, 87 n. 53, 94–5, 133, 172
    n. 139, Exx. 5.12b, c, 5.13
  quasi close 42, 65, 92 n. 69, 184,
    Ex. 4.1c
Draghi, Antonio 85 n. 47
Dufay, Guillaume 26, 27–9, 31–3,
  Exx. 3.1, 3.4b, 3.5a
Dunstable, John 20–21, 25, 185,
  Exx. 2.6a, 2.8, 7.1b

échappée xii, Ex. Pf
  chant 9, 10
  polyphony 16, 22, 24
  recitative 42–3, 60
  see also 2-3-1-(1)
English text 63, 136–7, 150, 154–6
  Boyce 135, Ex. 6.17
  Handel 86–7, 126–7, 164, 172 n. 141,
    Exx. I, 6.10c; Callcott 76, Ex. 5.4;
    Corri 156; Urbani 154–6, Ex. 6.23b
  Haydn 159–61, 164, 173, Ex. 6.27
  Mendelssohn 159, 161–3, 164,
    Ex. 6.28
  Pasquali 157, Ex. 6.24
  Urbani 154–6, Ex. 6.23
expressive appoggiatura, see
  appoggiatura

falling fourth, see downward fourth
Faure, Jean-Baptiste 165–6 n. 114

Ferrari, Giacomo Gotifredo 55 n. 27,
  139 n. 38, 147
fifths, see parallel perfect fifths
figured bass, see basso continuo
final cadence 49, 54, 58–9, 62, 68, 73,
  89–92, 123, 126 n. 14, Exx. 4.9b,
  4.11
fourth, see downward fourth
French text 24, 63 n. 1, 159, Ex. 2.7b
  Rossini 141 n. 43, 145
function:
  of appoggiatura: for accent or
    expression 114, 136, 152, 163–4,
    173–80, 187, see also appoggiatura
    (expressive, prosodic); in church,
    chamber, theater 123–5, 152–3, 175,
    187
  of cadence types 47–52, 65–7, 88–92,
    175, see also brief cadence; delayed
    cadence; final cadence
Fux, Johann Joseph:
  brief cadences 79
  cadenza truncata 54, 90–91
  counterpoint 41
  editorial appoggiaturas 172
  punctuation 90–91

Galliard, John Ernest:
  broken cadence 54, 55 n. 25, 89,
    Ex. 4.9
  notated appoggiaturas 124
  see also Agricola; Tosi
Galuppi, Baldassare 86 n. 49
García, Manuel Patricio Rodríguez 139,
  165, 169, 170 n. 131
Gardiner, John Eliot 80, 123
Gasparini, Francesco 83 & n. 37, 85
  n. 46, 86 n. 48
German text 63, 73, 87, 94, 136–7, 150,
  156–63, 168, 175
  Bach, J.S. 127, 129–34, 164,
    Exx. 5.9–5.11, 6.11, 6.13–6.16
  Graupner 96, Ex. 5.8
  Hahn 69, Ex. 5.3a
  Haydn 159–61, 164, 173, Ex. 6.27

German text (*cont.*):
Hiller 151–2
Keiser 96, Exx. 5.6, 5.7
Mendelssohn 159, 161–4, Ex. 6.28
Rolle 157–8, Ex. 6.25
Schubert 158–9, Ex. 6.26
Telemann 68, 114–25, Exx. 5.2, 5.12, 6.2–6.4, 6.8
Gluck, Christoph Willibald 63, 93–5, 100–101
appoggiatura 145
downward fourth 138 n. 34
operas 74
Alceste 145
Ezio 80
Telemaco 80
grace-note value, *see* appoggiatura
Graun, Carl Heinrich 92 n. 69, 165
Graupner, Christoph 63, 93–102 *passim*, Ex. 5.8
Greene, Maurice 135 n. 30
Gregorian chant, *see* chant
Grossin, Estienne 20–21, Ex. 2.6*e*
Grout, Donald Jay 107 n. 77, 170

Hahn, Georg Joachim Joseph 69, 70–72, 83, 108 n. 80, 121–2, Ex. 5.3, Fig. 3
Handel, George Frideric 73, 82, 86–7, 92–102 *passim*, 165, 167, 172, 186, 187
appoggiatura 123, 125–7, Ex. 6.10
cantatas 83 n. 37, 86, Ex. 6.10*b*
operas 63, 85–6, 188; *Arminio* 126, Ex. 6.10*a*; *Flavio* 78; *Orlando* 74 n. 15; *Rinaldo* 94, 100, Ex. 5.13; *Tamerlano* 74 n. 13, 86
oratorios 63, 77, 86–7, 165, 188; *Israel in Egypt* 77, 164; *Jephtha* 76, Ex. 5.4; *Joseph* 87 n. 53, 126–7, Ex. 6.10*c*; *Messiah* 1–2, 76–80, 91, 155, 164, 168 n. 124, 188, Exx. I, 6.23*b*; recordings 80, 123; *Theodora* 156
Passion 87
Hansell, Kathleen Kuzmick 55 n. 26, 79 n. 30, 171

Hansell, Sven Hostrup xiii, 55 n. 26, 70 n. 9, 79 n. 30, 83 n. 38, 90 n. 64, 170 n. 134
harmony xii
polyphony 30, 32, 38
recitative 43–4, 48–9, 58, 60–62, 66–7, 79–81, 89–90, 101–2, 105–7, 110, 176–9, Figs. 1, 4; Bach, J.S. 133; final chord 64, Fig. 2; harmonic rhythm 100–101, 110; polychordal 52–3, Ex. 4.8
see also authentic cadence; basso continuo; brief cadence; deceptive cadence; delayed cadence
harpsichord 105–8, 110–11
see also basso continuo; instruments; keyboard; secco recitative
Haydn, Joseph 93–102 *passim*, 141, 165, 174–5, 187
appoggiatura 140–43, 147–8, 155, Fig. 6; noncadential 140–41, 147–8; to single note on *bia, mia* 142, 148
operas 63, 142–3, 147–8, 165; *La fedeltà premiata* 142; *L'incontro improvviso* 142–3, 148; *Lo speziale* 93–100 *passim*, 142, Ex. 5.14; *La vera costanza* 142
oratorios: *Applausus* 75, 141, 173, Ex. 6.19; *The Creation* 2, 159–60, 165, Ex. 6.27; *Il ritorno di Tobia* 142, 148; *The Seasons* 159–61
Heartz, Daniel 170
Heinichen, Johann David 56–9, 68–72, 74 n. 13, 74–5 n. 16, 82–3, 88, 89, 91, 108 n. 80, 121, Exx. 4.10, 4.11, 6.9*a*, *b*, 7.1*e*, Fig. 3
Herbing, August Bernhard Valentin 156
Hiller, Johann Adam 137 n. 34, 151–53
Hogwood, Christopher 80, 123
Hymbert de Salinis 25–6, Ex. 2.9

imitation 34
Dufay 28–9, 31–2, Exx. 3.1*b*, *d*, 3.4*b*
Josquin 29–30, Ex. 3.2
Obrecht 32–3, Ex. 3.5*c*

instruments:
  polyphony 23, 34
  recitative 105–9, 110–11; Bach, J.S.
    134
  see also accompanied recitative; basso
    continuo; brief cadence; deceptive
    cadence; delayed cadence;
    harpsichord; keyboard; organ; secco
    recitative
Italian text:
  polyphony Exx. 2.7*a*, 3.1*c*
  recitative after 1700 63, 136–9, 138
    n. 35, 145, 155, 163–4; Ferrari 147;
    Handel Exx. 5.13, 6.10*a*, *b*; Haydn
    142–3, 147–8, 159, 173, Ex. 5.14;
    Mozart 148–50, 164, 167–8, Exx.
    5.15, 6.22, 6.29–6.31; Pacini 145–6;
    Ricci 146, Ex. 6.21; Rossini 141
    n. 43, 143–5, 164, Exx. 5.16, 6.20;
    Scarlatti 96, Ex. 5.5; Urbani 154–5
  recitative before 1700 42–7, 51–6,
    59–61, Exx. 4.1–4.4, 4.6–4.11

Josquin des Prez 26, 29–30, 36,
  Exx. 3.2, 7.1*c*

Keiser, Reinhard 63, 73, 92–101 *passim*
  operas 74 n. 13; *Die grossmütige
    Tomyris* 87, 89, 91, 93, 101–2,
    Ex. 5.7; *Nebucadnezar* 87
  Passion, St. Mark 94, 100, Ex. 5.6
Kellner, David 68, 70–72, 89, 90 n. 64,
  91, Fig. 3
keyboard 81, 82, 105–9
  see also basso continuo; harpsichord;
    instruments; organ; secco recitative
Klein, Herman 164 n. 112, 165, 167–8
Knapp, J(ohn) Merrill 78, 170 n. 134
Kollmann, Augustus Frederic
  Christopher 108, 153
kurtze Resolution 56–9, 69, 70–72, 107,
  Ex. 4.10, Fig. 3

Lablache, Luigi (Louis) 139, 143, 166
  n. 114

Lanciani, Flavio Carlo 85 n. 45
Landi, Stefano 43 n. 8, 45 n. 10, 53
  n. 21
Landini cadence 16, 20–21, 24, 26, 31,
  32, 33–4, Exx. 2.1*b*, 3.4*a*, 3.5*c*
Lasser, Johann Baptist 151, 152
Latin text:
  chant 7–8, Exx. 1.1–1.8
  polyphony 23–4, Exx. 2.3–2.5, 2.6,
    2.8, 3.1, 3.3–3.5, 3.7, 3.8
  recitative 124 n. 16; Carissimi 48,
    Ex. 4.5; Haydn 141, 173, Ex. 6.19
leaping passing-tone, *see* passing tone,
  leaping
Legrant, Johannes 20–21, Ex. 2.6*d*
Leo, Leonardo 85, 86 n. 48
Libert, Reginaldus 24, Ex. 2.7*b*
Lichtenthal, Peter (Pietro) 139–40 n. 38,
  169
Logroscino, Nicola Bonifacio 84 n. 42

Mackerras, Charles xiii, 140 n. 38, 143
  n. 50, 155 n. 91, 168, 169
Majo, Gian Francesco 145
Mancini, Francesco 85 n. 44
Manfredini, Vincenzo 143 n. 150
Marazzoli, Marco 43 n. 19, 48 n. 16
Marpurg, Friedrich Wilhelm:
  authentic & deceptive cadences 91,
    166–7
  falling fourth in feminine cadences 93
    n. 70, 137
  falling third in masculine cadences
    151
  few appoggiaturas in theater 153
  final bass note on strong beat 100
  preference for delayed cadence 74–5
  quasi close 42
Mattheson, Johann 89–91, 101
Mazzocchi, Virgilio 43 n. 9
melodic framework:
  aria 62, 178–9
  chant 5, 8–13, 183
  homophony 186
  polyphony 16–18, 30–32, 35–8,

melodic framework (*cont.*):
  Exx. 2.1, 2.2, 3.6
  recitative 42–50, 59–62, 64–6, 103–5, 120–23, 178, 184–5, Exx. 4.1–4.4, 5.1, 5.17, 6.1, 6.9, Figs. 1, 2
melodic sequence, *see* sequence, melodic
melody xi–xii
  chant 5–13
  polyphony 15, 17–23, 24–6, 27–33, 35–8; *see also* sequence, melodic
  recitative 42–9, 60–62, 92–5, 109–11, 113; voice and accompaniment combined without appoggiatura 103–5, 110, Ex. 5.17; combined with appoggiatura 121–3, Ex. 6.9; *see also* **1-3-1-(1); 1-7-5-(5); 2-3-1-(1); 4-3-1-(1); 5-3-1-(1); 7-3-1-(1);** appoggiatura; brief cadence; delayed cadence; melodic framework
Mendelssohn, Felix 77
  oratorios 159
    Elijah 161–3, 164, 165, Ex. 6.28
    St. Paul 161–3
Monteverdi, Claudio 45 n. 10
Mozart, Wolfgang Amadeus 63, 92–102 *passim*, 165–9, 171, 175
  appoggiatura 148–50, 167–73; noncadential 148, 166–7, 170, 171, 176–8, Exx. 6.29, 6.30; to single note on *Dio* 142–3 n. 50
  Messiah arrangement 79
  Neue Mozart-Ausgabe 79, 169–72
  operas 188; *Don Giovanni* 164, 165–6, 168, 172 n. 140; *La finta semplice* 148–9, Ex. 6.22; *Idomeneo* 148, 149–50, 170, 172, 176–9, Exx. 6.30, 6.31; *Lucio Silla* 79, 94–102 *passim*, 171, Ex. 5.15; *Le nozze di Figaro* 104–5, 164, 167–8, 168 n. 124, 171, 184–5, 188, Exx. 6.29, 7.1*f*

neighbor note xii, Ex. P*a, b*
  chant 9
  polyphony 16, 22, 24

Neumann, Frederick xiii, 128 n. 15, 129 n. 19, 130 n. 21, 140 n. 38, 169, 171, 172
noncadential ending, *see* appoggiatura; quasi close
nonharmonic tones, *see* ornamental or nonharmonic tones

Obrecht, Jacob 32–3, 35 n. 8, Ex. 3.5*c*
Ockeghem, Johannes 26, 32–3, 34, Ex. 3.5*b*
Old Hall Manuscript 18–20, Exx. 2.4, 2.5
opera 1, 41, 47, 49, 54, 82, 86, 88, 123, 125, 134, 136, 175, 179, 187, 188, Fig. 6
  French 63 n. 1
  key signature 83 n. 37
  see also Cavalli; Gluck; Handel; Haydn; Keiser; Mozart; Rossini; Scarlatti; Telemann; theatrical style
oratorio 1, 41, 82, 85, 123, 136
  Carissimi 48–9
  Draghi 85 n. 47
  Porpora 84 n. 42
  Rolle 157–8
  see also Bach, J.S.; church style; Handel; Mendelssohn; Scarlatti
organ 105, 107–8, 111
  see also basso continuo; instruments; keyboard; secco recitative
ornamental or nonharmonic tones xii, Ex. P
  chant 8–9
  recitative 152, 153, 156, 167, 169, 175, 178
  see also anticipation; appoggiatura; cambiata; échappée; neighbor note; passing tone, leaping; suspension
ostinato 34
  Josquin 29–30, Ex. 3.2

Pacini, Giovanni 145–6, 163
Palestrina, Giovanni Pierluigi 26, 31–2, 34–7, 41, 183, 184, 186,

Exx. 3.4*c*, 3.7, 3.8
Pallavicino, Carlo 85 n. 47
parallel perfect fifths:
  Bach, J.S. 119, 127–9, Exx. 6.11, 6.12
  Telemann 116–20, 128, Exx. 6.3–6.7
Parrott, Andrew 80, 123
Pasquali, Nicolo 106–7, 157, Ex. 6.24
Pasquini, Bernardo 85
passing tone, leaping Ex. P*d*
  chant 9, 10
  polyphony 19, 22
  recitative 60, 110
  see also **4-3-1-(1)**
Passion 109, 136
  Graun, C.H. 165
  see also Bach, J.S.; church style;
    Handel; Keiser
Paumgartner, Bernhard xiii, 169
Pergolesi, Giovanni Battista 63, 95
Peri, Jacopo:
  Euridice 43 nn. 5 & 8, 45 n. 10, 46
    n. 13
Perti, Giacomo Antonio 85 n. 45
Pinnock, Trevor 80, 123
plain recitative, *see* simple recitative
Pollarolo, Carlo Francesco 85 n. 44
polychordal 52–3, 83, Ex. 4.8
  see also Corelli clash; harmony
Porpora, Nicola 84 n. 42, 86 n. 49
Power, Leonel 18–20, 31, Exx. 2.5, 3.3
prosodic appoggiatura, *see* appoggiatura

Quantz, Johann Joachim 74, 88, 109,
  129, 169
quasi close (Quasischluss) 42–3, 46, 49,
  50, 60–62, 63 n. 1, 65, 90–92, 92
  n. 69, 116 n. 5, 133, 148–9, 172
  n. 140, 176–8, 184, 186, 188 n. 3,
  Exx. 4.1, 6.22*b*, 6.30, Fig. 1
  see also **4-3-1-(1)**; appoggiatura
    (noncadential); downward fourth

realization, *see* basso continuo
recitative, *see* accompanied recitative;
  secco recitative; simple recitative

recitativo semplice, *see* simple recitative
Rellstab, Johann Carl Friedrich 137,
  151–3
repeated-3 cadence 43–4, 49–51, 60–62,
  65, Exx. 4.2*b*, 4.6*a*, Fig. 1
replaced first 1, *see* appoggiatura
rhythm:
  polyphony 22–3, 26, 27, 34
  recitative xiii, 46–7, 95, 99–101, 110–
    11, 134, 143, 144, 155, 156, 175–6,
    184; brief cadence 51–2, 56–9, 68–
    72; change from brief to delayed
    73–4, 75–82, 187, Figs. 2, 4;
    harmonic 100
  see also rhythmic structure
rhythmic structure:
  polyphony 17–18, 35–7
  recitative xiii, 64–7, 109–10, 187,
    Exx. 4.1–4.4, 5.1; Bach, J.S. 134
  see also authentic cadence; brief
    cadence; broken cadence; deceptive
    cadence; delayed cadence; quasi
    close; repeated-3 cadence; unbroken
    cadence
Ricci, Luigi 146–7, 163, Ex. 6.21
Rockstro, W(illiam) S(mith) 166
Rolle, Johann Heinrich 157–8, Ex. 6.25
Rossi, Luigi 43 n. 9, 45 n. 10
Rossini, Gioachino 93–101 *passim*, 143
  appoggiatura 143–7, 155, 163, 164,
    167, 173, 174–5, 187, Ex. 6.20,
    Fig. 6; noncadential 140–41, 147
  cantata in honor of Pius IX 147, 163,
    164, 173
  operas 63, 145 n. 58, 165, 173; *Il
    barbiere di Siviglia* 164; *Le Compte
    Ory* 145; *La donna del lago* 144;
    La gazza ladra 140 nn. 39 & 42;
    Guillaume Tell 141 n. 43, 164;
    L'italiana in Algeri 94, 95, 100,
    109, 144, 169 n. 130, Ex. 5.16;
    Mosè in Egitto 139 n. 36;
    La scala di seta 143–4, 145, 163,
    Ex. 6.20; *Le siège de Corinthe* 141
    n. 43, 145

Sacrati, Francesco 43 n. 9
sacred style, *see* church style
Sartorio, Antonio 46 n. 12, 48 n. 15
Scarlatti, Alessandro 63, 73, 87, 93–101
   passim, 105, 123
  cantatas 57, 83 n. 37, 84
  operas 170; *Dafni* 50; *Gli equivoci
    nel sembiante* xi, 50; *Marco Attilio
    Regolo* 52, Ex. 4.7*b*; *Il Pompeo* 50–
    51, 54, 55, 56, 74 n. 13, 84, 95,
    Exx. 4.6, 7.1*d*; *La principessa fedele*
    91, 94, 95, 99, 100, 106–7, Ex. 5.5;
    La statira 46 n. 12, 52, 99, Ex. 4.7*a*;
    Telemaco 84 n. 41
  oratorios 85 n. 43
Scheibe, Johann Adolph 91–2, 100
   n. 72, 134, 137, 157
Schubert, Franz 158–9, Ex. 6.26
Schulz, Johann Abraham Peter 92 n. 69,
   158
secco recitative 77, 81, 82, 84, 104,
   105–9, 111, 187
  Bach, J.S. 127
  Boyce 135
  Handel 86
  Keiser 87
  Rossini 144
  speaking recitative (Urbani) 154
  see also harpsichord; instruments;
   keyboard; organ
secular cantata 85, 123
  anonymous printed by Heinichen 56–
   9, 89, Exx. 4.10, 4.11
  Bach, J.S. 127, 129–34, Exx. 6.13,
   6.15
  French 63 n.1
  Handel 125–6, Ex. 6.10*b*
  Pasquali 157, Ex. 6.24
  Scarlatti 57, 83 n. 37, 84, 89
  Telemann 72
  see also chamber style
sequence, melodic 28–9, 34, Ex. 3.1*c*
shake, *see* trill
Shakespeare, William (1849-1931)
   166–7, 171, 175, Ex. 6.29

Shaw, Watkins 78–9
simple recitative 105
  see also secco recitative
Smith, Erik xiii, 140 n. 38, 169
Spanish text 59
speaking recitative, *see* secco recitative
Stölzel, Gottfried Heinrich 90–91, 100
Stradella. Alessandro 85
Stravinsky, Igor 188
structure, *see* rhythmic structure;
   melodic framework
Sulzer, Johann Georg 92, 137, 151, 157
   n. 96
suspension 16, 17–18, 20, 30, 35–6,
   Exx. 2.1*e*, 2.2*b–d*, 3.6

Tagliavini, Luigi Ferdinando xiii, 169
Taylor, Franklin 166–7, 175
Telemann, Georg Philipp 63, 82, 88,
   92–102 *passim*, 169
  cantatas 68–72, 79, 89, 113–20, 174–
   5, 179, Ex. 5.2*b*, *c*, Fig. 6
  Harmonischer Gottes-Dienst 72, 83
   n. 37, 84, 87; appoggiatura 114–
   16, 125, 136, 167, 187, Ex. 6.8;
   noncadential appoggiatura 115,
   128, 136, 179, 187; parallel fifths
   116–19, Exx. 6.3, 6.4
  Musikalisches Lob Gottes 73, Exx.
   6.6, 6.7; parallel fifths 118–20
  operas 57 n. 31, 68–72, 87, 120–22,
   Exx. 5.2*a*, 6.9*d*; *Der geduldige
   Socrates* 72, 79, 87 n. 58,
   95–101 *passim*, Ex. 5.12; *Der
   neumodische Damon* 79, 87 n. 58
  oratorio 74 n. 15
  *Singe- Spiel- und General-Bass-
   Übungen* 87, 108; parallel fifths
   116–17, Ex. 6.5; performance of
   brief structure 57 n. 30, 68–74,
   79, 83, 88, 120–22, 127, 175, 187,
   Exx. 5.2, 6.9*d*, Fig. 3
text, *see* English, French, German,
   Italian, Latin, or Spanish text
theatrical style 67, 88–9, 105, 175

Rellstab 152
Tosi 123–5
see also opera
thorough-bass, *see* basso continuo
Torres y Martínez Bravo, Joseph de 59, 88
Tosi, Pier Francesco 169
  absence of appoggiaturas 123–5, 153, 175
  cadenze tronche 53–6, 64–7, 79 n. 30, 89, 92, 124
  trills 43 n. 9, 89, 126 n. 14
  see also Agricola; Alençon; Galliard
trill (shake) 126 n. 14
  Agricola 138
  aria 178–9
  brief cadence 125–6
  delayed cadence 130–31
  noncadential endings 133 n. 27, 138
  repeated-3 cadence 43
  unbroken cadence 43–4 n. 9, 89
  see also Tosi

tronca, cadenza, see *cadenza tronca*
Türk, Daniel Gottlob 75–7, 80

unbroken cadence 184–5
  French 63 n. 1
  polyphony 17–22, 24–6, 27–30, 36, Exx. 2.2c, d, 2.6, 2.7, 3.1
  recitative 44–9, 50–51, 60–62, 88–9, 103, 120, 124, Exx. 4.3a–c, 4.4a, 4.5, 4.6b, d, Figs. 1, 2
Urbani, Peter 76, 137 n. 34, 154–6, 163, 175, Ex. 6.23

Vaccai, Nicola 140 n. 38
Velut, Gilet 31, Ex. 3.4a

Wagenseil, Georg Christoph 84 n. 42, 138 n. 34
Westrup, Jack Allan xiii, 48 n. 14, 70 n. 9, 78, 170 n. 134

Zacharie, Nicola 24, Ex. 2.7a
Ziani, Marc'Antonio 85 n. 45